Personalising Library Services in Higher Education

Personalising Library Services in Higher Education

The Boutique Approach

Edited by

ANDY PRIESTNER and ELIZABETH TILLEY
University of Cambridge

ASHGATE

Published by
Ashgate Publishing Limited
Wey Court East
Union Road
Farnham
Surrey, GU9 7PT
England

Ashgate Publishing Company
Suite 420
101 Cherry Street
Burlington
VT 05401-4405
USA

www.ashgatepublishing.com

Andy Priestner and Elizabeth Tilley have asserted their moral right under the Copyright, Designs and Patents Act, 1988, to be identified as the editors of this work.

British Library Cataloguing in Publication Data
Personalising library services in higher education : the
  boutique approach.
  1. Academic libraries--Aims and objectives. 2. Public
  services (Libraries)--Case studies.
  I. Priestner, Andy. II. Tilley, Elizabeth.
  027.7-dc23

Library of Congress Cataloging-in-Publication Data
Personalised library services in higher education: the boutique approach / [edited] by Andy Priestner and Elizabeth Tilley.
    pages cm
  Includes bibliographical references and index.
  ISBN 978-1-4094-3180-0 (hardback) -- ISBN 978-1-4094-3181-7 (ebook) 1. Academic libraries. 2. Libraries and colleges. 3. Public services (Libraries) 4. Academic libraries--Case studies. I. Priestner, Andy. II. Tilley, Elizabeth, 1959-
  Z675.U5P473 2012
  027.7--dc23

ISBN 9781409431800 (hbk)
ISBN 9781409431817 (ebk)

Printed and bound in Great Britain by the
MPG Books Group, UK

CONTENTS

LIST OF FIGURES AND TABLES

FIGURES

TABLES

PREFACE AND ACKNOWLEDGEMENTS

The aim of this book is to examine the potential for implementation of a more personalised, or 'boutique', approach to delivery of information and library services in the Higher Education Sector. We believe there to be considerable mileage in a boutique library model, inspired by the practices of the boutique hotel industry, that as well as prizing uniqueness and individuality above uniformity and consistency recognises the value of connecting with our users on a less generic, more personal wavelength. We believe this approach has particular merit at this time, as we continue to seek to be relevant and engaging in the face of significant challenges such as funding cuts, heightened user expectations and rapid technological change. It is our conviction that 'going personalised' is a practical and viable roadmap for librarians and information workers in this 'Age of the Individual'. We hope this book will offer useful guidance and insights into successful adoption and implementation of this approach.

We would like to thank Lyn Bailey (Classics Faculty, Cambridge) for reading the manuscript and suggesting amendments; Kirsty Taylor (Judge Business School, Cambridge) for additional ideas on application of the approach; Claudia Luna (Judge Business School, Cambridge) for assistance with the final edit; attendees of the 2011 symposium on personalised libraries at Homerton College; our chapter and case study writers for their contributions; and each other for patience and forbearance.

Thanks are also due to Dymphna Evans of Ashgate Publishing.

Andy Priestner,
Elizabeth Tilley

Cambridge,
January 2012

CONTRIBUTOR BIOGRAPHIES

ANDY PRIESTNER (EDITOR)

Andy Priestner has worked in both the academic and public library sector since 1994. He is currently Information and Library Services Manager at Cambridge University's Judge Business School where he has made radical changes to resource provision and service levels. He was Chair of the UK's Business Librarians Association from 2006–2010 (which was rebranded and relaunched during his tenure) and is also active in European business librarianship. In 2007 he was awarded a teaching excellence award by the University of Oxford. In 2010 he led the 23 Things social media programme for Cambridge University library staff. He has recently made contributions to two forthcoming books on marketing and information literacy. He regularly blogs about business librarianship and the profession in general as 'libreaction'.

ELIZABETH TILLEY (EDITOR)

Elizabeth Tilley has worked in small, specialist academic libraries since 1997. As well as learning to tackle all aspects of librarianship, her previous career as a trained teacher has helped to inform much of her work in libraries. Her first post as librarian was in the Earth Sciences Library where she was responsible for developing a tailored skills programme for undergraduates and adopting an information commons space. Currently working in the English Faculty Library, she has spent three years working out what it is that English students and faculty need and want and has made many changes to the library service – policies, look and feel, teaching, and use of space – in order to tailor the service appropriately. Elizabeth is committed to the profession and has been active at both national and international levels via CILIP and is currently Candidate Support Officer for CILIP's CDG Eastern Region group. She is a Fellow of the Higher Education Academy.

MICHELLE BLAKE

Michelle Blake currently works as Head of Relationship Management at the University of York where she is responsible for Academic Liaison, Applications Support Training and Communications & Marketing. She previously worked at the London School of Economics where she was responsible for overseeing the Academic Support Service and the Institutional Repository, LSE Research Online. She was involved in the European Commission-funded project NEEO, which has developed a multilingual portal called Economists Online. Before that Michelle worked in university libraries in New Zealand.

ANGELA CUTTS

Angela Cutts has worked in Education libraries in Cambridge for a number of years, beginning her career at the Cambridge Institute of Education where she was responsible for the Resources Centre. In 1997 she became School of Education Librarian in charge of a split-site library service. In 2004–2005, having previously been appointed Faculty Librarian, she successfully organised the merger of three separate library collections to create the Faculty of Education Library, which serves a large and diverse readership of academic and research staff in addition to full-time, part-time and distance students.

HELEN EDWARDS

Helen Edwards started work at SKOLKOVO Moscow School of Management as Library Project Manager in September 2009 with the task of setting up a brand new business school library from scratch. Prior to this she was Head of Information Services at London Business School where she worked in various roles for nearly twenty-five years. She is a former president of the European Business Schools Librarians' Group (2005–2008) and an honorary fellow of CILIP. She blogs for the Russian business media.

VERONICA LAWRENCE

Veronica Lawrence is Learning and Teaching Support Librarian at Goldsmiths, University of London, where she is responsible for the work of the Library's Subject Team. Her contribution to this volume relates to work that she did while she was Liaison Librarian at Nottingham Trent University Library (1997–2008). She is particularly interested in the development of creative ways of engaging students in the information-finding aspects of their university work.

TATUM MCPHERSON-CROWIE

Tatum McPherson-Crowie is currently the Liaison Librarian to the three schools of Education, Educational Leadership and Religious Education at the Melbourne Campus (Victoria) of Australian Catholic University. Her current research interests focus on libraries, literacies and lifelong learning, and the ways in which libraries can respond to the changing nature of academic work. She has undertaken studies and participated in presenting papers at international conferences in art, literature, museology, librarianship and lifelong learning worldwide. In 2012 she was a visiting doctoral candidate at the University of Cambridge, and is currently completing her PhD at Australian Catholic University.

CHRIS POWIS

Chris Powis is currently Head of Library and Learning Services at the University of Northampton after spending much of his career in subject librarianship. He has written and spoken on learning and teaching in libraries for many years and was awarded a national teaching fellowship in 2004. He is also a fellow of CILIP, but still harbours faint hopes of becoming a double England international in football and cricket.

BEATRICE PULLIAM

Beatrice Pulliam is Library Commons Librarian for Technology & Access at Providence College, USA, where she has managed library technology, access and interlibrary loan services since 2007. She has a Master of Science in Library & Information Science from Simmons College and a Bachelor of Arts degree from the University of Michigan. Beatrice has led many of her library's new technology initiatives (most recently mobile, augmented reality, and so on) and has a special interest in integrating emerging technologies and user services, and staff development.

JANE SECKER

Jane Secker is the Copyright and Digital Literacy Advisor at the Centre for Learning Technology at LSE. She provides advice, support and training to staff in all aspects of copyright, e-learning and digital literacy. She is Conference Officer for the CILIP Information Literacy Group, a member of the RIN Information Handling Working Group and a member of the UK Working Group on Copyright. Jane has published widely, including most recently *Copyright and E-learning: A Guide for Practitioners*, published by Facet in 2010. She was recently project manager for the JISC project DELILA, which was about sharing open educational resources in the field of digital and information literacy. Jane is a fellow of the Higher Education Academy and teaches digital literacy classes to staff and PhD students at LSE. She has a PhD from the University of Wales, Aberystwyth, where she is an honorary lecturer in their Department of Information Studies.

DAVID STREATFIELD

David Streatfield is Principal of Information Management Associates, a research, training and consultancy team now specialising in evaluating library and information service impact. He is an independent impact consultant to the Global Libraries Initiative funded by the Bill and Melinda Gates Foundation, and has acted in a similar capacity for the International Federation of Library Associations and other bodies, as well as working on various UK and overseas research and consultancy projects. With his colleague Sharon Markless, David is preparing a new edition of their book *Evaluating the Impact of Your Library*, to be published by Facet next year.

EMMA THOMPSON

Emma's career in libraries began with a Saturday job as a teenager in Belfast. Her current role is Liaison Librarian for the University of Liverpool Management School, and she chairs the Business Librarians Association (http://www.blalib. org). After employment in private and public sector Business Information Services, Emma worked at the University of Plymouth: first as a subject librarian for Business and Law, and later managing the Business and Languages Information Service, a specialist library within Plymouth Business School.

TIM WALES

Tim Wales is currently Head of Library at the London Business School – successor to fellow contributor to this book, Helen Edwards. His chapter draws on his previous work as Associate Director (E-Strategy) at Royal Holloway, University of London Library services where he was responsible for library systems, e-resource management and Open Access. Tim also worked at the Open University Library for eight years as a business and technology subject librarian as well as a bank researcher and trade journalist. He has published articles on a range of professional librarianship topics including veterinarian information needs, alumni support and e-library systems.

KERRY WEBB

Kerry Webb is Deputy Librarian of the English Faculty Library at Oxford University, and was previously an information officer at the university's Said Business School. A chartered librarian, she has worked in the academic library sector for over ten years. Kerry has a strong reader services bias and an aptitude for devising marketing materials for the promotion of library services to readers. She has a particular interest in the field of information literacy in higher education. In 2011 she received a teaching award from the university in acknowledgement of her contribution to learning and teaching at Oxford.

MARGARET WESTBURY

Margaret Westbury is the Projects Officer for Information and Library Services at Judge Business School. Before that, she worked in several academic and public libraries, including an online university and the Library Program for the Bill and Melinda Gates Foundation. She has an active interest in using new media and social technology to enhance and change library services, and is especially interested in virtual reference, website design and library marketing.

NICOLA WRIGHT

Nicola Wright has extensive experience in library management gained in academic and research libraries including the British Library, School of Oriental and African Studies (SOAS) and Imperial College, London. Nicola has a background in collection management, coupled with information services delivery and the use of technology. Much of her career has focused on evolving traditional library services into an integrated digital service environment. Nicola joined LSE Library in 2008 from Imperial College where she was Project Manager for the UK Research Reserve. In 2011 Nicola was appointed as Deputy Director of LSE Library Services.

CHAPTER 1

INTRODUCING THE BOUTIQUE APPROACH
ANDY PRIESTNER AND ELIZABETH TILLEY

CHALLENGES AND THREATS

Today library and information services operating in the higher education environment are arguably facing the most intimidating range of challenges and threats in their history: the higher (and different) expectations of users, the breakneck pace of technological change, the emergence of social media, and, perhaps most significantly, cuts in government funding following the global economic crisis. Taken together these elements have the potential to dictate a very uncertain future for the academic librarian and the libraries in which they operate.

The majority of today's academic librarians do seek to innovate, to secure their ongoing value to their user populations. They have embraced social media and mobile technologies, grasped the opportunity to teach in the classroom, and integrated themselves into the research process at their institutions. They are sold on their roles as publishers and facilitators and recognise that it is no longer enough to simply act as collectors and curators. They understand the importance of moving beyond the library walls, of connecting with digital natives whose information skills have proved to be very different to, but not necessarily better than, the previous generation. They are convinced that we must both market ourselves and our services within our institutions, and ensure that we are identified as responsible for the provision of resources such as e-journals and e-books. In short they recognise the need for us to be visible and relevant to our institutions, and that advocacy is an essential component of their day-to-day work.

Now this is all well and good, but there is a sense that, while all of the above is certainly laudable, it does not necessarily constitute a strategic or planned approach to change, or a 'transformative agenda', as mapped out by Sue McKnight in Facet's *Envisioning Future Academic Library Services* (McKnight 2010). Rather than adhering to a recognised process or model, we librarians are increasingly 'having a go' at a bit of everything, sometimes, rather inevitably, with mixed results. We seem to end up trying to do too much and, as a result, do little of it very well. We also do not have time to evaluate our activities, or to check that they are actually bearing fruit. Moreover, there is a danger that, while offering such a multifaceted service, we ironically fail to remember the user in all of this. Yes, in a broad sense, all of this activity is 'for the user', but when put under the microscope, specific users and their needs may have got lost along the way. Ask yourself the following questions:

- Do you amend every teaching session you give to suit the needs of different user groups?
- Do you segment your marketing efforts to ensure your message hits home with everyone?
- Do you present many and varied opportunities for users to connect with you on a one-to-one basis?
- Do you know the student lifecycle and present an appropriate point-of-need service at each relevant juncture as a result?
- Or does your service more closely resemble a generic approach, whereby some of the mud you fling against the wall sticks, but most of it slides down?

We all know that 'one size does not fit all', but sometimes time, money or occasionally lack of imagination lead us to offer a service suggesting that we have not grasped that fact.

Of course the other huge problem is that more onlookers outside the profession are reaching the conclusion that librarians and libraries have had their day, however scant or flawed the evidence. We are customer focused, our physical space is still important, all information is not available for free on Google, and we do have the IT and design skills to respond to the demands being placed upon us, but all too often the opposite conclusion is reached. Is there anything we can do to turn the tide?

Finally, there is the compelling argument that all we are currently achieving by integrating with today's multiplatform, multimedia age is adding to 'the noise', especially if we are not truly thinking about or targeting our messages and just blogging, facebooking or tweeting in order to climb on the bandwagon.

A New User-centric Model

It was these kinds of questions and concerns that led us to start talking about developing a more user-centric model applicable within academic librarianship that could serve as a foundation for any librarians seeking to maximise their resources and reach and the usage, popularity and understanding of their service. This model would respond to the widespread recognition that in today's world the individual is 'king', has higher expectations of service, expects their voice to be heard and responded to, and is freer than ever to create, access and use information, but would simultaneously play to the skills and outlook of academic librarians and prove their ongoing relevance and value. The elements instinctively led us to draw up a model focusing on personalised and local information delivery to individual users that could be described as highly tailored, unique and reactive. This model could also realistically accept that such an approach is inevitably shaped by how and where the service sits within the context of a wider library system, and the prominence and value of collaborative and centralised elements within that environment. It would, in short, meet the demands of today's users and embrace the components of the modern information world, actively treating them as opportunities rather than threats.

LESSONS FROM THE HOTEL INDUSTRY

Our direct inspiration for this new approach was the concept of the boutique hotel. Although hoteliers have never been under threat in the way that librarians are now, back in the early 1980s they were beginning to recognise that there could be another, far more lucrative, way of meeting customer needs. When forging their new approach they looked to high-end fashion retail and specifically clothing boutiques that prized uniqueness and individuality above uniformity and consistency. Transposing this model to the hotel industry, new hotels began to emerge, first in London and San Francisco and later throughout the world, that embraced a new way of thinking about customers, services and facilities: boutique hotels. Boutique hotels sought to provide a level of service and experience that simply could not be matched by the homogenous Hilton and Radisson hotel chains, by making specific customer needs their number one priority. Boutique hotels by definition seek to be different to each other, but they can generally be characterised by the offering of a seamlessly intuitive and highly personalised service focusing on every detail of a guest's stay. Compelling architecture and design also have an important part to play, with much made of the history of the hotel, the luxurious nature of the environment, or a particular theme reflected in the décor and layout.

One of the best-known examples of a boutique hotel is New York's Library Hotel, which is described in its promotional literature as follows:

> *Fashioned from a landmark 1900 brick and terracotta structure, this boutique treasure has been beautifully restored into a small luxury New York City hotel of the highest caliber. An oasis of modern elegance ... its attentive staff provide a thought-provoking experience to sophisticated leisure and business travellers with a passion for culture and individual expression. (Library Hotel 2011)*

Each of the Library Hotel's ten floors is dedicated to a different class of the Dewey Decimal Classification system, with each hotel room representing a different subdivision of those classes, meaning you can stay in, for example, the Dramatic Literature room (800.004), which has playbills decorating the walls and a bookcase of relevant tomes. This particular boutique hotel has certainly struck a winning formula and was recently voted the Best Luxury Hotel in the US.

Such has been the success of the boutique hotel concept that, as these establishments have become more prominent and widely recognised as profitable, somewhat inevitably the big hotel chains have tried to get in on the act, unveiling upscaled versions of the approach with hotels billed as 'boutique' that nevertheless cater to many guests in the same way, for example the Radisson Blu Edwardian chain.

THE FIRST BOUTIQUE LIBRARIES

Despite the obvious parity with libraries, in respect of putting user needs first, the adoption of boutique by the library sphere took some time; indeed, it has never been fully embraced. It was not until 1999 that the first 'boutique library' opened its doors. This library was the brainchild of Singapore's National Library Board (NLB), who were seeking to reinvigorate their public library services by attempting to make them more relevant and appealing. Having elected to focus upon the specific needs of a specific group of customers following a national reading survey, the result was 'library@orchard' in the city centre, aimed squarely at the young adult market. Initial concerns about catering to just one user group dissipated rapidly due to high usage by, and glowing feedback from, the target customers. 'Library@orchard' was used as a testbed for new products and services, and due to its success the NLB decided to open a second boutique library in 2002, this time with a subject focus on the performing arts: 'library@esplanade'. Following a serious promotional campaign, 'library@ esplanade' saw some 14,000 visitors through its doors on the first day alone! Although 'library@orchard' is currently closed (as the building lease came to an end) there are plans to reopen it, while 'library@esplanade' continues to thrive. As an aside, it seems likely that the NLB partly chose to go with the boutique moniker because the city is synonymous with boutique shopping, with the gleaming Takashimaya mall on the famous Orchard Road being the destination of choice for high-end shoppers.

The world's third boutique library opened in Christchurch, New Zealand in August 2005: the Parklands Boutique Library, which was put together by a team of people who 'worked on every aspect of the library building and service' and sought a space that was 'flexible, adaptive, stimulating and dynamic' (Thompson 2006). This is, and was, a library designed with its different user communities in mind, exemplified by its innovative time zone concept, which is intended to break down traditional library barriers and personalise the times of use. Named zones include: 'Play' (time for preschoolers to be able to make noise); 'Revive' (time for adults to relax and enjoy the quiet environment); 'Breakout' (time for homework help and study support); 'Relax' (time for everyone at the weekends); and 'Connect' (time for specific community groups). Rather than just arbitrarily naming zones, the visionary individuals behind the Parklands project were keen to connect on a personal, even emotional, level with their customers, with a view to offering them an experience as much as a service:

> *Moving to the north end of the building you find yourself in yet another zone, the 'Easy Zone/Te Whanui' (community). Being in this part of the library feels like you are sitting in a magazine spread. With a wonderful outlook onto the sculpture garden it is full of light and warmth ... with warm winds wafting through the enormous wall of opening doors, you can transport yourself. (Thompson 2006)*

One other notable boutique element was an intention to have staff roving, mingling and engaging with customers at all times.

BOUTIQUE AND THE ACADEMIC SECTOR

It is both interesting and surprising that these three highly successful libraries appear on the face of it to be the only libraries to have ever been conferred with the term boutique. Despite one or two scant mentions in library and information literature post 2005, most notably in Dewe's *Planning Public Library Buildings*, in which boutique libraries are cited as a viable alternative to monolithic central libraries and specialised facilities that 'should be housed close to those who would make most us of them' (Dewe 2006: 68), it seems the boutique name just did not catch on. Whether this was because people were uncomfortable with the word or with the approach in general is unclear.

It is perhaps more of a mystery that the terminology did not break through into the academic sector, especially given that it boasts a larger number of specialist subject libraries than the public sector, with unique collections and users with more specific needs. The relevance of 'the boutique approach' to the academic sector was so readily apparent to the authors of this book that their first piece on the subject (Priestner and Tilley 2010) was pitched as a defence of subject librarians, especially as they have become an increasingly threatened breed in recent years (with severe restructuring at Bangor University, swingeing staff cuts at London Business School, and many job losses at London Metropolitan University, to name just three examples). The article also highlights how there have been disappointing trends, following centralisation, towards standardising services in order to make specialist subject libraries generically familiar and appropriate to everyone, rather than celebrating those existing services that embraced a unique, tailored and highly customer-focused approach that was greatly valued by their users. Exploration of such scenarios led to our recognition that the boutique approach could be applied across higher education as it is more about taking a view on service strategy than about the existence of specific collections. The distillation of what we mean by boutique is detailed in Figure 1.1.

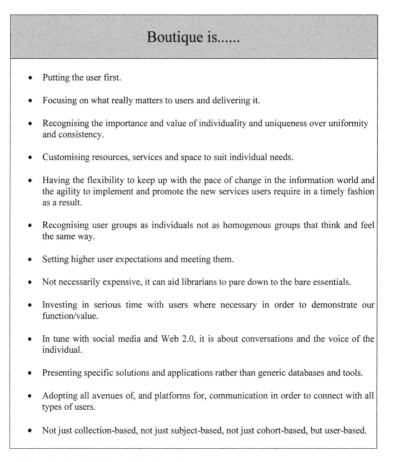

Figure 1.1   A distillation of the boutique approach

MODELS OF LIBRARY SERVICES

The question that many librarians might ask is, why develop a model at all? Do we really need it? Social science methodology follows a typical path by firstly, observing and subsequently identifying, trends and themes in the world around us, and secondly, formulating hypotheses, theories or indeed models against which to further measure other scenarios to establish whether a model is simple enough to be applicable. A model describes observed current practice and, by definition, it is a simplified representation of reality. It could be argued that, by the time models are developed and services benchmarked against it, they merely represent a paradigm shift that has already gone by, and therefore have limited application. However, if the model can be dynamic and practical, as well as descriptive, it provides a convenient mechanism for planning service development.

We feel that the boutique model (Figure 1.2) is a simplistic but clear reproduction of the structure in many academic libraries. Its three component parts are not immovable; they would evolve and change over time and between services. Ultimately, designing a model provides a pragmatic solution for creating a visual representation of the key contributors to a successful boutique library. The underlying emphasis in the boutique service model is that personalised services are crucial for the user. Of vital importance was the need to ensure that application of the concepts across the academic library sector, irrespective of current structures, was possible; in other words, to realistically contextualise boutique within an institutional framework whether part of a federated library service, a large university library or a standalone library.

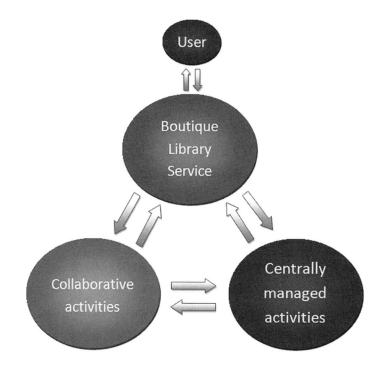

Figure 1.2   The boutique library model

Figure 1.2 shows the original boutique model as first proposed. The model can be interpreted differently without the basics changing. Services will differ from each other in terms of the extent to which they are characterised by boutique, or collaborative or centralised services; there will inevitably be an imbalance in reality between the component parts. Variations will exist depending upon reporting lines, structure and autonomy. An imbalanced model does not mean that a service is wrongly managed or structured; benchmarking your service against the model merely demonstrates the extent to which your service may be skewed in any one of the three directions or whether it is balanced. For example, you may work in a service that is centralised, with little ability on your part for autonomous decision making, but you are able to work collaboratively with colleagues. An analysis of this kind should lead managers to ask questions about their service and consider the impact it is making.

Some aspects of the model may be misunderstood: for example, centralised decisions may be required to approve a personalised approach; there are many centralised services that we could not be without; boutique is not about collections, it is about the service that we offer. This issue and many more were discussed at a national symposium, Personalised Library Services in Higher Education, held in March 2011, and we return to them throughout this book.

The second model we developed expanded upon the personalised nature of the boutique model. Figure 1.3 details what a personalised or boutique service looks like. This model again can be a very useful benchmark against which to measure library services to ascertain the extent to which they are personalised. The model does not assume that services will change necessarily; it merely illustrates typical aspects of a library that had adopted a boutique approach.

The physical representation of the boutique model (Figure 1.2) was challenged at the symposium in 2011 in two ways. Angela Cutts, who has also written a case study for this book, suggested an alternative 'jigsaw' model: this model considered the connections and relationships between the components. It is an alternative that managers of the particular service concerned felt was a more accurate representation of their current practice. Secondly, members of the symposium proposed an alternative position for the user, being convinced that they should be at the centre of the model, therefore demonstrating how the user interfaces with all aspects of service provision. However, we deliberately elected not to position the user at the centre of the model as we firmly believe that the user does not need to see, or understand, the often-complex, behind-the-scenes relationships that exist – the collaborative activities and the centrally managed activities – but instead they need to experience a seamless and excellent front-of-house service. The user *could* be placed in the centre of the model if it makes people feel more comfortable, but the whole point of boutique is putting the user first anyway.

Figure 1.3   Typical components of a boutique, or personalised, library service

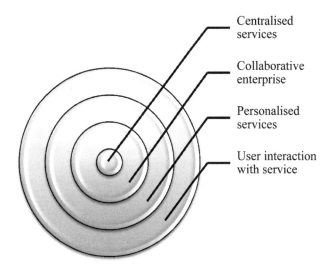

Figure 1.4   Alternative boutique model proposed by Tilley, 2011

Figure 1.4 illustrates a possible variation of the model that we proposed, but one where once again the user would see and experience what is relevant to them, would not be put off by the lack of relevancy of other parts of the service, and would sense that their individual needs were being addressed.

In this model each aspect of service delivery is given equal space and merit. Some element of core centralised services are part and parcel of all academic libraries. The LMS, the catalogue or the discovery system are all intrinsically central to our activities. Collaborative enterprise is something many of us naturally 'do' in our day-to-day lives. You only have to examine the responses to a 'crowdsourcing' query on Twitter to know that there are colleagues out there providing help to each other all the time. More formal collaborative endeavours exist, but many of them are still grassroots activities and work the better for this. As soon as collaboratively focused activities become rooted in bureaucracy, the impetus and enthusiasm behind the activity often fade. This is not to say that collaborative enterprise is essential to the personalised service working at its best – as would be the same for any of the parts of the simplistic alternative model outlined above – but it might make you think about what collaboration is going on in your service and where collaboration might assist with, for example, saving time developing a new technology. Personalised services are of course what we are focusing on in this book and, as we firmly believe that it is this aspect of our service that users find most beneficial, they are naturally placed closest to the user in this model. Users must be the most important aspect and this book will continually emphasise that they are 'king'. We want our users to experience the benefits of our personalised services, as we truly believe that this is what they want or need. But be the judge of this yourselves. As you read this book, bear these models in mind. They will be referred to regularly, as will the component parts of the boutique model, and you might want to work out which elements of the models fit your service the best, or decide whether they will help you transform your library into one fit for those we serve.

In the final analysis, however, perhaps it is best to think of the models as informing a philosophy or approach. This should help us to think about how we are viewing our users and how we are delivering services to them. If our time is spent in knowing our users well and finding out what they need, we can personalise and tailor those very things that in another service would be ignored.

SCOPE OF THIS BOOK

The boutique approach and its potential for application to real academic library services is the focus of the rest of this book. Each chapter considers broad areas of library service where aspects of the approach are most relevant. Contributors address their topics using their own experiences in the area of academic librarianship. In a number of instances they are well regarded as experts in their particular fields. There is an international flavour in the book, with representation from contributors working in Australian, American and Russian library services. The issues explored in each chapter are as follows:

- The core issue of communication is examined by Andy Priestner, who strongly advocates the value of face-to-face contact with library users and of behaving as welcoming hosts rather than salespeople, before going on to detail a wide range of practical personalised communication strategies.
- Library spaces need to reflect the personalised services that we offer, and this can be achieved in many different ways. Beatrice Pulliam considers the impact of the information commons on changes to space in academic libraries in the USA. She compares examples of changes made in two different higher education institutions to boutique principles.
- Can the 'philosophy of boutique' be applied to technology strategy? How personalised can e-delivery be? Tim Wales explores these questions and specifically examines demand-driven e-book acquisition and implementing discovery systems, based on his experiences at Royal Holloway.
- Bespoke teaching approaches are considered by Chris Powis. The learner must be at the heart of the learning experience, and it is this all-important aspect that Chris takes as his starting point before examining the implications of this for teaching in libraries.
- The application of the boutique approach to research activities. Jane Secker considers the relationship of research needs to the development of research activities. She considers how the approach that has been taken within the London School of Economics Centre for Learning Technology, for research skills training, reflects many of the personalised components of the model.
- In her chapter on marketing personalised services, Emma Thompson advises us to get to know our market and to correct assumptions about what we actually offer and do along the way. She encourages experimentation and harnessing in-house talent, and, most importantly, engaging in market research and segmentation with a view to improving our services.
- One of the key criticisms of the boutique library approach is that it costs too much: it is too intensive a user of staff time and resources, and this alone will prevent services from adopting the boutique approach. This is an important aspect to consider in the current economic climate. Elizabeth Tilley looks at a number of the issues that surround the costing of such a service and dispels some of the myths along the way.
- David Streatfield, well known for his work on impact and library services, considers what impact is and how to measure it in a boutique context, an aspect essential to, and at the heart of, any successful library service.
- Finally, we explore how to actually go about implementing and managing a personalised approach. How do you start along this path and what are the practical considerations you need to consider? This chapter also explores

the place of honesty and realism in our services and how librarians could be ideally positioned in the 'Age of the Individual'.

In addition to these chapters there are two sections containing practical case studies showcasing boutique in action in libraries in the UK and beyond, offering ideas for successful application of personalised library services.

We hope that you enjoy this book. We are firm believers in the concept of personalisation as the way forward in libraries today. We are convinced that it is financially manageable and that applying boutique principles could prove to be the lynchpin of a successful service. The £9000 per year student will need to feel cosseted, appreciated and heard; the services that we create, maintain and sustain for them will be essential to our institutions and our survival.

REFERENCES

Dewe, M. 2006. *Planning Public Library Buildings: Concepts and Issues for the Librarian*. Aldershot: Ashgate.

Library Hotel. 2001. Library Hotel Manhattan [online]. At: http://www.libraryhotel. com/ (accessed: 10 September 2011).

McKnight, S. (ed.) 2010. *Envisioning Future Academic Library Services: Initiatives, Ideas and Challenges*. London: Facet.

Priestner, A. and Tilley, E. 2010. Boutique Libraries at Your Service. *Library & Information Update*, 9(6), 36–9.

Prime Minister's Office, Singapore Government. 2004. Excellence at Work: Evolution of the Boutique Library [online]. At: http://www.ps21.gov.sg/ Challenge/2004_01/work/dmg.html (accessed: 20 June 2011).

Thompson, S. 2006. The Parklands Boutique Library Christchurch. *Australasian Public Libraries and Information Services*, June [online]. At: http://findarticles. com/p/articles/mi_hb3315/is_2_19/ai_n29271283/ (accessed: 20 May 2011).

CHAPTER 2

FACE-TO-FACE VALUE: PERSONALISED COMMUNICATION STRATEGIES
ANDY PRIESTNER

> *Everyone wants to be treated as an individual.*
>
> Jan Carlzon, Scandinavian Airlines

Personalising library services and, more specifically, personalising communications with our library users, is often misconceived as basic activities like adding student names to library induction packs or mail-merging email messages to specific individuals, but it can and should mean much more than that. Approached imaginatively it has the opportunity to be a holistic approach to your entire service, a strategy that prioritises user needs and personal experience of information and library provision above all other concerns.

The arrival of email and the internet in libraries in the early 1990s and their subsequent wholesale adoption to a point at which we can now barely remember what it was like to run libraries without them, has provided librarians with numerous opportunities and challenges. However, one of the barely examined downsides has been our increasing failure to consider our users as individuals, with a marked decrease in face-to-face or personal communication. How often do we sit apart from our users in out-of-sight workrooms and offices sending out generic email after generic email about our services, resources and training sessions, kidding ourselves that they are: (a) being read, and, even less likely, (b) being understood? Not that the print and CD-ROM world of the pre-1990s constituted the glory days of librarianship, far from it, but back then at least we had one crucial thing that many of us do not have now: direct connection with all of our users (although it should be remembered that this connection was largely prompted by the fact that users had no choice but to come to us, as at that time we were only able to offer *in situ* resources).

In today's online world, information can be communicated as text, audio, images or video; however, none of these formats is as rich or productive as face-to-face communication (Nicholas and Rowlands 2008: 97). Face-to-face communication will always have the edge over online communication as it allows us to convey information both verbally and non-verbally.

Examining the mechanics of the face-to-face communication process in detail, we can identify that when individuals converse in this way the exchange incorporates a *transmitter* (who frames and sends the message) and a *receiver* (the person who receives and interprets the message). The information that the transmitter chooses to 'send' is coloured by their personal motivations, objectives, traits, values and prejudices. This is termed *perceptual filtering*. The receiver does their own perceptual filtering when interpreting the message. This process, which can be further complicated by physical, social and cultural factors, inevitably leads different people to receive and interpret the same message in a completely different way. However, there is the opportunity in a face-to-face context to enhance or reinforce meaning through verbal and non-verbal cues such as intonation, facial expressions, posture and eye contact. There is also the opportunity to check understanding through feedback mechanisms such as head-nodding, restatement and summary. When broken down and examined in these component forms and processes, as well as standing out as the richest of our communication channels this face-to-face medium is also revealed to be multilayered, complex and, most of all, versatile.

So what happens when communication takes place in an online setting, then, say by email? Naturally, the message is immediately denuded of many of its component elements, including all the non-verbal cues (or clues), and both transmitter and receiver are constrained by a context that can only take away from, rather than promote understanding of, the communication taking place. When current sociocultural trends are added into the mix, such as the tendency to scan rather than read, decreased attention spans, the prevalence of text-speak, and inboxes that are fuller than ever, it is something of a wonder that any meaningful communication takes place at all via this medium.

However, it would be wrong to dismiss online communication wholesale, as some research has shown that during a meeting of two individuals online 'hyper-personal' bonds can sometimes be established, whereby individuals might establish strong connections with each other, for example by asking more direct questions than might occur in a face-to-face setting (Tidwell and Walther 2002: 319–20). In general, though, unlike online communication, the face-to-face approach allows individuals to transmit information with the least ambiguity possible and with the added benefits of immediacy, emotional content and instant feedback. Most importantly this personal contact offers the opportunity for a personal and positive impact that, more often than not, guarantees true understanding and engagement.

Is this chapter a call to arms, then, with a view to a Luddite-style revolution in which we throw our PCs out of our office windows (should we be lucky enough to have a window)? Well, yes and no. The internet has given us far more than it has taken away, but the fact is that in our twenty-first century information and library services it has arguably made us lazy. Not lazy in terms of our intention to offer

customer-centric services to our users that are genuinely relevant to their needs –
99 per cent of librarians would surely cite this as their avowed intent – but rather in
terms of the communication channels we have adopted to get this message across,
specifically over the last decade.

We offer brilliantly planned training sessions that are poorly attended because they
have only been advertised by email (that would be brilliantly executed too if we
only had an audience to attend them). We prepare intricate information literacy or
database tutorials and after uploading links to them on our websites are surprised
when no one uses them (regrettably some of us do not even check that they are
being used). We create Facebook groups in order to jump on the social media
bandwagon and populate the wall with dull robotic service announcements and are
surprised when only 27 people 'like' us.

All too often we are guilty of selling ourselves short by not taking enough time to
consider the best ways of communicating our offering to our users. Too often we
take the 'hit and hope' approach, despite the fact that we know full well that an
'all-students' email or a tired newsletter is not going to have the impact we need
it too. Too often we fail to be realistic about what will be read. And too often this
can mean that the activities in which we are engaged are not valued, or worse still,
because of our disconnection from our users, not valuable. An increasingly obvious
alternative is for us to make a fundamental shift away from the generic to the
personal, towards a service that actively embraces face-to-face communications
and a personalised mindset as a primary objective or mission.

LESSONS FROM OTHER INDUSTRIES

In his bestselling business book *Moments of Truth*, then president of Scandinavian
Airlines (SAS) Jan Carlzon outlined just how important personalised
communications were to his business, believing that to become a truly customer-
driven company you need to be a 'company that recognises that its only true assets
are satisfied customers, all of whom expect to be treated as individuals' (1987: 2).
Throughout his book he cites examples of his employees going the extra mile to
provide excellent personalised service to SAS customers (for example, by ensuring
the availability of specific dietary meals or reuniting them with tickets left in hotel
rooms). He terms these instances in which the customers receive the kind of superior
service that they will likely never forget as 'moments of truth':

> *Last year each of our 10 million customers came in contact with approximately
> five SAS employees. Thus, SAS is 'created' 50 million times a year, 15
> seconds at a time. These 50 million 'moments of truth' are the moments that
> ultimately determined whether SAS will succeed or fail as a company. They*

> *are the moments when we must prove to our customers that SAS is their best*
> *alternative. (Carlzon 1987: 2–3)*

Are we creating enough moments of truth? Are we a better alternative to Google? Are we genuinely connecting with our users, and if not, how can we engender more opportunities for moments of truth to occur?

Jonathan Tisch, CEO of Loews Hotels, in *Chocolates on the Pillow Aren't Enough*, also describes the importance of personalised communications to the success of his business:

> *In our industry, the key to attracting lifelong patrons is transforming*
> *customers into guests. This means that the hotel and all who work for it must*
> *behave not like salespeople but like hosts, with all the human qualities that*
> *implies – warmth, openness, generosity, welcome. And any organization that*
> *can capture this spirit, no matter what the industry, will create a growing body*
> *of loyal and appreciative patrons. (Tisch and Weber 2007: 44)*

Is this not exactly the sort of spirit we need to embrace in libraries today? We are all guilty, to a greater or lesser degree, of flogging products and services in the classroom as if we were salespeople. And sometimes this desperation to encourage awareness of the value of our resources and to ensure that products are used can be at the expense of real user needs. Put simply, we are finding ourselves engaged in more selling than hosting.

The Club Med (not to be confused with Club 18–30) holiday company model is another interesting and relevant example. Club Med's organisers, known as *gentil organisateurs* (or GOs), are on first-name terms with their guests, encourage them to divulge their opinions, have the autonomy to offer exceptional service, and treat each and every customer as an individual: each 'is a person with a character and a physical presence which can be described and identified.' What is more, GOs are never considered to be off duty and are always available for each guest 'to help them, play with them, or party with them.' Club Med cite the principal advantage of this individualised approach as a way of ensuring that changes to improve services can occur rapidly: 'the closer the GOs are to the guests, the better they can evaluate their needs and expectations in terms of service, and the quicker they can adapt the service to meet those expectations' (Horovitz and Panak 1992: 5–6). Another model we can seek to emulate?

CAN, AND SHOULD, WE GO PERSONALISED?

Five years ago I gave a presentation at a day-long workshop for PhDs at the University of Oxford that chiefly sought to reveal to them how much more information support and advice we could offer than they were actually asking for. At one point, the 50 or so attendees (who by virtue of their attendance at the event must already have been somewhat open to the prospect of library support) were asked who they currently went to for advice on the resources they should use for their research, using voting pads for their responses. No prizes for guessing that 'their friends' topped the list, while academics were second. Library staff came in a depressing fifth out of the six available categories, and sixth place was 'other'! The librarians present could not have received a stronger message that change was needed and during the informal event debrief there was recognition that we simply did not talk to PhDs enough or understand their needs, which were, on the whole, surprisingly basic. There was no question at all that we had the knowledge they needed; the problem was, and still is, the channels of communication used and our generic approaches to them as a discrete user group. It seemed obvious to us then that changing these channels and focusing on their specific needs was the only way of getting us higher up their hit list.

The most frequently levelled argument against 'going personalised' is the cost involved of all of this face-to-face time. One obvious response is to question the cost to us if we do not. Would we still have a service or staff at the level currently resourced if we continue as we are, namely underestimated, misunderstood and marginalised?

Another rejoinder is consideration of the overall value to any service of personalised activities. To use two specific examples, what benefits the library service more –

- Three hours spent with a faculty member in their office advising them on use of bibliographic software (which might feasibly create a library champion as a by-product of this training), or three hours spent reclassifying stock?
- Ten minutes talking to a student in a corridor about which database to use (which they might conceivably tell their friends about); or ten minutes' work on a user guide detailing changes to the library catalogue that might take as long as a day to complete in total (and which might never be read)?

The value and rewards reaped from face-to-face communication in terms of subsequent word-of-mouth recommendation and resultant service reputation are so startlingly obvious that it is a wonder that we spend as much time sitting in our libraries as we do. This is not to say that effective personalised communication cannot take place in our libraries, but that we must not forget that this is communication with established library users, people who by paying a visit to our territory are already accepting that we are the 'go-to guys' when they need help. What of those who never visit and underestimate our value? Should we be more actively seeking to connect with them in person?

What, though, of the small team or solo librarian? Once again this comes down to prioritising our activities. Would they be better employed engaging in face-to-face interactions beyond the library walls, rather than waiting for users to come to them? And who is to say this should not be most of their time? After all, plenty of libraries are now open to users for long periods without staff, with negligible security issues affecting stock or equipment, while self-service lending is now an accepted standard.

PRACTICAL PERSONALISED COMMUNICATION APPROACHES

If we accept that we do have to change and embrace personalised communication and that it is indeed time well spent, however big or small our team, how then do we make opportunities to connect in this way? Thankfully there are numerous approaches open to us and therefore little excuse for clinging to those safe but ultimately ineffectual generic communication methods that unfortunately seem to have become second nature to us.

Enquiry Points or 'Outposts' outside the Library

Situating yourself outside your library, preferably in a busy area, heavily populated by students and staff alike, can help you to reach those people who rarely or never visit the library. Positioning such temporary enquiry points near cafeterias or lecture rooms can also help you reach those people who would visit the library more (say at lunchtimes/breaks) if only it were nearer. All you need at this 'library outpost' is a seat, a small table, a sign and a laptop, but much more important than this meagre equipment is an engaged staff member, willing to make conversation and to connect with those who need the library's help. While this approach will undoubtedly yield enquiries at this outpost, just as important is the impression of commitment to customer service it makes, encouraging greater use of our assistance at the outpost, in the library, by email or other channels.

One-to-One Consultations

Offering one-to-one consultations with a view to better understanding and meeting information needs is a great foundation for a long-term and fruitful relationship between the subject and the library, albeit an option probably best to explore with academics, researchers and postgraduates rather than undergraduates (who are likely be intimidated by such concentrated attention). This sort of consultation should be viewed not only as an opportunity for the subject to express their needs but equally valid for library staff to advise them of relevant resources and services that would assist them in their research life. The desired, and somewhat inevitable, result is that the subject leaves the consultation replete with many more useful tools and ideas than they bargained for and, just as importantly, a deeper understanding of what it is we do. Although it is perfectly acceptable to offer such consultations by email, it is important that we recognise that for the best results we must try other routes as well and that might include promoting the opportunity in user groups or other appropriate meetings, through newsletters or blog posts or, perhaps best of all, volunteering a consultation in person.

Usability Testing

Inviting users to evaluate library websites, blogs or tools (preferably on neutral rather than library territory) is another excellent way of connecting with your users. As well as establishing user evaluation of a product, and therefore user need, it is of course possible (and sensible) to use the same opportunity to gather details of their more general information behaviour and service likes and dislikes. As well as engendering user buy-in to the product undergoing testing, the fact that their opinion is being sought also establishes a positive connection with your service. An incentive of some kind is normally required to lure attendees to sign up. Usability testing and focus groups (further below) are perfect opportunities to observe the 'Franklin Effect' in operation, the well-documented phenomenon whereby asking others to do you a favour leads them to be more positively predisposed to you in future.

Door Knocking

One of the most obvious means of engaging in face-to-face communication with academics and researchers is simply to go door-knocking. While this approach rarely results in an impromptu training session or consultation there and then, it nevertheless reminds those approached that we are available to help them and more than willing to visit them in their offices. Follow-ups from door-knocking exercises can be gratifyingly high. It is worth remembering that some academics are unwilling to openly volunteer their research shortcomings and, as a result, are keen to receive assistance in the privacy of their offices. Time of academic year, and of day, are also worth bearing in mind. Everyone is looking for a distraction at 4pm, so why not make ourselves that distraction?

Focus Groups

An obvious alternative to product-specific usability testing is a focus group on particular aspects of your library service. Once again the lure of a free lunch or a gift is a must. A focus group could be used to: establish opinion on your social media channels; assess how much of your service should be offered via mobile technology; or reveal what elements of your service are most valued. In order to ensure that this is a true personalised experience for attendees it is important that the focus group is not too large and that it is run in such a way that everyone has their say (and no one gets a free lunch without contributing!). It is also vital that, after the focus group, action is taken to make it clear that the contribution of attendees was listened to. Contact the participants individually by email, firstly to thank them and later to inform them of focus group outcomes. However, be mindful that there is little point in holding a focus group if you have no intention of implementing the ideas and suggestions that arise from it.

Library Surveys

Although user surveys can be incredibly valuable we librarians rely on them too much and often in preference to more direct communication approaches that could prove more illuminating. Surveys offer little opportunity for open and free feedback, and free text boxes on a survey are a poor substitute for asking open questions in person. Surveys are also inevitably skewed, as they are largely completed by library-friendly users. And worst of all, some of us distribute the same surveys every year and make little effort to act on the feedback received, usually because we think we know better and/or think the user does not understand why things have to be the way they are. As a wise library consultant once said, 'do less surveys and do more with the findings' (Chalmers, Liedtka and Bednar 2006: 191). This is particularly good advice if you choose to personalise your library survey process. After the survey end date simply invite a sample of those who have completed the survey to a one-to-one meeting to ask for additional contributions, but make it clear that they are not being invited to a 'telling off'! If you want to take this approach you will have to make sure that your survey is anonymous or ask respondents to enter their name if they are willing to be questioned further in person. You might be surprised as to just how many users are willing to contribute in this more direct manner.

Inductions

Best practice for start-of-year student inductions merits an entire book in its own right, but a great starting point is simply to make sure the session has interactive elements, such as discussion and group work to make it clear that you are interested in conversation and feedback. Standing up and talking to a screen for an hour as you demonstrate the catalogue and go through the library rules is a surefire way of alienating your new students. A freer format that seeks to engage attention and flag up our relevance is going to have more long-term value than an attempt to explain absolutely everything about your service in one go. Although the term induction almost exclusively makes us think of what we offer students alone, it is important that we do not underestimate the importance of inductions with new academics, researchers and staff as they join our institution. Ask your HR staff to automatically book a time for you with the new starter, preferably scheduled to take place in their office. This will offer the opportunity for you to demonstrate access to library resources remotely to iron out any local technical difficulties. This is a good idea as realistically this is how users will predominantly access your resources, and besides it demonstrates the library's presence and commitment outside of its physical environs. By all means offer a friendly one-to-one tour of the library as well, as it is likely to provoke some extra questions, but psychologically it is better to start on their territory rather than our own. A personalised induction of this type makes a great first impression.

Research Seminars

It is important that library staff emphasise their relevance to, and connection with, the research taking place at their institution. Attending research seminars, lunches or receptions provides an opportunity to speak to researchers face to face, contribute informed opinions and generally get to know your local research community. Who knows, your presence may even lead to collaborative research in which the library is a contributor or even partner.

A Library Film/Film Clips

The best library films are those to which users directly contribute with their opinions on your service. Naturally, peer recommendations are far more influential than anything we librarians might choose to say. In 2009 University of Warwick library staff handed over a video camera to a group of students and asked them to record their thoughts on the library there. The end result needed very little editing, feels entirely honest, and best of all required very little staff time to produce. The students were pleased to be asked to take part and several 'library champions' were created right there and then (University of Warwick 2009). This is the 'Franklin Effect' in operation again. At my own institution we recorded clips of students talking about the service to show to new students at their inductions and the response to these initial peer recommendations was similarly favourable.

Library Reps and Committees

Most courses nominate a library rep to stand on a staff–student library committee or similar. It is a good idea to arrange to meet these reps one to one early on in the academic year to make sure they know that their opinions are genuinely welcomed and that suggestions will be acted upon, but also to gently make sure they understand that they should act as a conduit for their classmates (some reps might not recognise this). If this meeting goes well then you have a readymade route into that course during the year. There is a danger that user committees can become unnecessarily formal. You should try to make such meetings as relaxed as possible, preferably with some refreshments. If the meeting is not welcoming enough, your reps may not return. It is also important that the time they give to this pursuit is verbally acknowledged during the meeting and that their contributions start the meeting rather than your own library update. After the meeting, it is worth: personally checking with your reps that they felt as though their voice was heard; clarifying anything that might have been confusing; and thanking them for coming. Of course, timely post-meeting action and updates to the reps (preferably prior to the next meeting) are crucial to the success of these relationships.

Ethnographic Research Interviews

Ethnography is an anthropological term for the examination of individual human societies, while ethnographers themselves research culture and behaviour from within those societies by engaging in 'participant observation'. While we cannot, and perhaps would not, wish to live among students again (!) we can usefully adopt ethnographic-style research in order to reach a better understanding of the pressures and problems they face. By approaching students in the common areas/library cafés we can ask them for their off-the-cuff opinions, via mini consumer research-style interviews (armed with a clipboard if you like), as to the library support they receive and identify areas where there is a gap between their expectations and our service. It is important that such exchanges value the student perspective and do not try to impose too much library structure or bias, and that reporting does not distort the views that are gathered, otherwise the purpose of this type of research is rather undermined. The best ethnographic interview would involve as much observing and listening as interviewing. It may be more appropriate for less threatening junior staff to conduct this activity or to employ – properly briefed – students to do this on the library's behalf.

Embedded Librarians

Embedded librarians fit neatly within this ethnographic approach and are now standard posts within US library services. In most cases the term embedded librarian refers exclusively to a staff member's online presence in a VLE or similar course management system where they are ready and waiting to assist their users: 'research action no longer swirls around neither the reference desk nor the library website, but in students' online learning space' (Tumbleson and Burke 2010: 974). Some of these embedded librarians never meet their students in person and are, in effect, entirely virtual librarians (see Margaret Westbury's case study), while others are embedded in both an online and face-to-face sense, offering one-to-one support, training sessions and an initial induction as the designated librarian for that course, as well as providing support via course platforms. The latter have the opportunity to employ a suite of personalised approaches and are positioned in such a way as to reach significant and valuable ethnographic understanding of the students under their care. Examination of the characteristics of course participants is vital (a form of market segmentation) before services are rolled out, and this can easily be achieved by engaging in dialogue with the relevant course administrators, lecturers, directors and, of course, students. The embedded approach has obvious potential for considerable collaboration, integration and innovation (Heider 2010: 119). At my current workplace I have elected to designate our six-strong team of professional and para-professional staff as embedded librarians across the school's programs for the 2011/12 academic year with the above pay-offs clearly in mind, and we are already reaping many dividends. It is worth noting that rather than using the term 'embedded librarians' here I have used the term 'designated support librarians' in order that students and staff can better understand what we were talking about from the off.

Reporting

While a library's annual report can never be personalised as such, the reporting of its contents – statistics, achievements, developments – should be, and much more frequently than once per year. The golden rule here is, do not wait to be asked for statistics on usage: gather them as a matter of course on anything that moves (and some things that do not) as you should be constantly using them both to secure your service financially and to advance your offering. Once you have them at your disposal make sure you 'bring them alive' before you present them to your stakeholders by analysing them and deriving trends, opportunities and failures. Everyone knows that you can use statistics to prove anything – no people more so than those who hold the purse-strings at your institution – so do not try to massage them. If a database or service is not getting enough usage, it has not earned its place and needs to go. You should be actively seeking opportunities to report these statistical findings at formal meetings, research events, the library committee/user group and meetings with your manager, but you need to do so accessibly and in a way that makes an impact on the audience in question by tailoring the content each time, just as you would a CV for an interview.

Communications with... Your Manager

One of the most important recipients of your personalised communications is, of course, your manager, especially if they are not a librarian themselves. It is important that you ensure that the content of your meetings with them focuses on what they need to know, not on every aspect of your management of the service. For instance, they may not really need to know that you are holding a booksale or deleting some grey literature – that is, after all, why they employed you (unless they are interested, in which case you can afford to put some meat on the bones). Describe developments, opportunities and projects, detail successes and failures and staffing issues, but most importantly of all prove to them that you can manage your budget and present solid statistically backed cases for more funds as and when you need to. Your relationship with your manager should be different to your relationship with anyone else in your organisation, so it is vital that you tailor your communication with them accordingly. It is the very essence of personalised communication to make the message right for one individual, so it should take you some time, and lots of keen observation of and listening to your manager, before you get this right.

Communications with... Your Team

It is all very well instituting approaches like those detailed above, but if you have disengaged individuals on your team who are not customer oriented then you need to spend significant time communicating with them before you 'let them loose' on your users. There are very few truly poor employees out there and the majority who are perceived as such are, more often than not, disenfranchised or misunderstood rather than difficult. Communication with your team members on a one-to-one basis, in order to learn about their frustrations, hopes and fears, and likes and dislikes, is the key to turning this around. Although you will find this experience time consuming and occasionally find their issues difficult to understand, if you do not invest time in them or put yourself in their position, you cannot hope to make progress. What most unhappy staff members are seeking is recognition, responsibility and variety, and empowering them to engage in personalised communications with your users, whether it be via enquiry points, focus groups or interviews, should tick all those boxes. Naturally you will need to communicate the aims and objectives of such approaches clearly as well as laying down some behavioural and practical ground rules, but you also need to allow staff members to feel their own way and have the freedom to make some decisions alone. You might choose to exercise your judgement as to which staff are better suited to certain activities, but remember it is very easy to underestimate team members, especially when the task is something they have not tried before. Just like your users, they will surprise you.

Not so much a Programme, more a Way of Life

The idea of always being 'on' (like those Club Med reps) is part and parcel of embracing the personalised approach and indeed the role of the advocate librarian. You need to be identifying and taking opportunities to engage in face-to-face communications throughout your working day in every environment and situation you find yourself in, and tailoring your message to groups and individuals accordingly, depending on their expectations and needs. Of course to do this well you need an intimate knowledge of your user population, and the only way of building this is to communicate with them. To communicate better, you need to communicate more.

PERSONALISING SOCIAL MEDIA

Although it is undoubtedly the route to the most fruitful results, a personalised communication strategy should not be constrained to face-to-face meetings alone. In fact there are many ways that we can personalise our message more in everything we do. A good example – which could be extrapolated to other non-face-to-face components of any service – is our approach to social media channels. When social media came along, it was hardly surprising that, after years of characterless email correspondence, many librarians simply transferred their impersonal and overtly formal communication style directly to these platforms and were surprised to discover that this approach got them nowhere. Soulless service or resource updates that could have conceivably been added by a robot do not an engaging Facebook wall or Twitter account make. What is often missing is personality. Only from this can true connection and dialogue spring. It may be time efficient to update Facebook and Twitter from Hootsuite, but it will not win you followers. For some engaging personalised Facebook walls (2011) check out:

- Jerwood Library Trinity Hall,
- Selwyn College Library,
- and, naturally, Judge Business School Library Services.

Library service blogs also have a tendency to be discouragingly flat. Social media is all about expressing your voice so your blog absolutely needs to have one too. Bloggers agree that the most engaging posts are written in an active voice in jargon-free plain English, as if talking to a friend, and are composed of short readable paragraphs with a compelling opening. There is an awful lot more to penning good blog posts than these basic elements, but they make for a useful start. The key is simply to invest your writing with warmth and character.

The stark fact that we librarians are not currently succeeding when it comes to social media can be derived from the fact that, during a four-hour discussion about researchers' use of these channels, conducted by Emerald for a recent report, librarians were not mentioned once. Our provision of workshops on using Twitter for research would be an obvious way of addressing this.

IDENTIFYING CHAMPIONS

One of the best outcomes of personalised communication is the creation of library influencers or champions who are so excited and impressed by what you are doing, that without prompting they will advocate on behalf of your service with other institutional stakeholders. By adopting some of the practical face-to-face communication approaches detailed above, champions should be a natural by-product. The 'Ladder of Loyalty' model (Figure 2.1), first conceived and developed by relationship marketers, is a useful way of thinking about the effect that our connections can have on those we come into contact with, and how they might change in relation to us as a result over time (Barber and Wallace 2010: 9).

CHAMPIONS

CLIENTS

CUSTOMERS

PROSPECTS

SUSPECTS

Figure 2.1   The ladder of loyalty

SCHMOOZING

Like it or not, face-to-face communication does come down to being prepared to schmooze: to notice people, connect with people and thereafter stay in touch with them. But how do you feel when you read the word?

> *Maybe it sounds smug, unctuous, oily, slimy. It sounds frankly, like 'oozing'. Schmoozing is far from slimy, but 'oozing' actually isn't a bad description of what a schmoozer does. A schmoozer slides into opportunities where none are apparent, developing friendships from the slightest of acquaintances. Through formless, oozy, schmoozy action, a schmoozer moves slowly but inexorably towards his or her goals. (Lerner et al. 2002: 7)*

Making communication for personal or, indeed, service gain does not sit comfortably with us librarians, perhaps because we have always been confident that what we have to offer speaks for itself. Unfortunately in today's multiplatform multimedia environment we face a great deal more competition than we once did and letting the service speak for itself can leave it ignored and misunderstood. By schmoozing – sliding ourselves into opportunities and building relationships within our institutions – we have the potential to open our service up to a wider engaged audience sold on the benefits and relevance of what we have to offer. Yes, it requires confidence, and no, it might not come as second nature to us, but schmoozing, or networking, its duller, more gauche cousin, is the key to getting our services on the radar.

On the 'M' Word Marketing blog Kathy Dempsey recently mused about the need for librarians to embrace schmoozing and referenced an influential New Jersey library director:

> *Joe is a soft spoken man with an easy going personality. When this guy walks through his town, he knows just about everyone he sees. And they know him. Why? Because he has spent years building relationships. Before budget cuts started hitting his library hard, he invited influential community members to form an advocacy committee. They volunteered. He's on his way to ensuring a voice for his library will be at the table when budgets are being discussed. (The 'M' Word – Marketing Libraries 2011)*

This is an important reminder that schmoozing does not necessarily mean the 'hard sell'; more than anything else, it is about making and maintaining connections. Kathy's example is also a reminder that we need to ensure we schmooze enough in these financially straitened times in order to have readymade advocates fighting our corner. Schmoozing is not a dirty word; in fact, it could be a means of ensuring our survival.

LISTENING

It is very easy to forget that listening is a fundamental part of face-to-face communication. If we do not spend time listening to our customers, and finding out about their needs rather than second guessing them ourselves, the service we provide can never fully hit the mark. In the same way, for the strategies detailed above to be successful, they require equal amounts of receiving and transmitting.

It is very difficult for us librarians not to assert that we know what is best for our users, which is perhaps why we transmit, or broadcast, so much, but the bottom line is that we need to listen to our consumers more and respond accordingly, even if we do not particularly like what they are saying. Sticking our head in the sand, ostrich like, or upbraiding users for not using our resources properly or at all, is never going to increase engagement. The information is out there if we would only gather it by taking the time to listen.

It is also worth noting that listening is not a passive state. Good listeners, either consciously or subconsciously, do some or all of the following: make extensive eye contact to ensure the speaker knows they are being understood; nod and smile to show their interest; offer minimal verbal responses along the lines of 'Oh really?'

or 'I'm with you'; and after the speaker has finished, ask questions demonstrating that what they have been saying has been understood and assimilated.

Many people happily volunteer that they are hopeless at small talk, but this is partly because they incorrectly think it is their role in these situations to fill the conversation void, rather than starting a conversation, for example, about how someone else is thinking or feeling. A good 50 per cent of a conversation should be about us listening, if not more. The more we take interest in someone else, the more able we are to understand them and make a connection with them again in the future.

In *How to Win Friends and Influence People*, Dale Carnegie famously states: 'You can make more friends in two months by becoming interested in other people than you can in two years by trying to get other people interested in you' (1981: 52). This eloquently sums up the approach we need to take if we are going to build fruitful relationships with our users and create those much-needed library champions.

IMPRESSION MANAGEMENT

If we are going to be engaged in more face-to-face outreach, there is a strong argument that we also need to pay more attention to how we are perceived by our users when we interact with them. The sociopsychological theory of 'Impression Management', which examines the potential for having greater control of, and influence over, social interactions, may help us in this regard.

Impression Management, or IM, was first coined by Erving Goffman, who explored the motivations behind the way humans chose to present themselves in a social setting, using the metaphor of a play to further his ideas. In response to Shakespeare's famous line from *As You Like It*, 'All the world's a stage, / And all the men and women merely players', Goffman stated, 'All the world is not, of course, a stage, but the crucial ways in which it isn't are not easy to specify' (1959: 72). Goffman sought to tease out when and why we choose to perform and the fact that we may not always be presenting our true selves. Goffman's theories recognise our conscious or subconscious attempt to make a particular impression or encourage a certain perception with a view to influencing behaviour by virtue of what we say, what we do, non-verbal communication, and what we wear. By choosing to control and become more aware of the signals we send and receive, we are engaging in Impression Management.

IM is not without its detractors. Some argue that it is nothing short of manipulation, refusing to accept its validity and stating that it reduces trust and generates suspicion. Others, however, see IM 'as no more than an extension of an understanding of how others see us [that] causes interactions to run more smoothly' (Roberts and Rowley 2008: 39). As we librarians are regularly and consistently underestimated and misunderstood, more active recognition of how our actions and words are expressed, through conscious impression management, can only serve to enhance our message.

BACK TO THE BOUTIQUE MODEL

As with all other activities, communication approaches can be improved if the three components of the model – boutique, collaboration and centralisation – are in appropriate balance.

Successful personalised communication is very 'boutique' as it requires a unique and highly tailored approach that recognises the importance of interactions with individuals. Ideally it requires knowledge of users if not by name then certainly of what they are likely to need due to the demands of the particular course of study they are following.

Collaboration with other library staff, both within and without your institution, is vital if this sort of personalised approach is to be pulled off. This can ensure wheels are not being unnecessarily reinvented and the same mistakes are not re-enacted with modifications that are appropriate to our specific users. Through sharing of experience and working together we can devise better ways forward. Having said that, we librarians have a tendency to gather all the available evidence before trying something new, and while collaboration definitely has its place sometimes it is better to go out and, to borrow from Nike, 'Just Do It'.

Although personalised communication approaches do not have to be expensive to implement and are eminently achievable as a centralised strategy – provided there is a will at a senior level to take a significant change of approach – they are more likely to emerge at a grassroots level among separate autonomous libraries and librarians simply because they require agility, flexibility and, most importantly, direct contact with academics, students and staff who are not necessarily established library users.

CONCLUSION

In essence we need to become more adept at personalising our communications. Continuing to blithely do 'business as usual' – broadcasting generic messages, as we have done for the past decade – is a sure path to obsolescence. It is time we dropped the generic in favour of the specific and sought to tailor our communication to individuals to ensure that our relevance and value is understood at such a crucial point in the profession's timeline.

TOP TIPS

- Stop sending as many generic emails to your library users. Now!
- Set up a library 'outpost' to improve service visibility.
- Actively offer and promote the availability of *one-to-one* consultations with your users.
- Invite users to take part in usability testing and focus groups, and feedback to them later.
- Go door-knocking outside the library.
- Institute follow-up consultations after library surveys to source more qualitative information.
- Make sure that start-of-year inductions are interactive and that you converse with the audience.
- Connect with institutional research and researchers.
- Arrange inductions with new staff and faculty that take place in their offices.
- Have students create a library film or record student testimonials.
- Connect with library reps in person and value their contributions.
- Consider employing an ethnographic research approach.
- Embrace an embedded or 'designated support' librarian initiative.
- Record statistics meticulously and bring them 'alive' when defending your services.
- Personalise communications with your boss.
- Invest in your team by offering them significant communication responsibilities.
- Ensure your social media channels have character and voice.
- Consider how you and your service are perceived and let it inform your approach.
- Do not assume you know what your users want – actively listen to them.
- Embrace all opportunities for communication, 'schmooze', make and maintain connections.
- Communicate better by communicating more.
- Match your message to your user group.
- Talk less, listen more.

REFERENCES

Barber, P. and Wallace, L. 2010. *Building a Buzz: Libraries and Word-of-Mouth Marketing*. Chicago, IL: ALA.

Carlzon, J. 1987. *Moments of Truth: New Strategies for Today's Customer-Driven Economy*. Cambridge, MA: Ballinger.

Carnegie, D. 1981. *How to Win Friends and Influence People*, rev. edn. New York: Pocket Books.

Chalmers, M., Liedtka, T. and Bednar, C. 2006. A Library Communication Audit for the Twenty-First Century. *Portal: Libraries and the Academy*, 6(2), 185–95.

Goffman, E. 1959. *The Presentation of Self in Everyday Life*. New York: Anchor.

Heider, K.L. 2010. Ten Tips for Implementing a Successful Embedded Librarian Program. *Public Services Quarterly*, 6(2/3), 110–21.

Horovitz, J. and Panak, M.J. 1992. *Total Customer Satisfaction: Lessons from 50 European Companies with Top Quality Service*. London: Pitman.

Jerwood Library, Trinity Hall. 2011. Facebook Group, Facebook [online]. At: http://on.fb.me/vVdwbf (accessed: 20 June 2011).

Judge Business School Library Services. 2011. Facebook Group, Facebook [online]. At: http://on.fb.me/s1OPvu (accessed: 20 June 2011).

Lerner, M., et al. 2002. *Vault Guide to Schmoozing*. New York: Vault.

Nicholas, D. and Rowlands, I. (eds) 2008. *Digital Consumers: Reshaping the Information Profession*. London: Facet.

Roberts, S. and Rowley, J. 2008. *Leadership: The Challenge for the Information Profession*. London: Facet.

Selwyn College Library. 2011. Facebook Group, Facebook [online]. At: http://on.fb.me/vhvfvi (accessed: 20 June 2011).

The 'M' Word – Marketing Libraries. 2011. *Six Principles of Influence* [online]. At: http://themwordblog.blogspot.com/2011/06/six-principles-of-influence.html (accessed: 20 June 2011).

Tidwell, L. and Walther, J.B. 2002. Computer-Mediated Communication Effects on Disclosure, Impressions, and Interpersonal Evaluations: Getting to Know One Another a Bit at a Time. *Human Communication Research*, 28(3), 317–48.

Tisch, J. and Weber, K. 2007. *Chocolates on the Pillow Aren't Enough: Reinventing the Customer Experience*. Hoboken, NJ: John Wiley.

Tumbleson, B.E. and Burke, J.J. 2010. When Life Hands You Lemons: Overcoming Obstacles to Expand Services in an Embedded Librarian Program, *Journal of Library Administration*, 50(7/8), 972–88.

University of Warwick. 2011. Student Perspective of the Library [online]. At: http://www.youtube.com/watch?v=LJxbnZ9yR0o&feature=youtu.be (accessed: 12 June 2011).

CHAPTER 3

LIBRARY SPACE AND DESIGNING FOR A BOUTIQUE LIBRARY SERVICE IN THE USA
BEATRICE PULLIAM

INTRODUCTION

In the twenty-first-century library, evolving expectations and study habits of college students regularly compete alongside budget woes, aging infrastructure and obsolescing equipment, making designing personalized spaces and services in libraries no minor consideration. This chapter will take a closer look at the viability of Priestner and Tilley's 'boutique library model' (Priestner and Tilley 2010) through the lens of current library commons trends and recent library space renovations at Providence College in Rhode Island.

Providence College, founded in 1917 in Providence, Rhode Island, is a private, predominantly undergraduate, liberal arts, and Catholic institution of higher learning. Phillips Memorial Library provides information and research resources to a user community of over 5,000 students. The library is housed on three levels in a building that was constructed in 1969, has a collection of over 350,000 books and journal volumes, and contains more than 100 public desktop computers and laptops available for use.

BRINGING UP 'COMMONS'

More than a decade after Donald Beagle (1999) first conceptualized the information commons framework in the library literature, the 'commons' model still endures as a starting point for innovative library design and service personalization. While the information commons, often used synonymously with library commons, defies a single definition, it may include many of the following characteristics:

- amalgam of emerging technology, student services and/or learning support in one physical space (usually in a library, but not required).
- flexible, café-like spaces and seating for learning and collaboration.
- tiered approach to service delivery (heavy use of well-trained student/

support staff to triage and/or troubleshoot issues).

- self-service options (for example, scanning stations, self-checkout, and so on).
- ancillary services for other groups of users (for example, faculty, graduate students, and so on).

In the early days of converting library spaces into library commons, it was customary to direct renovation efforts towards updating and increasing the variety of technology equipment and maximising the number of computing seats available to library users. The commons of a decade ago often resembled large computer labs. These spaces, while well suited for accommodating large numbers, were not naturally conducive for collaborative work or other learning experiences. Many libraries are now taking a second look at the use of their commons environments. In a recent article on meeting the needs of the 'Net Gen' college student (students between 18 and 22), Joan Lippincott, Executive Director of the Coalition for Networked Information (CNI), and a leading researcher on Net Gens and higher education learning spaces, offers one possible solution to libraries struggling to remain relevant in the digital age: become the campus leader in promoting 'a close connection between digital content, technology, and academic and professional work' (Lippincott 2010: 28).

The progression from library to learning commons illustrates the evolving nature of the commons model and a marked shift in focus towards users and the more personalized services they demand. Perhaps inspired by Foster and Gibbons' (2007) ethnographic study of how University of Rochester undergraduates approached research in 2005, a growing community of researchers and librarian practitioners has also begun tracking and reporting on the study habits of students on college campuses in the United States. Librarian practitioners have subsequently used the results of their own local studies to step up enhancements to services and user experience in libraries.

In an effort to position themselves as more responsive to students, many libraries develop technology tools that offer personalized and useful solutions relevant to their users. Librarians in North Carolina State University's Learning Commons (NCSU Libraries 2011) developed the GroupFinder tool, a popular web-based service that enables students to find their fellow students and study groups in its multilevel, often bursting-at-the-seams library. This understanding of how students utilize the space in your library as well as a clear vision of the type of experiences you wish to provide is vital. Keeping your students at the forefront of your space planning (it is, after all, *their* library) will help you to remain relevant.

Learning principles have also been evolving, and include a change in the view of the student as passive participant (traditional learning via transmission) to growing support for the student as active learner (using constructivist learning principles) through the integration of 'interactivity and social engagement' (Brown and Long

2005). Examples of wider adoption of these trends include more regular use of group work and social media tools such as wikis and blogs, which have been shown to foster critical enquiry and collaboration.

Academics and college administrators have also taken an interest in the topic and there are now conferences devoted to modern learning space design practices and theory. Learning space design is also increasingly prevalent in the learning literature. In 2005, in an investigation of the important intersection between space, technology, pedagogy and student learning, Educause, an organization leading advancement of higher education through the intelligent use of technology, devoted an entire e-book to case studies showcasing innovative learning space design practices.

'COMMONS' IN THE UK AND AUSTRALIA

The commons movement is not exclusive to libraries and institutions in the United States. Researchers and administrators in higher education within the UK and Australia have also been very responsive to new trends in collaborative and learning space development. Recognising that there is no single solution to engaging today's or rather tomorrow's learners, more decision makers in the UK and Australia have also been embracing learning space design methodology that offers flexibility to educators and learners alike and promotes transformative learning experiences.

A 2006 report on designing spaces for effective learning published by the Joint Information Systems Committee (JISC) further illustrates the shift across several UK higher education institutions towards the development of open and flexible learning spaces that aim to inspire and motivate students to achieve more academically. This report also shows case study participants placing emphasis on customer-focused spaces with a high level of customization, and often adopting a 'learning-can-happen-anywhere' approach (unintentional and deliberate) through the use of flexible, portable furniture and placement of seating throughout facilities.

'[C]hanges in furniture layout can assist learners' navigation around a building' (JISC 2006), while also encouraging specific activities in a space. The intentional use of flexible seating and reconfigurable spaces accomplishes two important things: it aids in future-proofing facilities and shifts more autonomy to the students using the space. Passing more control to the primary users of your spaces encourages them to take the lead in crafting their own learning experiences.

THE BOUTIQUE HOTEL AS AN ASPIRATIONAL EXPERIENCE

While the idea that a well-designed learning space can be inspiring is still gaining traction in libraries, boutique hotels have long been at the forefront of aspirational design and cultivating personalized experiences for their client–guests. In the 1980s Ian Schrager, co-creator of the legendary Studio 54 nightclub, and credited as one of the architects of the boutique hotel concept, opened one of the first boutique hotels in New York (Morgans Hotel Group 2011). Schrager's boutique brand eventually extended to such enterprises as the Delano in Miami and St Martin's Lane in London. Hallmarks of the Schrager experience included attentive staff, luxurious modern design that extended beyond the lobby to guest rooms (with a price list in case you wanted to purchase a lamp in your room or the latest music playing in the elevator), and a website that extends the personalized experience virtually (including complimentary Wi-Fi for reservations made using the mobile site). There were also other personal touches such as high-end spa toiletries for guests, interesting art and a library with CDs and DVDs. The boutique hotel became the destination.

Can your library become a destination for your users beyond the normal transactional activity associated with library use? Let us take a look at a few different library spaces and examine how they fit into Priestner and Tilley's boutique library components model.

THE ACCIDENTAL BOUTIQUE LIBRARY?

The transition from library to 'library+commons' at Providence College has been incremental. The first phase of the transition began in 2006 with the transformation of the reference desk and underutilized office space on the main level of the library. In 2010, the library embarked on its first formal collaboration with the college's Information Technology (IT) Department, another key service partner on campus. While both departments had been working quite well together on an informal basis for years, this undertaking provided an opportunity for two groups with different reporting lines (the library under the college's provost and IT under the college's chief financial officer) to pool their collective expertise.

The initiative in 2010 also marked a big shift away from a heavy focus on technology to service and experience. At the same time as the library and IT initiative was underway, underused office space on the first level of the library was repurposed for faculty use. Both areas had a soft launch in the fall of 2010 and have been very popular. The following section will describe recent transformations and then examine them in the context of the 'boutique library' approach.

Transition from Library to 'Library+Commons'

In 2006, with staff buy-in and input on a rebranding strategy, and only a small investment in furniture and technology equipment, an imposing marble-topped 1970s-era L-shaped reference desk and office space were repurposed and the 'library+commons' at Providence College was born. The general goal in developing the 'library+commons' model at Phillips Memorial Library was to retain the best of what makes traditional library services so sustaining – books, of course, and helpful, personal interactions at service points, while ratcheting up the technological resources (hardware and software) and enhancing existing learning spaces (for both collaborative and individual study). When monies are limited, it becomes even more important to use existing resources and spaces creatively. The lack of a large funding stream also had an unexpected benefit: it kept us flexible and, in hindsight, in a better position to change spaces as needs changed.

Throughout the library other more personalized micro-spaces soon followed, further allowing students to select or design their own library experience from an array of options, including: the quiet zones in the second-floor alcoves along the periphery of the library for more individual or reflective study; living rooms, clusters of soft seating on first and second levels, perfect for taking a break with friends or catching up on email or reading; group study rooms, first-come-first-served spaces with computers, large tables and whiteboards for collaborative projects and group work; and a presentation rehearsal space, fitted with a projection screen, projector, whiteboards and reconfigurable seating.

Many of Priestner and Tilley's boutique library components listed below (Priestner and Tilley 2010) were evident in the 'library+commons' at Phillips Memorial Library, even in 2007:

- Customer focused: librarians, staff and students working in 'library+commons' are cross-trained, friendly, eager and able to assist students with research questions (of varying breadth and depth) and basic technical support issues.
- Trendsetting and reactive: the library is a technology leader known for using and integrating emerging technologies and being responsive to student needs (regular use of Web 2.0 tools, making new technologies available to students, extending hours during exam periods).
- High degree of autonomy: in this instance, control now rests with the student. They can readily create their own experiences in the library by choosing from a variety of study and workspaces available.
- Unique services and resources: with additional staff in place, the library now offers interlibrary loan (ILL) services during all hours of library operation and begins providing wireless connection service to students, a welcomed alternative to IT Help Desk, which did not have extended hours.

Staff also log service transactions at all service points, including number of requests for wireless assistance.

- Personalized: librarian outreach extends to students outside the library (outpost in student café), with online research guides customized for specific courses, assignments and subjects.
- Convenience: library is centrally located, open very late (until 2.00AM most days) and with the majority of key services available all of the hours the library is open (116 hours per week).

During this first phase, hourly headcounts, especially during peak exam periods, served as proof of heavy use of the new personalized spaces. The ability to extend a popular service such as ILL to seven days per week was also well received by patrons (students and faculty). Tracking service transactions at all service points gave staff data to mine to identify opportunities for further personalization and enhancement of services going forwards. Data collected on wireless assistance requests, coupled with our success triaging many more tech issues in house, raised our stature on campus as natural partners with IT.

More broadly applied, where the trendier hallmarks of the one-stop shopping (and possibly too cookie-cutter?) model of the earlier learning commons were often hardware and funky furniture, Priestner and Tilley's 'boutique library' approach keeps it local by retaining the customer and highly tailored services at the core of any planning.

Popular mantras of 'just-in-time' and 'point-of-need' (usually included in discussions about 'Net Gen' students and library services) suddenly seem to have more teeth. Further, libraries that can tap into the 'local' needs and devote considerable time to thinking about how to deliver more unique services to patrons may finally be able to offer tangible evidence of their relevancy to student learning at their institutions.

The following short case studies demonstrate the application of local, personalized strategies in service changes.

The TecHub at Providence College

Background   The development of the TecHub space was the culmination of several meetings between the library and IT staff, marking the first formal collaboration between the two departments. In the spring of 2010, the college hired an outside strategy consultant to facilitate the first meeting. Having an external party run the initial meeting kept both departments on an equal footing and the process objective.

The chiefs of both departments challenged staff to come up with ways to improve services (by expanding support) without spending a lot of money. The central outcome for the joint collaboration was to harness collective expertise to provide students with a quality college 'experience'. When the departments discussed what values they shared and considered important, the following bubbled to the surface:

- Both groups support teaching, learning, research and campus life.
- Both groups are customer focused (having a service-level agreement to delivering excellent patron service).

In response to the challenge of expanding support and services to students at little to no cost, the departments first looked for the 'low-hanging fruit'. The departments agreed that creating an outpost of the Help Desk in the library fit the bill and would allow both groups to leverage what they had already been doing well, separately and informally, while having a direct and positive impact on service.

Implementation   The decision was made to locate the remote Help Desk in the lower level of the library that was already scheduled to undergo a separate renovation. Before the TecHub, the lower level of the library was a dingy, poorly lit space with mismatched furnishings that, despite not having undergone an upgrade in 30 years, was still a heavily used destination for students looking to work in groups away from the quieter areas of the library. Because the library already had dedicated 'stations' where patrons could get various types of support (research, access, digitization, and so on), the TecHub and Tech Station (the renamed help desk) spaces were developed as further continuation of the 'library+commons' transformation.

The TecHub offers Herman Miller flexible tables and seating for 70; a multifunction color copier/scanner/printer; a walk-up charging carrel; six dual-boot Mac Minis; three large flatscreen monitors; large collaborative workspaces with privacy screens; mobile whiteboards (nearly everything in the TecHub is on wheels and can be easily reconfigured); soft seating with tablet arms, ottomans and Arcadia Hush chairs (Furniture Fashion 2011); gourmet coffee, beverage and snack machines; and robust wireless and power. A recently renovated presentation space is also located in the TecHub. Additionally, the TecHub is the setting for library resource demos and drop-in instruction session events.

The Tech Station, which offers tech and tiered research support during the majority of library's hours of operation, is staffed by cross-trained library and IT students. At the time of writing this chapter (summer 2011), IT graduate assistants will also staff the Tech Station. In addition to two dual-boot iMacs for Tech Station staff, the Tech Station has seating for eight to accommodate more involved tech support and informal instruction, and a large flatscreen monitor that runs a mirrored digital content loop (from the digital display screens on the first level of the library) powered by Concerto software (Concerto 2011).

To date, assessment of activity on TecHub space is largely quantitative, comprising hourly headcounts in the TecHub and presentation space by student staff, as well as LibStats, an open-source web-based service transaction tool for libraries, to capture requests for assistance at the Tech Station. Reliance on student staff for data collection is not without challenges, and requires close monitoring and consistent communication by student supervisors. So far, the maximum number of students in the TecHub space during an hourly count has been 48 – that is, approximately 70 percent of the total number of seats available. IT-trained students working in the TecHub also use an online ticketing system to report more complex technical issues – for example, backend problems related to printing or networking that cannot be resolved by library staff – to IT and media services staff.

We recognize the need to gather data that more accurately reflect how students are using the space throughout the library's hours of operation, and are currently investigating how to better collect this information. The extent to which more personalized delivery of services is possible, using, for example, mobile technology, would be interesting to pursue in micro-spaces such as the TecHub.

The Faculty Commons

A second similar implementation is the Faculty Commons, which was launched in the fall of 2010 in an infrequently used office area. Though still in its nascent phase, it offers faculty dedicated space and privacy for focused research and scholarship endeavors. Nestled between the Digital Publishing Services lab and a first-floor quiet zone, this space has three large workspaces/desks, a conference table, computers, a scanner, printing, telephones, whiteboards and a refrigerator stocked with water. Faculty frequently use the new space to do research and meet with students and as a satellite office.

The space is a welcoming, comfortable, personalized customer-focused area, with faculty receiving prompt responses from library staff. There is a regular 'Lunch and Learn' to introduce them to new technologies such as iPads. A loan service for laptops, iPads and netbooks that is unique to this group of users exists alongside this learning service. The space is intended for faculty alone and they have a high degree of autonomy in their use of the area. It is a convenient space for faculty, centrally located on campus with the space available during all hours of library operation.

The Research Bar at Marlboro College

Marlboro College, Vermont, founded in 1946, is a small, private, coeducational liberal arts college of approximately 300 students and 40 faculty, and an average classroom size of seven to eight students. In size it is quite different from Providence College, and has different needs. Marlboro College prides itself on offering a student-centred education where students work with an advisor to develop a personal plan of concentration. Its library, Rice-Aron Library, is no exception. It maintains an open-door policy 24 hours per day and uses an honor system to handle circulation of materials (they have opted to place several self-checkout stations throughout the library and use a single merged service point to handle other questions).

At the same time, the library was in sore need of instruction space. Without its own computer cluster or dedicated classroom space, its only option was a computer lab without a projector that was also not bookable, making it a challenging and distracting environment for teaching and learning. With a gift from an anonymous donor, the library converted the fortress-like, traditional circulation desk that was gathering dust into much-needed instruction space, and renamed it the Research Bar. With its stone top and under-counter lighting, the underutilized circulation desk already resembled a moderately swanky hotel bar.

The Research Bar is fitted with a large ceiling-mounted projection screen, a portable digital projector and locking laptop cart for storing the netbooks and projector, two iMacs, ten Ubuntu netbooks (in keeping with the library's open source philosophy) and mini-mice, eight barstools, and several chairs for the lower wings on each end of the bar. One lower wing has an iMac and functions as a service point workstation, and the other contains another iMac and is used as the library's very first public access workstation. The portable laptop cart and projector help to keep the Research Bar a flexible micro-space, enabling it to be easily transformed from an informal laptop bar to a hands-on teaching and learning area within minutes. When it is not being used for instruction, the Research Bar is often used as a social study space.

To Emily Alling, Rice-Aron Library Director, a positive trade-off to conducting instruction sessions in an open area is that a key function of the library is now very transparent. Alling frequently hears the following from passers-by when instruction workshops are in session: 'I didn't know that librarians teach!' Says Alling: 'We don't keep a gate count, as we lack gates; but anecdotally, the space definitely feels more vibrant and inhabited: the tumbleweeds are gone.'[1] Alling and her team are looking to develop other micro-spaces including additional reading/study space, a space for presentation practice, and a learning booth for language instruction and videoconferencing with instructors.

MEASURING CASE STUDIES AGAINST THE BOUTIQUE COMPONENT MODEL

How do the changes to services in the case studies described above measure up against the boutique components model? Table 3.1 looks at two of the case

---

1   Private correspondence, 2011.

Table 3.1   Evaluating TechHub and Research Bar against boutique principles

Boutique Library	TecHub@Providence College Library	Research Bar@Marlboro College
Customer-focused	Dedicated staff trained to be first responders to a variety of tech issues (computers, productivity, classroom support, a/v, etc.) and provide tiered research support	In the new space, staff better able to meet students and faculty where they are, and offer demos of online services via portable projection setup
Highly tailored	Librarian-led 'Hungry for Knowledge' series, a menu style selection of 40 half-hour intro sessions to new library databases and e-content	Librarians now able to offer instruction and workshops in dedicated new space
Trend-setting & reactive	Use of interactive digital display to deliver content and information to patrons; cookie and beverage breaks during exam periods	Impromptu gathering place for language study groups, chess games, tea parties and town residents after recent Hurricane.
High degree of autonomy	Students feel like they 'own the TecHub' and can decide how they will use the flexible space; staff have ability to reconfigure space for different audiences (e.g., informal instruction, presentations, and social events) and authority to tweak services (flexibility to experiment and ditch services that do not work)	Students use Research Bar as social-study space when workshops not in session. Openness of campus reinforced and supported in activities at the Research Bar
Unique services & resources	Walk-up wireless assistance and tech support; password resets and printing assistance	Space also used by peer-tutors, Career Services and other library staff for other workshops (drop-ins, resume workshops and library orientation for new students and faculty)
Personalized	On demand 1-2-1 training available from peers, librarian or staff	Nice, comfortable place to collaborate, relax or work
Convenience	Students and faculty can now receive most Help Desk services in TecHub at hours convenient to them	One stop shopping for reference help, tailored instruction workshops, quick lookup and self-checkout

studies, TecHub and Research Bar, evaluating the new services against aspects of the boutique component model. In nearly every respect there is a close fit with the model.

DELIVERING BOUTIQUE 'EXPERIENCES'

While there has been a shift away from the age-old stereotype of libraries as book and print journal repositories, designing services around the concept of 'creating experiences' for users is not the norm for libraries. Libraries tend to focus on technology solutions (usually complex third-party proprietary technology) and are not inclined to think of the services we provide as commodities. User experience is still largely considered the domain of those in business or technology.

In an ACRL 2011 conference report on a study measuring user experience satisfaction in academic libraries, Steven Bell, incoming ACRL president, details the WOW experience, a concept used by the retail industry to describe a very positive 'unique and memorable experience that creates (customer) loyalty' (Bell 2011). Five major indicators of a WOW experience mapped to boutique library service features are illustrated in Table 3.2.

Table 3.2   WOW indicators mapped to boutique library service features

WOW indicators	Boutique service features
Engagement: being polite, caring and genuinely interested in listening and helping	Customer focused
Brand experience: appealing design and atmosphere making customers feel they are special	Unique services and resources, Personalized and Highly Tailored: Services are just-in-time and delivered at point-of-need
Problem recovery: efficiency in resolving problems and compensating customers	Customer focused
Executional excellence: outstanding knowledge of the products and ability to explain them	Subject specialism: Speaks to high-level of cross-training, level of expertise
Expediting: helping speed the process to save customers time and sensitivity to their time constraints	High degree of autonomy, subject specialism and Personalized: Staff understand 'local' needs of community and have flexibility and skill to troubleshoot and resolve issues promptly

These WOW indicators could also serve as a tool for measuring the effectiveness of boutique library services and overall user satisfaction. Bell's study does not endorse one-size-fits-all solutions, but instead recommends that, when designing a user experience, the experience should be customized to local user needs and culture.

CONCLUSION

The incremental transformation at Phillips Memorial Library from a traditional, high-touch library environment to a 'library+commons' has had the unexpected benefit of allowing us to observe how various areas of the library have been used and develop more tailored services for patrons. Formal collaboration with another campus service partner permitted us to pool resources and creativity in order to achieve a positive and direct impact on service delivery and satisfaction via the TecHub, and now other departments are looking to join in new collaborations.

In the fall of 2011, four high-tech classrooms were due to open in the TecHub level of the library, further positioning us as a centre of academic life on the campus. More micro-spaces are in the works in the future, including a multimedia studio and the ReSearcHub, which will involve the creation of a comfortable and inviting space for patrons seeking librarian consults and conversion of the existing reference desk area into a flexible patron desk. The library is also committed to continued development of services for faculty.

We should also investigate how our existing mobile services (for example, mobile library site, catalogue and database apps) and social media tools might be integrated into the boutique model and more personalized service delivery in the micro-spaces described in this chapter.

Librarians, students and faculty viewed the Research Bar implementation at Marlboro College as a success. Traffic in the new space has increased dramatically and, more importantly, unintended use by other departments (for example, Career Services and Academic Support Services) has led to new collaborations and further strengthens the library's standing as *the* destination for a variety of services and activities.

All three examples of library services illustrate that the boutique approach is scalable to accommodate different service modes (for example, in person, online and mobile), types of institutions and organizational cultures and should work well as a checklist when designing tailored services for users.

TOP TIPS: SOME PRACTICAL TAKEAWAYS

- Buy-in: Get it. Staff are likely to feel more ownership and invested in the change if they are involved in the planning process.
- If you do not have money in your budget to hire a strategy consultant, look for similar expertise within teaching faculty or administration. The experience may lead to future collaborations.
- Keep your services local. Do not be afraid to experiment, but make decisions based on what is happening at *your* institution or the needs of your community of users.
- Leverage the expertise and feedback from the best focus group you'll ever have: your student staff and student users.
- Be open to the unintended uses of your space. This may lead to other opportunities to provide or expand services.
- Do not discount the value of your website or other virtual environment (Facebook, and so on) as a 'boutique' service. According to the 2010 OCLC Perceptions of Libraries report, 'fast and easier' wins out over authoritative and accurate as 83 percent of college students still choose search engines when beginning research (OCLC 2010). This represents yet another missed opportunity to create a positive experience for users accessing your services online.
- Survey your community for feedback and qualitative evaluation of boutique services. Make evaluation an ongoing part of service development.

REFERENCES

Beagle, D. 1999. Conceptualizing an Information Commons. *Journal of Academic Librarianship*, 25(2), 82–9.

Bell, S. 2011. *Delivering a WOW User Experience: Do Academic Librarians Measure Up?* Paper, ACRL 2011 [online]. At: http://www.ala.org/ala/mgrps/divs/acrl/events/national/2011/papers/delivering_wow.pdf (accessed: 1 July 2011).

Brown, M. and Long, P.D. 2005. Trends in Learning Space Design, in Oblinger, D. (ed.), *Learning Spaces*, Educause, 9.1–9.11 [online]. At: http://www.educause.edu/learningspacesch9 (accessed: 1 July 2011).

Concerto Digital Signage. 2011. Concerto [online]. At: http://www.concerto-signage.com/ (accessed: 1 July 2011).

Foster, N. and Gibbons, S., eds. 2007. Studying Students: The Undergraduate Research Project at the University of Rochester [online]. At: http://hdl.handle.net/1802/7520 (accessed: 1 July 2011).

Furniture Fashion. 2011. Hush Lounge Chair by Arcadia Contract [online]. At: http://www.furniturefashion.com/2008/06/11/hush_lounge_chair_by_arcadia_contract.html (accessed: 1 July 2011).

JISC. 2006. Designing Spaces for Effective Learning: A Guide to 21st Century Learning Space Design [online]. At: http://www.jisc.ac.uk/publications/programmerelated/2006/pub_spaces.aspx (accessed: 1 July 2011).

Lippincott, J. 2010. Meeting Millennials' Needs. *Journal of Library Administration*, 50(1), 27–37.

Morgans Hotel Group. 2011. Morgans Hotel Group (formerly Schrager Hotels) [online]. At: http://www.morganshotelgroup.com/ (accessed: 1 July 2011).

NCSU Libraries. 2011. GroupFinder [online]. At: http://www.lib.ncsu.edu/dli/projects/groupfinder/ (accessed: 1 July 2011).

OCLC. 2010. College Students, Perceptions of Libraries, Context and Community [online]. At: http://www.oclc.org/reports/2010perceptions/collegestudents.pdf (accessed: 1 July 2011).

Priestner, A. and Tilley, E. 2010. Boutique Libraries at your Service. *Library & Information Update*, 9(6), 36–9.

SECTION 1

STUDENTS AS CONSULTANTS: SKOLKOVO MOSCOW SCHOOL OF MANAGEMENT
HELEN EDWARDS

SKOLKOVO Moscow School of Management is a new international business school offering MBA and executive education programmes with the focus on leadership, entrepreneurship and emerging markets. The MBA and executive MBA programmes are international and conducted in English with about three quarters of the students from Russia and former CIS countries. The library project started in summer 2009 when I joined SKOLKOVO as Library Project Manager with the brief to establish the library and set up services for students and researchers.

A key function of the library is to support the experiential project work that is central to the SKOLKOVO programmes. On the MBA programme students work in teams in Russia, India, China and the USA to address real issues in the public and private sectors. Recent projects include a new road construction project for the Ministry of Transport; advising a major Indian charity on healthcare provision for low income populations; and working with a Chinese supermarket group on product positioning and real estate management. In addition, two research groups, based in Moscow and Beijing, focus on emerging markets and infrastructure issues.

Two challenges are identifying appropriate content for the library and setting up library services to meet the needs of students, staff and researchers. In both cases the boutique approach, with its focus on tailored content and services, has significant advantages.

Content

Many business databases are sold on a universal access, unlimited use basis. Wide research interests are often associated with large institutional size. However, at SKOLKOVO we need a model where specialised content can be secured as required, often in circumstances where the topics are not known much in advance and subject to frequent change. We want the facilities of a large research library but without the cost of blanket subscriptions.

An early task for the library was to introduce SKOLKOVO to major database suppliers and work with them to identify alternative models. Arrangements include the use of usage statistics to agree tiers of cost, set up in advance in the contract with specific review points; short-term licensing arrangements for individual researchers and project groups for access to specialised resources; purchase of individual market research reports on project subjects; and, of course, heavy use of pay as you go for articles and the purchase of individual books and subscriptions (print and electronic) on request.

The philosophy is that the first call on the library budget should be the articulated needs of users today. Immediate legitimate requests are prioritised, researched and funded with budget allocated for this very purpose at whatever time in the financial cycle they appear. The library environment is designed to expose users to a range of business resources, but the expenditure, as much as possible, needs to be closely linked to actual usage. The fact that Russia is a new market for many suppliers no doubt assists in their willingness to discuss new business models more suited to the school's population.

SERVICES

Time is at a premium in business school programmes that are packed with lectures and seminars, activities and group work. Many of the students have not had previous experience of using business databases, and past exposure to library services have not led to any great expectations. Excellent availability of seminar rooms on the new campus means that students have a wide choice of places to meet and study. It soon became apparent that generic library introductory sessions, all-purpose library news and standardised guides held little interest. Indeed, the announcement of the arrival of the opening book collection of 2,000 new English language titles led to only seven loans in the first two weeks.

The first set of projects provided the opportunity to engage the students with the library. Project work involves student contact with high-level personnel from government and business in areas with which they are largely unfamiliar, and the project directors are keen that the students be properly briefed. In effect the students are acting as management consultants and need the kind of support offered by commercial environments.

The first step was to create library project pages within Basecamp, the project management environment used for project communications, with a set of resources for each project. These pages form the basis of the library session held for the students during the project induction phase. Relevant books are also brought to the information sessions and issued there and then. The library is positioned as the repository of western knowledge and as a node in the wider information network, also comprising the local information provided by the project host and the students' own networks.

This approach encourages students to share their information needs with the library, reinforced by the knowledge that library staff have knowledge of their projects. Enquiries are taken at face value, as they would be in a professional environment, and without worrying about the possibility of 'spoonfeeding'. Ensuring exposure to information is more important. In practice direct provision of content from databases, together with a note about how the information was sourced, has served to increase independence and skills. The dialogue also forms a connection with the students, who sometimes follow up by issuing LinkedIn invitations to library staff.

Another advantage of the emphasis on project support by library staff is that it forces a critical look at the databases and resources. Database vendors quote impressive numbers and extensive coverage, but this does not mean that the information actually needed can be found in the products. The project focus provides an additional measure of usefulness over and above usage statistics and offers the ongoing opportunity to test library resources against real needs. Deep web searches, use of print reference works and making contact with other specialised libraries are also important.

While focusing on specific project requirements the library sessions are also used to introduce generic library skills. Project pages together with a library session are set up for each new module, allowing a phased introduction of new sources and research skills over the course of the programme and matching the requirements of project work. In addition to participating in the induction for each module, library staff also attend the presentations at the end of the projects. This enables informal evaluation of the use of information resources.

A similar model is also being applied to staff. The library supports key business functions by highlighting relevant material, forwarding articles and reports, and creating resource pages. As staff tend to have long-term ongoing interests, good use can be made of RSS feeds and Twitter updates to pick up on new content for staff alerting.

The library works with the Communications Department to publicise library resources on the school social media sites by contributing regular short articles about new books and topical business issues. The advantage of this is that the library content is juxtaposed with all the other school content reaching an audience who might not sign up to a library blog. Users are already interacting with the school Facebook site and thus are more likely to 'Like' or comment on the library content also. Also noted is a marked increased demand for material selected for highlighting and recently to requests for more articles for Russian business sites.

SKOLKOVO library's approach to services is to focus nearly all effort on supporting specific projects and known research and staff interests. Budget is prioritised to meet expressed needs. The actual usefulness of subscribed resources to contribute to projects and research is continually evaluated. The production of generic library materials is minimised and general-purpose sessions are not held. Content is positioned where the users go: project sites and social media. Time is further freed up by reducing administration, for example by buying shelf-ready books together with their catalogue records and taking advantage of the productivity gains inherent in the use of Web 2.0 technologies. Even library opening hours are matched where possible to programme schedules and the presence on campus for part-time students.

Coming to an environment with little expectations among students and staff for library services, there is no comfort zone of an established user base with independent habits of library use. Without explicitly identifying and trying to meet specific user needs, there is the real danger of resources sitting unused while the library remains on the periphery of the student experience and ignored by staff.

RESEARCH POSTCARDS AT THE LONDON SCHOOL OF ECONOMICS
MICHELLE BLAKE AND NICOLA WRIGHT

BACKGROUND

The London School of Economics and Political Science (LSE) has around 9,000 students; of these, just over half are postgraduates. Students are drawn from around 140 countries and overall about two thirds of LSE students come from outside the UK. LSE actively focuses on continuously developing and enhancing the research environment for this cosmopolitan student body.

Like many universities, LSE is taking action to respond to the feeling of isolation that is sometimes experienced by PhD students (Ali and Kohun 2006, Hawley 2003, Park 2005) and a range of activities are being undertaken by the academic support departments to address this concern. In the library, we believe we have a key role to play in supporting students' work and contributing to a sense of community among the PhD student group. The creation of a new post in June 2009 gave us the opportunity to review our research support services and to develop a portfolio of tailored services specifically for PhD students. We felt we needed to find new ways of making contact with research students (who can be here for three to six years and longer if they take up an academic post) so that we could promote our services effectively. Our aim is to build long-term effective relationships that will develop as their research progresses.

Each LSE department, research centre and group has a dedicated professional librarian, known as an academic support librarian, who has knowledge of the subject and the information resources available. We believe that we have valuable help to offer and we want to establish a meaningful two-way partnership, not simply a system where the library bombards the students with an indiscriminate and overwhelming plethora of information.

All relationships begin with an introduction and we needed to find an effective and attractive way of making contact with new PhD students.

RESEARCH POSTCARDS

These are double sized and detachable along a perforated line. The student keeps one half of the postcard and returns the other half to the library with their contact details and research interests. The postcards were created in time for the start of the 2009/10 academic year and were aimed at new PhD students. We launched the research postcards at the school-wide PhD induction held at the start of October and they proved an effective icebreaker for academic support librarians to approach new students.

The research postcards were designed with two purposes in mind. Firstly, they are a way for academic support librarians to introduce themselves to new students. A very simple message on the postcard highlights the research support services offered by the library and gives contact details. Secondly, the postcards ask PhD students to give brief details including their name, email address and academic department. They are also asked for information about their research topic and keywords. The students send these back to the library and the relevant academic support librarian responds with some initial feedback about their research topic. This includes information about resources the library has that may be useful (including archival material, print and electronic collections), search tips (for any complex databases), help with keywords, and other libraries of relevance.

OUTCOMES

We knew we wanted to be able to offer personalised and value-added services, but in order to do this academic support librarians would need dedicated time to deliver them. It was only because of changes we made in how the library's help desk service was staffed that personalised services such as our research postcards were possible.

The postcards have proved to be very popular, with a 39 per cent response rate of first year PhD submitting a postcard in the first year and over 50 per cent in the second year. The amount of time required for academic support librarians to complete the feedback for students has been monitored and has proven to be very cost efficient especially when assessed alongside other services we offer. The cost of delivering the research postcards was 50 per cent less than the previous Help Desk service and also demonstrated a much higher value from our users.

The success of the research postcards was evaluated in a number of ways including a survey of PhD students who submitted a postcard in the first year. We found that 76 per cent of students who returned a postcard felt that the response they received from their academic support librarian was useful. One student commented: 'Thank you so much for this document. This an excellent starting point. I was actually wondering where else I could find resources, after Google, Google Scholar, or Google Books.' In addition, over 90 per cent of respondents said that they already had contacted, or that they would contact, their academic support librarian again in the future. Another student said: 'Thank you very much for sending me this very useful document. I think I will spend a couple of weeks looking at all these databases and then request a meeting with you in order to sharpen my research.'

The student feedback has been useful in helping to assess the impact of the service. It is clear that PhD students have mixed levels of research skills and there is a definite need for skills training from the library. This is supported by two recent RIN reports (RIN 2008, 2011). Since introducing the research postcards the library has seen greater uptake of its dedicated six-week information skills course MY592. Academic support librarians also have greater numbers of PhD students booking one-to-one research consultations. The research postcards support and promote both of these services.

Along with other services the library offers for PhD students, the postcards were submitted as part of the successful bid for LSE to become a doctoral training centre. The profile of the library has also been raised within the school and as a result of these services the library has been invited to take part in school-wide projects that it may not otherwise have been involved in. This included the development of the first PhD poster exhibition as well as further embedding of sessions for undergraduate and masters students who as a result of using tailored services have seen the benefits for their own research. Additionally, schools are keen for their own students to receive instruction in areas that the library can support.

FUTURE

Like any service, our research postcards will need to be reviewed periodically to make sure that they are still meeting the needs of our PhD students and adding value. For us they have been very successful, but it should not be underestimated how much time they can take up. For a very small library this type of service may not be sustainable. To be effective the postcards must be introduced at the start of the academic year, a time that is already extremely busy for academic support librarians, and the turnaround time for responses must be relatively quick or they lose their impact. We have found that the spin-off benefits do make this investment worthwhile.

REFERENCES

Ali, A. and Kohun, F. 2006. Dealing with Isolation Feelings in IS Doctoral Programs. *International Journal of Doctoral Studies*, 1 [online]. At: http://ijds. org/Volume1/IJDSv1p021-033Ali13.pdf (accessed: 17 February 2010).

Hawley, P. 2003. *Being Bright is not Enough.* Springfield, IL: Charles C. Thomas.

Park, C. 2005. War of Attrition: Patterns of Non-Completion Amongst Postgraduate Research Students. *Higher Education Review*, 38(1) [online]. At: http://eprints. lancs.ac.uk/118/1/war_of_attrition.pdf (accessed: 17 February 2010).

Research Information Network (RIN). 2008. *Mind the Skills Gap: Information Handling Training for Researchers* [online]. At: http://www.rin.ac.uk/ our-work/researcher-development-and-skills/mind-skills-gap-information-handling-training-researchers (accessed: 17 February 2010).

Research Information Network (RIN). 2011. *The Role of Research Supervisors in Information Literacy* [online]. At: http://www.rin.ac.uk/news/role-research-supervisors-information-literacy (accessed 1 November 2011).

BOUTIQUE AT THE FACULTY OF EDUCATION
ANGELA CUTTS

The Faculty of Education (FoE) is one of over 100 departments of the University of Cambridge located some distance from the rest of the university. It has 80 academics, 30 research staff and approximately 1,200 students, the majority of whom are part-time, PGCE and distance students. These students rely heavily on the Faculty Library as they are either learning to teach or teaching while undertaking academic study and under severe time constraints.

The Education Library is the first port of call education students turn to. Considering their use of information resources within the context of the university, the relationship between students and library provision can best be illustrated in Figure C.1. This demonstrates that while making use of the local services in the Faculty Library users also make use of centrally organised systems, such as the library management system and the provision of e-resources that are delivered via the virtual environment. All four elements in the diagram interconnect, but students are probably most unaware of collaborative activities such as those undertaken by library staff. However, they often benefit indirectly: for example, the FYI Faculty Library blog (2012) was produced following staff involvement with 23Things Cambridge (2012).

Over the last five years the Faculty Library has developed a personalised approach to service delivery. It provides a highly specialised education collection, both physically and electronically via a VLE, and has four professional library staff with considerable subject knowledge and experience in a team of 6.6 FTE. There is a strong emphasis on customer service in all aspects of provision, which is highly tailored to different types of course. Library staff are encouraged to be creative and reflective practitioners, constantly aiming to improve services to courses as well as to individual students and academic staff of the faculty. The librarian is directly responsible to the head of faculty and is therefore able to make quick decisions in response to course and student needs. CamTools (2012), the Cambridge in-house VLE, has been developed to provide information and resources tailored to each type of course via a Faculty Library site, with direct links to relevant e-books, e-journals and databases, saving PGCE, part-time and distance-learning students

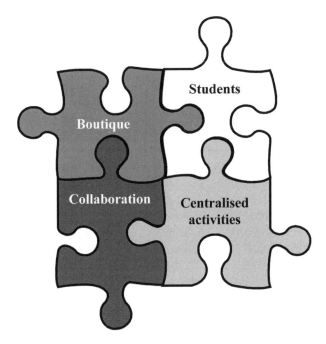

Figure C.1   The University of Cambridge Faculty of Education boutique model – Angela Cutts 2011 (after Priestner and Tilley 2010)

valuable time in navigating the complex electronic world. Relationships with academic staff and students are central to the success of the service and these are honed through extensive communication, both personally and via email, Twitter, text and the FYI blog. The library is located in the heart of the faculty, next door to Homerton College where many undergraduate and some postgraduate students are based, forming an education sub-campus within Cambridge.

This 'boutique' approach has been successful so far in the faculty. Although the number of active faculty borrowers has decreased slightly over the last five years, the use of the library service has increased, both physically in terms of footfall and virtually as reflected in the usage of the VLE (147 unique and 248 repeated visits on 10 January 2010 following research skills sessions for groups of PGCE students).

There has been a domino effect in the demand for tailored services from academic staff, as they have seen groups of students benefit from online workshops or subject-specific resources on the VLE. The resulting increase in library/academic staff interaction provides library staff with better knowledge of course content, leading to improved services that are timely and relevant.

Indications that this approach is successful include the rising number of unsolicited positive comments sent via email or in person (138 positive unsolicited responses in 2010/11, compared to 74 the previous year), and course evaluations also reveal high satisfaction rates (the percentage of PhD students rating the library as excellent or very good rose from 83 to 88 per cent in the last two years). Some faculty courses are externally inspected; in January 2011 Ofsted found the faculty PGCE courses overall to be outstanding, with no recommendations for improvement. The library team have a close working relationship with these courses and consequently tailored services are highly developed, particularly for the Primary PGCE. Quite independently, Ofsted described the way PGCE courses were delivered as personalised, targeted, flexible and tailored, and the library service was described by local managers and examiners of the Primary PGCE as 'highly tailored to our specific needs, constantly developing, and essential for an effective course'.[1]

Most library staff appreciate the professionally stimulating working environment that this approach creates. They enjoy the challenge of needing to be 'on the ball' in aiming to satisfy and anticipate different information needs. Others are concerned that this approach may create too much pressure at times. All staff find the good working relationships with academic staff and students rewarding.

However, there are also tensions inherent in our delivery of this model. A flexible, responsive and proactive approach to delivering services requires high-calibre staff with similar qualities, which are often not those traditionally associated with librarianship. Tailored services require more staff time than generic ones: for example, inductions and online research skills sessions are embedded into course structures, tailored to particular assignment topics, and delivered in teaching locations across the faculty, in small subject groups and at times to suit attendance patterns, which can be early evenings or Saturday mornings. The emphasis on timely and relevant communication to different courses also takes thought and planning. The 'boutique' approach in this context is dependent on being able to sustain both the quality and number of professional staff in the library team.

New technologies have greatly enhanced our ability to deliver tailored services to large numbers of students, which would have not been possible on the same scale before VLEs, social media, and so on. These electronic media also require staff time to maintain, with associated problems of balancing staff time delivering both electronic and traditional services. Education students have a strong preference for print, despite extensive use of e-books (in 2010/11, six of the top ten most used e-books in the university were education titles), so the pressure to provide and operate an excellent physical library remains, while simultaneously maintaining and developing electronic services. Inevitably there is some work that we no longer have

---

1   From an Internal Faculty memorandum, 'Faculty of Education – Library Provision', a commentary from the Course Manager and Chair of Section 1 (Assignments) Examiners, *Early Years and Primary PGCE Course* (1-page document, not available online).

time for; we have neglected the assessment of older material and the development of an educational archive; and we never have enough time to stocktake, but we are very quickly made aware of anything that goes missing through the reservation system, and losses are low.

Overall the 'boutique' approach currently serves the faculty extremely well, although there are questions about whether it is sustainable. The emphasis on tailored services means that library staff time and effort is focused on what is wanted and required by students and academic staff, not wasted on resources that will not be used, or services provided out of context. The result is an easy-to-use service, delivered in cooperation and partnership with the faculty, that saves time, contributes to raising achievement, and is highly valued by the majority of students and academic staff.

REFERENCES

23 Things Cambridge. 2010 [online]. At: http://23thingscambridge.blogspot.co.uk (accessed: 28 March 2012).

CamTools. 2012 [online]. At: https://camtools.cam.ac.uk/ (accessed: 28 March 2012).

Faculty of Education Library Blog. 2012. FYI: For Your Information [online]. At: http://edfaclib.wordpress.com/ (accessed: 28 March 2012).

Ofsted. 2011. University of Cambridge: Initial Teacher Education Inspection Report [online]. At: http://www.educ.cam.ac.uk/courses/pgce/downloads/2011_ofsted.pdf (accessed: 28 March 2012).

Priestner, A., and Tilley, E. 2010. Boutique Libraries at your Service. *Library & Information Update*, 9(6), 36–9.

PERSONAL SPACE FOR STUDY: MEETING REAL NEEDS
ELIZABETH TILLEY

The University of Cambridge is full of many libraries (well over 100) with all sorts of varied and interesting nooks and crannies for students to use for studying. The search for the 'perfect desk' has been documented in a recent short film created to give new students to the university some idea of how to discover the spaces that exist in this specialist library environment (Cambridge University 2010). With all the variety of spaces to choose from, searching for a great place to work does not take long. Library staff work hard to be creative with the facilities at their disposal and students have a wide choice available to them. Anecdotal conversations with students reveal that many regularly 'library-hop' using different spaces at different times of the week or year. They are used to moving around between the spaces depending on their love of light, atmosphere, view, where their friends are, or just using space to be efficient in their use of time. Others prefer a regular spot in the same space and will arrive early in the day to ensure that they get the prized location. In some of the smaller libraries, especially those in the colleges of Cambridge, it is common at certain times of the year to find students 'colonising' their favourite study spaces, quickly settling in and adding personal touches such as photographs or cards, relevant quotes, and notes from friends who know that they work in that particular place. These spaces quickly lose their anonymity.

However, taking it to another level in terms of personalising study space, there is a particular specialist library offering a service that has even more obvious parallels with boutique hotels. Services offered at a typical boutique hotel are all about personalising the experience for their users and making them feel special. It is about the visitor feeling cosseted, special and unique, with hotel management keen to ensure that their visit is memorable. The boutique library approach seeks to do the same for users of the service and with the provision of study space is endeavouring to invoke experiences that build positive memories for students. These positive memories will help provide the library champions for the next year's fresher group or, in the case of a close-knit research community, the knowledge that a visit to the library will be a positive experience.

Tyndale House is an international centre for biblical research to which scholars from around the world visit for varying lengths of time. There may be up to fifty scholars studying in the community at any one time. An integral part of Tyndale House is the library, which houses an excellent collection of academic Biblical Studies books and journals.

As a specialist library, Tyndale House is in a unique position of having a focused clientele who need specific resources that they cannot easily get elsewhere. The context is one of a community where service is exactly what it means it is: the action of helping someone. Staff know users by name and have a clear understanding of their well-defined needs. Services that develop as a result of this knowledge 'fit' the users – there is a sense of a favourite coat that fits well, is practical and yet luxurious, is yours and yet is willingly lent out to whoever needs it most. One particular service that Tyndale offers to its users is the ability to book a desk in the library for their personal use for the duration of their visit. There is a booking system as scholars often plan their time in Cambridge well in advance. The desk spaces belong to those who have booked them, from one week to three years; the books that get piled up on the desks from the nearby shelves 'belong' to the user. There is simply an understanding that if someone wants a particular item they borrow it for a short time leaving a polite note to inform the current 'owner' of the book. The space belongs to the researcher for the duration of their visit, but being the environment that it is, they are also expected to contribute to maintaining the space. So students must empty the bins at their desk, they help library staff with stock check, they re-shelve the books they are finished with, and they take a turn making tea for the community at large. The students rent the study spaces and so the experience is not free. However, renting the spaces seems to ensure that there is a commitment on the part of the user to maintaining the space that they work in and the surrounding resources.

This library demonstrates how use of space can be personalised and tailored for a particular group, ultimately based on understanding the context or community within which it is based. There is also an interesting assumption that providing a service that is so personalised is at its most successful for the user when there is a price to pay – not just in the 'rent', but in the form of an expected contribution to the service. Personalising the space offered in this library creates an atmosphere that fosters research and learning. The ownership of the space, and service, is important, and this approach meets a very real user need. This last point is the ultimate goal in personalising services.

REFERENCES

Cambridge University. 2010. The Perfect Desk. At: http://www.youtube.com/watch?v=3hjzNNvaELA (accessed: 10 March 2012).

CHAPTER 4

LIBRARY TECHNOLOGIES FOR BOUTIQUE SERVICES
TIM WALES

INTRODUCTION

In this chapter I examine the latest library technologies at the time of writing – Summer 2011 – and test them against the central tenets of the boutique approach to see whether they complement or contradict each other. I draw on two specific practical case studies from my own experience at my former employer, Royal Holloway, University of London Library Services (RHULLS), and also illustrate how easy it is now to set up a boutique library service from scratch thanks to web technologies. My focus is very much on practical and pragmatic practitioner experience including the odd discussion on the future of technology, in the hope that this book delivers both immediate value and insight to the reader and a record of the current thinking about UK academic library systems.

In essence, I see five technology-driven services for boutique libraries to harness, whether delivered from a central or boutique library service:

- demand-driven acquisition (specifically e-books, but other e-resources in future).
- Discovery (systems, interfaces and content).
- virtual enquiry and training services.
- social media services (blogs, wikis, Facebook, Twitter, and so on).
- mobile devices/library content delivered to mobile devices.

Table 4.1 illustrates how these technologies potentially map onto the features of a boutique service using Priestner and Tilley's (2010) boutique library components model.

Of course, depending on the set-up of the service and the demands of the parent institution, there are also other technologies that the boutique library service could offer or support in part or whole:

Table 4.1   Library technologies and boutique service features

Technology type	Subject-specialism	Customer-focused	Highly-tailored	Trend setting & reactive	High degree of autonomy	Unique services & resources	Personalised	Convenient location
Demand-driven e-book acquisition	✓	✓	✓	✓	✓	✓	✓	✓
Discovery system	✗	✓	✓	✓	✓	✗	✓	✓
Virtual enquiry/ training	✓	✓	✓	✓	✓	✓	✓	✓
Social media	✓	✓	✓	✓	✓	✓	✓	✓
Mobile devices	✓	✓	✓	✓	✓	✓	✓	✓

Note: Comparison as of July 2011

- Current Research Information System (CRIS): to support national research assessment exercises, researcher (performance) management, external benchmarking and open access.
- Content repositories: subject-specific content in different forms (article, book chapter, thesis, and so on) ideally populating external subject repositories automatically to provide one single point of deposit for researchers. Can be open or closed access and can encompass other discipline specific special materials. Also includes learning object and reading list repositories.
- Research data archives: these may be part of content repositories (above) or a separate system. Not necessarily limited to science disciplines.

Stretching the boutique hotel analogy further, the equivalent of the Bang & Olufsen stereo in each room could be the installation of Smart Blade shelving as at the Biomedical Sciences Library at the University of Cardiff (Fortune 2010). This intelligent library shelving uses RFID tags in local book collections to monitor the actual location of a book and flag its whereabouts to the user using a copy of the library catalogue, ideally on a mobile device. The shelving flashes to take the user to the right location. How many users can operate this at one time without confusing each other remains to be seen, but it can fit into a low-use boutique library, albeit at a high price. Or maybe it would be the Espresso Book Machine (2011) with print-on-demand technology in the foyer that delivers a user a copy of an out-of-print book while they wait? No more waiting for an interlibrary loan from the British Library and no need for the library to stock little-used items on shelves anymore. Both of these technologies are prolonging the life of print resources in the hybrid library, but in truth the future is likely to be around the core technologies that I discuss in more detail below.

INSTITUTIONAL CONSIDERATIONS

On the face of it, there seems to be a contradiction in terms in speaking of a boutique service and a large-scale library system or technology, but it is my assertion that the best examples of web technologies in the retail sector offer personalised boutique services to the individual even if they are built at scale. The key one is Amazon, as it is offering the same products as libraries and is often cited by users as the service to which libraries should aspire (especially in speed of order delivery). Later in this chapter, I compare Amazon functionality against the new RHULLS LibrarySearch system. And, in terms of tailoring the boutique library collection to meet the boutique user needs, there are now new and proven approaches available from e-book suppliers that put the user firmly in the driving seat, powered by clicks and digital rights management (DRM). Social media and Web 2.0 and the expectation of self-service in everyday life have all led to the user wanting to be in control.

The key issue for boutique libraries with the application of such technologies and processes boils down to autonomy and this in turn relates to organisational structure. If the boutique library is a satellite or site library of a larger library service, can it have its own library management system (LMS) or search systems? To what extent is it possible or desirable for the larger library's systems to supply a separate instance or data-feed for a boutique library to customise? Also, might not such a move countermine the search experience for a user, and what about dedicated technical resource or e-resource management (ERM)?

On the face of it, it is rare that a boutique library, in the UK academic sector at least, has the organisational autonomy necessary to have control over its key technologies. A 2009 survey of the Business Librarians Association membership underlines this fact even for the traditionally autonomous business libraries (75 per cent of members were actually 'business sections within an integrated university library', 16 per cent were libraries within a university business school, and only 8 per cent were truly standalone). Instead, a boutique library is reliant on the parent or umbrella library service. How, therefore, in the age of a decreasingly hybrid library, can it hope to offer a boutique service if it cannot shape the way e-content is made available to its users? It is not going to be feasible to adopt its own system in the current climate of cuts and 'shared services' so therefore there is pressure for the central systems to be able to offer boutique-like services at scale, allowing the user much more control than has been the case in the past over the e-library. This benefits all users of the library rather than just the small subset of users who use one particular 'boutique'. On the other hand, social media technologies offer boutique libraries the freedom they need to put a tailored 'front-end' onto all services and content, whether locally or centrally provided, with a direct communication channel to their end users.

A review follows of specific technologies alongside relevant examples where put into practice.

DEMAND-DRIVEN E-BOOK ACQUISITION

'Demand-driven' or 'patron-driven' acquisition is a new business model for providing access to e-books. Libraries have traditionally purchased content on a 'just in case' basis, purchasing books in advance of anticipated needs to ensure that books are in stock when users need them. However, when purchasing in advance it can be difficult to predict exactly which titles will be needed, and studies from other libraries show that up to 55 per cent of titles purchased are never borrowed (Cornell University Library 2010), which is clearly poor value for money. Conversely, sometimes the library does not have the titles students want, or does not have enough copies to meet demand, resulting in poor student satisfaction.

Consequently, academic libraries in the US and UK have experimented with a 'just-in-time' approach, taking advantage of the potential of e-books to provide instant access to create a demand-driven acquisition model:

- Details of e-books available from book suppliers are loaded onto the library catalogue. When a user searches the catalogue, these e-books appear in their search results as if they were already part of the library's collection.
- If a user clicks on the link to one of these e-books, they can read it for free for up to five minutes. If they choose to continue reading after five minutes, the library pays a rental fee (typically 5 to 10 per cent of the full price of the book), which gives the reader temporary access to the book for a few days.
- If the book is requested a second or third time, the library again pays a rental fee. If the book is requested a fourth time, it is automatically purchased and the library is charged the full price of the book. The library now owns this e-book and all readers can use it whenever they like with no further fees.

This model aims to deliver the content users want, when they want it, and to avoid spending funds on acquiring content that is never used. No money is spent on books that are never used, while lower-price rental fees provide access to books that are only used once or twice, and the library only purchases books for which there is ongoing demand.

However, this does mean that money is spent on providing readers with temporary access to books that are not added to the library's collection – similar to spending more money on interlibrary loan requests at the expense of purchasing. Furthermore, any books purchased through this model are more expensive, because the total cost to the library includes the full price of the book plus three rental charges.

Case Study 1: Royal Holloway's Demand-driven Acquisition Pilot

To test this emerging business model, RHULLS (2011) ran a pilot study of demand-driven acquisitions, working with the supplier EBook Library (EBL 2011) during the busy end-of-term period in November/December 2010. Funding of £10,000 from the Student Textbook budget was allocated to support the project. Details of 30,000 e-books were loaded to the library catalogue, and during the study almost 1500 of these e-books were viewed, almost 900 were rented, and 37 were purchased.

Analysis   Although it ran for a short period, the pilot study has provided some useful data on RHULLS users' title selection. The overall level of demand, and consequently the rate of spend, was much higher than expected. It was initially hoped to run the study to the end of March 2011, but the funding was exhausted in just over five weeks. This was partly a consequence of the timing of the study – November is one of the busiest months for use of the library and its online resources, so demand was probably higher than it would have been at other times of the year. It may also reflect the high level of detail of the catalogue entries that were provided for the books, which may have helped users to discover more e-books that were relevant to their subject.

Of almost 1500 titles that were viewed, over 500 books were used for less than five minutes and therefore did not trigger a rental charge to the library. This may be because users found that the books were not relevant to them, or that five minutes was sufficient to retrieve the information they needed. Some users may have briefly viewed the e-book, and then decided to borrow a print copy to read in more detail. Whatever the reason, the ability to provide preview access to full-text e-books without charge is of value both to students deciding what to read and to academic staff wishing to preview a book before recommending it for purchase.

About 50 per cent of the e-books purchased were titles already held in print in the library. This demonstrated that the user-driven model is not just about providing access to titles not held by the library, but can also be used to provide instant access to additional copies where the library's print copies are out on loan, or to provide users with the option to use an e-book in preference to print, or to get 24/7 access to books even when the library is closed. Finally, the high number of rentals compared to purchases demonstrated that the demand-driven acquisitions model is not simply a new model for purchasing e-books, but is also about exploring user-driven rental. The pilot study provided an opportunity to investigate the best-value way to provide content to users, and to explore whether short-term rental actually provides better value than purchasing content that is used rarely or not at all.

In terms of the boutique model, this case study demonstrates how centrally managed activities can provide a local *tailored* boutique service, offering 'mass customisation'. The next challenge will be how to pipe such content into a local plethora of mobile e-book reading devices and smartphones.

Next Steps   Having already analysed where purchased e-books overlap with library print holdings, some of the rented e-books may be purchased for the library collection if funds are available. The e-strategy team will be monitoring usage of the e-books purchased during the pilot study, to see whether they are used on an ongoing basis. RHULLS will also consider a second phase in the 2011/12 academic year, to determine whether demand-driven acquisition could be run on an ongoing basis as a complement to the current model of selection-based purchasing.

However, it is clear that the rate of spend during the pilot study is unsustainable, and would need to be slowed in any future implementation of user-driven acquisition. This could be achieved in part by reducing the number and maximum price of titles made available to users through the library catalogue. For example, a focus could be made on key subject areas and key academic publishers, or the selection limited by date of publication. Various criteria can be used to select which books are added to the catalogue, and to ensure that the range of titles is closely matched to the needs of RHULLS users.

There are also options to adjust the rental/purchase criteria, for example increasing the number of rental requests that are paid before a book is purchased. Since rentals are cheaper than purchases this may slow the rate of spend, but it would also mean that the library spent an even higher proportion of funds on temporary access and acquired less content for its permanent collection. Conversely, decreasing the number of rentals would result in more purchases, but would probably increase the rate of spend. As noted above, determining an appropriate balance between rental and purchase is difficult and would require ongoing monitoring and assessment. Finally, it is possible to exercise greater control over both spending and title selection by mediating rental and/or purchase requests, as has been adopted at the University of East Anglia. Under this variation of the user-driven model, rather than granting immediate and automatic access to e-books at the end of the five-minute free preview, requests to read the e-book must be approved by a member of library staff. The library can choose whether all requests are approved, or only requests above a set price threshold. The library can also choose whether to offer a rental or to purchase a book straight away without paying for rentals, which gives more control over the allocation of funds to rentals versus purchases.

However, this approach has a number of disadvantages for library staff and for users:

- The library catalogue would include a mix of some e-books that the library has already purchased, which are immediately accessible to users, and 'e-books on demand', which would need to be requested by users. To avoid causing confusion and frustration to users:
  a) the catalogue would need to distinguish between available e-books and mediated e-books,
  b) we would need extensive publicity,
  c) we would need training for helpdesk or enquiry staff.
- Users would have to wait for access to a mediated e-book, and by the time access was granted they may no longer need the book (especially at weekends).
- Library staff would need to set criteria for approving or denying requests, and administer all requests.

This option would fundamentally change the nature of the project, since it no longer offers instant 'on demand' access. However, with high demand but limited funding, it is the only option that is sustainable in the long term, and other libraries that have piloted user-driven access have opted for this model.

Discussion   Key points to be made:

- There was a highly tailored selection by users, but would RHULLS librarians have chosen those 37 titles? Yes, for the 50 per cent already available in stock in print perhaps.
- The free five-minute preview option accounted for 33 per cent of use, so why do we not just load in thousands of titles into LMSs with this activated (or the Google Books equivalent)?
- The ratio of loans to purchases chosen was unsustainable – do we want to add in a mediated option or is the small percentage of likely rejects worth the staff time spent in mediating requests?
- Do boutique libraries need to have their own LMS in order to operate this?

Those university libraries that are further down this route than RHULLS have made some interesting decisions. Northampton has decided to upload 150,000 e-book records into its catalogue each year and uses a script to hide those e-books that have not been bought once the pot of money set aside for purchase has been used up. Newcastle has put in over £75,000 to their scheme and UEA has opted to switch on the mediated purchase option in order to act as a way of forcing users to think whether they really need the book for a longer period of time – hardly any requests for purchase are turned down.

Although there is quite considerable scope to customise the pool of books available for the single boutique library, unless the library has control over its systems it is unlikely that the boutique library will have much say over this centralised service. But from the user perspective, it is an example of where the back-office machinations are irrelevant as the user is getting what they want there and then, provided of course that the publisher has made a deal with the respective supplier. This issue is also relevant when considering making such e-book content available on whatever mobile device the user happens to have with them.

DISCOVERY SYSTEMS

Discovery systems are a new generation of library systems inspired by Google search architecture of massive content indexes. They are built around a central index of licensed third-party content and local content feeds (for example, from the library catalogue and institutional repository) offering speedy searches from one single-search box and faceted deduplicated results lists. Marshall Breeding (2010) provides an excellent summary of what Discovery systems should offer our users and why they have become the next big thing for academic libraries in the twenty-first century:

> *A great Discovery interface should operate in a mostly self-explanatory way, allowing users to concentrate on selecting and evaluating the resources returned rather than struggling through the search tools that the library provides. Explaining the idiosyncrasies of the brand names of the publishers and providers from which we acquire information resources in wholesale often becomes the focus of information literacy and bibliographic instruction. Since so many library users consume the products we offer from outside our library buildings, having more intuitive tools to deliver library resources that do not require special training represents a valuable advance in the state of the art. The ability to assemble into a single index all the books, journal articles, and other collection components, in my mind, represents one of the most significant breakthroughs in library automation in recent decades.*

Case Study 2 below details another library technology implementation at Royal Holloway, this time an attempt to customise a Discovery system for local needs while harnessing the power of its central content – a classic illustration of both 'mass personalisation' and the tensions inherent within the boutique model. Then at the end of this chapter we compare the RHULLS system against Amazon to determine how well current state-of-the-art library technology compares against best-of-breed commercial equivalent.

Case Study 2: Implementing a Discovery System

RHULLS decided to implement the Summon Discovery System from Serials Solutions in 2010 on the basis of quality of interface, cost, space, content and API availability against two other competing systems. Summon is a 'Software as a Service' system, which means it is hosted remotely on behalf of RHULLS. A beta version of the service went live in September 2010, but it was evident that, in order to truly offer an integrated and powerful search-and-browse experience to the user, additional work would be required to implement a Discovery layer on top of Summon data that would combine Aleph account functionality and OpenURL resolver data with Web 2.0 functionality for users to personalise the service to meet their needs. School of Management students, for example, had requested the ability to review and rate individual e-resources, something that was not available in the 'vanilla' Summon interface at the time.

Having had prior experience of implementing an open source interface layer on top of a proprietary Ex Libris system (Grigson et al. 2010) and conscious of the first successful implementation of VuFind (2011) in the UK at the London School of Economics (LSE) for a new interface for their legacy SirsiDynix OPAC, the systems team were able to start work on a similar solution with Summon, this time using the VuFind open source interface developed by Villanova University's Falvey Memorial Library. Using VuFind meant that RHULLS could customise the Discovery interface to meet local needs and integrate additional local data and functionality with the Summon data API, including OpenURL resolver data via the SFX4 API and Aleph account management data via a web services combination of the Aleph X-Server and RESTful API.

The main challenges were (a) configuring the VuFind software to work comprehensively with Aleph as RHUL were one of the first Aleph users to contemplate using VuFind in this way, and (b) handling the complexities of the emergent architecture created from installing VuFind on top of an existing Summon implementation rather than implementing them simultaneously. Principally this meant that our indexing of all of our data sources was being done by Summon in the cloud rather than locally by the VuFind Solr search engine – this complicates data exchange and means there is a 24-hour delay in changes to catalogue data appearing to the end user. The final challenge was working out how to offer decent e-resource browse lists by subject and by title as these had not been indexed in the catalogue before. The Xerxes installation had very good browse capabilities and we needed to offer something similar without needing to maintain the MetaLib software to deliver it. A MediaWiki (2011) approach was identified as used by the University of Huddersfield with their Summon implementation. The benefit of this approach was that additional information and screenshots could be added to each e-resource entry for the first time and the wiki interface was easier to maintain than in the past. The downside of this approach was that we would be diluting the goal of a single interface for users combining search and browse functionality – they would still have to contend with the VuFind interface and MediaWiki interface (and possibly the old customised interlibrary loan interface in the Aleph OPAC). Nevertheless this was still a 50 per cent reduction in the number of interfaces RHULLS users had to cope with!

In the tradition of open-source community, any refinements and development had to be tested and incorporated into later releases of the master version of the software available from vufind.org – but this did mean that we could benefit from the wider development community when we hit problems. There is an overhead in version control in keeping track of local changes to the source code against the original.

Discussion   From a boutique library point of view, this case study illustrates the tension between the centrally managed activities and the local (boutique) activities with a twist – the centrally managed activities (search and browse) are actually in the cloud externally. VuFind was implemented to enable more local control of such activities, but how local can such control be? Could there be a business and management version (interface) to a subset of the centrally managed content and an arts and humanities version? This is exactly the kind of skinnable interface being promoted by EBSCO (2011) with their EBSCO Discovery product. Would boutique libraries have the capacity to build their own open source installations? Unlikely, but, depending on their relationship to the institution and institution library service, they could subscribe to their own if the local needs were very specific. This may be required in any case for non-standard user support such as alumni and executive education clients. A boutique business school library may require a separate Discovery system anyway in order to guarantee ring-fencing of content access from the standard academic licensed content. As these products are effectively subscriptions and hosted services, the ability to switch and cancel is much easier than with locally installed systems.

Having read Case Study 2, it will be recognised that, from a boutique library viewpoint, Discovery services are unlikely to ever be able to offer a single Discovery interface to all boutique library content. The London Business School Library, for example, subscribes to very specialist financial information datasets such as those provided by Bloomberg commonly used only by City financial institutions for investment analysis. These were not designed for the academic market and not priced for the academic market, and there is no driver yet in the City for single-interface searching. The volume, complexity and non-textual nature of such datasets would not lead them to be integrated into the predominantly textual knowledge bases of library Discovery systems. The boutique library therefore still needs to maintain and administer such services separately from the rest and facilitate their use (often in a very restricted way due to strict license conditions). Nonetheless, there is still value in the London Business School in replacing its federated search system with a Discovery system to take advantage of its speed and more comprehensive searching for its textual dataset subscriptions even if the high-value market research content used heavily by business schools has yet to be licensed by the Discovery system providers.

VIRTUAL ENQUIRY AND TRAINING SERVICES

Under the banner of 'research support', enquiry and training services are often the 'de facto' justification for a boutique library. Technologies to support them have been around for over ten years now and have become a stable part of library web presences. They are a very good example of how technology can assist a library to offer a tailored service at scale and distance, replicating the traditional one-to-one reference interview or one-to-one session at a user's desk or group training session. They are also an example of a very cheap or free technology that can be owned at local level.

With regard to so-called 'web-chat' or virtual enquiry services, customisation of service icons can fit in with boutique library sub-brands very easily and the number of operator licences can fit onto local staff patterns and rotas. The icons can also have the so-called 'Heineken effect', reaching parts of the institution that other central library services cannot reach, such as specific VLE pages or portal pages.

The challenge of such services is when the service needs to extend its opening hours beyond normal times and staff contracts have not yet been adjusted to fit. Then the library service has to move to a consortial virtual reference model as offered by OCLC's QuestionPoint (2011) that in effect offers cloud-based virtual librarian services through the different time zones of member libraries. This then dilutes the ability to offer a boutique service as generic support becomes the norm.

Virtual training software can be split into two different types: (1) screen capture software, and (2) conferencing software. I have written extensively about screen capture software elsewhere (Robertson and Wales 2008: 365–81), outlining the pros and cons of using the technology at the Open University Library. Free screen capture software exists and I believe it still has a place for quick visual aids. Collaborative conferencing software for education offers virtual classrooms with shared whiteboards, discussion rooms, shared presentation spaces, breakout spaces, recording, and so on, and plugs into the institutions' virtual learning environment. For a boutique library these technologies offer the ability to produce tailored content at point of need to specific user demands. But there is often tension from centrally managed services wishing to create generic tutorials and enquiry support to reduce the maintenance overhead and proliferation of the cottage-industry approach.

In the age of user-generated content such concerns are becoming increasingly irrelevant. For both technologies may be compromised by the documented tendency for our users to avoid using librarians or their proxies as sources of help and guidance (CIBER 2008). This is why renewed emphasis on creating simple and effective Discovery systems is key for all libraries, boutique or not. We provide the tools and data and see which ones work and are in demand.

SOCIAL MEDIA SERVICES

Here too are examples of internet technologies being seized upon by boutique libraries as an opportunity to offer customised tailored content, released from the confines of a corporate content management system or a rigid library website (or institutional communications) structure. They are increasingly all about 'impression management' or 'corporate reputation management'.

However, a 2010 Research Information Network report suggests that academics are not yet incorporating them systematically into their research practices as the benefits of doing so are not clear. The amount of engagement with comment and RSS feed features of such tools is often restricted to the most technology literate academics. As ever, it is very hard for librarians to get the right amount of credible feedback on such services to be able to evaluate their efficacy and utility.

Blogs

Although blogs were intended to be (and started off as) interactive journals, a recent trend has seen them become a simple form of web content management or speedy content broadcasting and the blog has replaced the existing library website as the primary web communication channel. This makes sense as blogs enable local control over websites with tagging imposing a structure on content alongside a traditional top bar navigational structure with breadcrumb trails to help the user orientate themselves through the content. User interaction is a bonus but not a prerequisite. Blogs may be hosted outside the institutional domain with their own domain name or within the domain as an embedded part of an existing website. The presence of these micro-sites has led to inevitable territorial disputes between libraries and institutional marketing, press and IT web teams over who has jurisdiction over branding, look and feel, and content control. The best diplomatic tactic for libraries in this situation is to offer to be the blogging testbed for the institution as a whole as it is likely that the university websites will become even more blog-like in the future. Boutique libraries that have multiple websites and subject blogs are likely to find these unsustainable on a per reader basis.

Facebook

Facebook sites take the boutique library online where the users are, but even so it is very hard to create and maintain a two-way relationship with users and Facebook page sites (as opposed to Facebook personal sites). Bells and whistles can be added in the form of widgets such as JSTOR and library catalogue search boxes or LibraryThing (2011) feeds, but there is no hard evidence to suggest that such tools are being used heavily or that the library's web presence should become solely its Facebook one. Nonetheless, provided the staff overhead of maintaining the Facebook page is kept low by means of content feeds, a Facebook page provides a quick PR and marketing win for the boutique library.

iTunes U

Specialist libraries such as HEC Library, Paris are also starting to load their own training content onto ITunes U to complement the learning material offered by the parent institution – this is an excellent method for libraries to establish a credible presence in the so-called walled gardens of third-party marketplaces and platform providers and for them to demonstrate politically their value to their own. It also helps the library contribute to their institutions' mobile platform strategy as a content provider. The user benefits from being able to access content on demand at a time of their choosing and on their preferred device. Quality control is vital as there is no hiding place for out-of-date training materials on iTunes U.

Twitter

Having started off mainly as a professional networking aide, Twitter (2011) is now a core utensil in the boutique library's communications toolbox. As with Facebook, it offers a new means of targeting communications directly at the end user and gaining direct feedback, whether in new followers, retweets or direct messages. Tweets are also indexed in Google, so contributing to search optimisation for the source library. Twitter news feeds are starting to replace RSS feeds on library websites – the latter never proving popular with end users, the former perfect for short sharp service bulletins that can get lost on a busy library website. Thanks to Twitter's API, a whole infrastructure of support tools is now available too to help libraries extract maximum value from their tweets.

The discipline Twitter engenders of communicating within a fixed number of characters mitigates the profession's tendency to produce too much textual support information. As with other social media, the library will have to justify its own Twitter account alongside that of its parent institution. But retweeting allows the central press/communications department to pass on library communications under the main brand.

In the near future, we are likely to see relevant tweets indexed into library news sources datasets and library systems generating tweets as well as text messages to users. Indeed, it will be interesting to see whether Twitter eventually replaces SMS as the primary consumer asynchronous text communication channel.

Wikis

As with blogs above, the purpose and possible applications of wiki technology is starting to evolve. Originally used as an internal knowledge management tool and replacing the old library intranet, offering online staff manuals and handbooks or collating practical sets of core internal web links, the continued success and sustainability of the Wikipedia (2011) model has led to libraries using the well-supported MediaWiki software for user-facing content provision. Case Study 2 contains an example of this: a MediaWiki e-resource browsing interface (with screenshots) developed by Huddersfield to replace their Ex Libris MetaLib-delivered equivalent. Although I briefly considered replacing a conventional library website with a library wiki site (open to registered editors as per the Wikipedia model) to offer the ultimate in a tailored, crowd-sourced library website, the increased use of assessed student wikis in VLEs is likely to be the main manifestation of user-facing wikis in an academic context at present, as pioneered by the Open University in their Moodle (2011) environment.

LIBRARY CONTENT ON MOBILE DEVICES

The success of the iTunes/iPhone/iPad model and the proliferation of e-book reading devices backed up by downloadable fiction content is leading to an expectation that academic libraries can and should offer the same. Esposito (2011) neatly summarises the bind in which librarians find themselves in this area. The fact that academic libraries have been offering e-books in many different forms for over ten years now counts for nothing. So often, the particular content that our users want is not made available to academic libraries by the respective publishers who are still trying to protect their print revenues. Also, a suite of different e-book platforms have sprung up with standard library authentication systems that are completely different to the iTunes/Amazon consumer e-book model. Up until now, the two markets (consumer and academic) have been completely different, but the availability of technology has started to blur the boundaries. As the Gartner (2010) analysts have noted, users expect to be able to use their own devices in a corporate environment without any trouble.

However, e-books offer a great opportunity for the boutique library to offer a personalised service. The absence of academic e-books on iTunes for now is not necessarily a barrier: focus is shifting to preloading selected (and highly tailored) course content onto mobile devices that can either be borrowed by users or given to them as part of the course offering they sign up to. This is analogous to the previous practice of higher education institutions providing key printed set books to students at the start of terms to take the pressure off limited library stock. The difference is that the new librarian skills sets relating to licensing and rights clearance can be applied to support the acquisition process here. The challenge for the institution is to ensure that they are not paying over the odds for the content (nearly zero cost in replicating the successive digital copies after all) and that usage rights are sufficiently flexible. Perhaps of less importance is the interaction of such content with other library systems.

The interplay between central and boutique services again comes into play here. Is the expectation that the e-resources librarian handles the rights clearance, or can this be devolved to a boutique level within an agreed set of conditions, standards and expectations?

It is too soon to say whether this is an evolutionary or revolutionary step. We do not know user preference for carrying a variety of devices: mobile phone, laptop and e-book reader against, say, mobile phone and tablet device. The technology does not last long and there is a massive overhead in keeping it current – there is a cupboard full of obsolete e-book readers at Royal Holloway. And new types of device in development have still to come to market, such as foldable electronic paper. The overhead in supporting these different types of readers cannot be overstated, akin to the overhead in supporting desktop PCs or lendable laptops with a continual cycle of software updates, content deletions, repairs and battery charging, not to mention testing against the latest browser or platforms.

Although US libraries have had a head start in exploring this area, there are various pilot projects underway in the UK investigating the viability of offering preloaded content to users via e-book readers. While projects such as ALPS are focusing on assessment tools on mobile devices in the medical disciplines, libraries like Queen's University Belfast have been experimenting with lending out a small collection of Amazon Kindles (catalogued and circulated as if normal library stock) with a limited number of Amazon-purchased e-books preloaded. Feedback so far has been mixed, with concerns around the range of content and specific e-book device. There are also increased staff resource overheads involved in maintaining the devices for circulation. This is a fast-moving field and the likes of Inkling for iPad are starting to address the issue of key textbooks in the HE sector not being available in traditional e-book forms. Even if not offering preloaded library content, there is a still a strong case for boutique libraries acquiring a couple of tablet devices to assist with roaming user support.

What about boutique library apps for smartphones? This is one area where centrally managed activities win out in the boutique model. Universities are employing companies such as oMbiel (2011) to create university apps that include basic library functionality. The service offering to the user would be very confused if boutique libraries were able to develop their own in the shadow of the parent institution. However, a compromise approach, in the absence of any initiative in this area from the host institution or library, would be for the boutique library to serve as the development arm for the institution to develop an initial library app with a third-party supplier that could form the basis of a bigger library app in future, following the principle of perpetual beta. Meanwhile library suppliers and publishers are already starting to offer direct-to-user apps bypassing the four walls of the library. The demand for these is likely to outstrip demand for any library specific app; the boutique librarian is left to know about them and support them as best they can.

BENCHMARKING BOUTIQUE LIBRARY TECHNOLOGIES

Having reviewed the technologies and read the case studies of how some of them have been implemented, it is tempting to think that our job is done. The truth is that the library community, boutique or not, is still not offering information services comparable to the best of breed in the commercial sector. I would like to illustrate this by taking Amazon as an example.

Amazon is perhaps not the obvious example of a boutique service against which boutique library can benchmark itself, but in my estimation it is the true example of personalised retail (and library-like service) delivered successfully at scale across the world. Amazon users get a personal experience tailored specifically to them based on their past transactions with the service. Depending where they live, they will also get regional variations where local laws and practices allow. For example, Amazon delivers a corporate service to libraries in the US but not in the UK. Similarly the Search Inside service respects regional publishing rights.

We should acknowledge the comments of Pariser (2011) at this point, who reminds us that (a) the personalisation services of Amazon and Google are not totally machine driven as a team of human editors is still required to overrule the results of algorithmic searches, and (b) users can get stuck in a so-called 'filter bubble', oblivious to information that lies beyond the set of information carefully tailored to their previous search behaviours (or moods or even state of health in the future). We'll have to see how the library Discovery system providers respond to these possible limitations.

In the meantime, how does the latest library technology compare against its commercial equivalent? Table 4.2 compares Amazon functionality and personalisation against the LibrarySearch Discovery system at Royal Holloway featured in Case Study 2. The outcome shows good progress, but there is still a way to go.

Table 4.2   **Amazon versus RHULLS LibrarySearch functionalities**

Functionality	Amazon	Library
Single sign-on and account management	✓	✓
Fast searching	✓	✓
Single search across all resource types	✓	✓
Faceted browsing across all resource types	✓	½
User reviews and ratings	✓	✓
More like this Users who bought x also bought y	✓	✗
Personalised recommendations and alerts	✓	✗
Downloadable e-content	✓	✓
Regional variations	✓	✗

Note: Comparison as of July 2011.

Some of the crosses or fractions by LibrarySearch are not a restriction of the technology itself but merely a limitation imposed by legacy data or systems constraints. For example, imposing a consistent institution-specific ontology across Royal Holloway data (as has been done at Open University Library) would facilitate the creation of a truly comprehensive faceted browse but would also require a new architecture with the creation of a middle-layer SQL database. Regional variations are unknown territories. VuFind does have regional interfaces available, but the challenge would be in offering content in the correct language (perhaps use of Google Translate via an API could help there) and also in respecting local licensing and copyright constraints.

However, the main limitation of Discovery systems in a boutique environment cannot be revealed by benchmarking against Amazon alone. This comes back to the specialist and complex nature of the information domains in which many specialist libraries operate. A business library is more than just books and journal articles: it includes specialist corporate finance and statistical databases, some such as Bloomberg still sold on custom terminals, a throwback to the earliest library retrieval systems from the early 1980s including large and complex financial data with their own search interfaces. At best, they will integrate with MS Office. There is not a lot of cross-data standardisation of these datasets and certainly the business model behind them is restrictive for the academic market – data would not be licensed separately for Discovery systems. And the same is true of chemical information in the likes of the Beilstein database. And in the engineering sector we have patents, standards, data sheets and physical properties to contend with, some more standardised than others.

So the boutique library user still has to contend with separate interfaces and perhaps still has to receive dedicated support for these, whether delivered by the librarians or the supplier's own set of trainers. Only if the corporate market wants to have consolidated Discovery, or these datasets are merged over a few years when their suppliers are taken over by larger conglomerates, is this situation likely to change. The current impasse in open research data in the academic community also indicates the complexities of trying to catalogue and archive this data in a consistent and retrievable way.

THE FUTURE

*I never think of the future. It comes soon enough. (*Albert Einstein (1879–1955) in Knowles 2009: 305)

It seems foolhardy to try to predict the future in light of Einstein's words above, but I believe it is necessary for a book chapter to extend its practical working life by flagging a selection of current developments in 2011, any one of which may impact on libraries in the next five years and therefore should be monitored closely by today's boutique librarians. Some are smaller in scale and impact than others:

- Augmented reality – this offers new life to the remaining print collections by offering users the ability to use their smartphone cameras to locate stock in the manner of Google Street View – with annotated classmarks and directions appearing on the live images. This requires RFID tags to work and phones with RFID readers embedded.
- National ERM or Shared Services initiative – a current SCONUL/JISC (2011) project is investigating the feasibility of a central data platform (known as Knowledgebase+) for HE libraries to manage their e-resources (primarily e-journals). This once again illustrates the tension between centralised library services and systems and the boutique library's desire to customise such services.
- Next-generation library management systems – Ex Libris (2011) launched its new workflow-based system, Alma, in 2011 with a two-year development phase with preferred partners and a full release expected in early 2014. It has been built from scratch as a SaaS with a new-system architecture and knowledge base at its heart. Apart from OCLC's and ProQuest's Web-scale Management Services, the alternatives will be open source LMS systems from the likes of Koha, Evergreen and Kuali (2011).
- E-paper – this has the most potential as a disruptive technology. This will provide an alternative to e-book readers and lend itself to easier custom publishing. Librarians could 're-intermediate' themselves by negotiating custom content with publishers and lecturers to load onto the paper directly. It will also replace smartboards and screens and display screens as the

primary means of displaying information to users in the physical learning space.

• Interactive 3D avatar software – it is already technically possible (Lionhead Studios 2009) for a self-learning computer-generated avatar to interact verbally and physically with humans and complex objects via 3D cameras. Once the cost of the technology comes down, these avatars could start appearing on reception and helpdesks as the boutique librarian of the future!

N.B. I recommend following the work of Breeding to see how close the above predictions come to fruition. He offers regular analyses and annual summaries of the 'state of play' of the academic library technology market.

CONCLUSION

This chapter has attempted to demonstrate that there are various technological solutions now available that are offering a personalised library user experience whether delivered centrally or locally. Although there is still work to be done to improve library search and browse in comparison with best-of-breed commercial systems and the e-book marketplace is still immature, a boutique library can now use a basket of technologies to differentiate itself. Unlike in the past four decades of library automation, these new technologies are increasingly free or subscription based so that the boutique library's technology strategy can be one of constant evolution or 'perpetual beta', no longer locked into the development cycle of monopolistic library management system using proprietary code. If something does not work it can be dropped or replaced by a different product (something already occurring in the UK Discovery system market as the first movers re-evaluate their initial system choice as the market develops).

This reality is amply demonstrated by Helen Edwards' case study in this book, in which she had the once-in-a-lifetime opportunity to build a boutique library from scratch and, within a limited budget, choose the resources and technologies she needed from many of those studied in this chapter. Would she have been able to do this relatively easily without a team of library systems officers even five years ago?

FINAL WORD – A CHOCOLATE ON THE PILLOW?

One of the memorable concepts from the Personalised Library Services Symposium convened by the editors in March 2011, was the signature trait of the boutique hotel – the welcome luxury chocolate on the pillow for all new guests entering their boutique suite for the first time. I left the event reflecting on what the equivalent of this could be in the boutique e-library and came up with the idea of a free piece of personalised e-content (iTunes download or voucher or e-book) relevant to the user's research topic. What would be your suggestion?

TOP TIPS AND PRACTICAL ADVICE

Discovery Systems

- Do not be put off by cost. Discovery systems can be as cheap as a subscription to a major aggregated e-resource subscription, especially for a three-year commitment (and lower JISC-banded institutions). There are also savings to be made from cancelling A&I subscriptions replicated in the Discovery systems knowledge base.
- The quality of your Discovery experience for your users boils down to the quality of your metadata and that of your suppliers. Do consider cleaning up both before you start (it can be outsourced) as there are no hiding places for rubbish data anymore and it will save a lot of work in the implementation process.
- If you wish to include data from specialist local or in-house databases, see if they can be configured to export data in OAI-PMH format as this will save a lot of technical time in future if they can.

Infrastructure

- Get your library service to implement a proxy server if they have not already done so, even if you have another authentication system! Library system suppliers such as Serials Solutions, Talis and OCLC (2011) are all starting to offer SaaS access management solutions using proxy server technology. And they can also be used to ring-fence services to special user types (Smith, Street and Wales 2007: 162–76).
- Discuss open-source solutions with your IT team and show them examples of successful implementations elsewhere. A modular mix-and-match approach may be best to begin with – for example, start with a local MediaWiki implementation then an open-source room-booking system then look at, say, an ERM module. Make the case for any tender or procurement documentation to be sent to open-source 'design-and-build' hosting companies as well as proprietary library systems providers.

E-books

- Link to Google Books from your catalogue records. It offers the simple browsable and 'chunkable' access to e-books that our users demand and shows how libraries can work with Google to meet user needs. It is a free alternative to paid-for catalogue enrichment services.

Social Media

- Do not be afraid to experiment with different social media, but try to use content feeds to eliminate manual effort in keeping them up to date. For example, an RSS feed from your library website or Twitter account can populate your service's blog and Facebook page.
- Use services such as TwInbox (2011) to setup automated Twitter searches to monitor for user feedback about your library or HootSuite (2011) to schedule your own service's Twitter messages to be sent outside of your normal opening hours.

Virtual Services

- Investigate ways of recording your training sessions and chunking them into discrete bitesize topics so that users can replay them at their leisure on iTunes.
- Be wary, however, of adding audio commentary to screen-capture sessions. It is better to rely on onscreen annotations and call-outs to keep maintenance and complexity cost down.
- Get the library or institution to invest in an online survey software subscription to enable quick polling of different user types and easy analysis of result.

ACKNOWLEDGEMENTS

The author writes in a personal capacity but would like to acknowledge the work of Royal Holloway, University of London Library Services staff for providing source material for this chapter: Anna Grigson for Case Study 1 and Peter Kiely and Graham Seaman for their work on Discovery systems described in Case Study 2.

REFERENCES

ABLD. 2010. ABLD 2010 Conference [online]. At: http://bit.ly/fgaKzQ (accessed: 21 August 2011).

BBSLG. 2009. Membership Survey 2009 [online]. At: http://www.blalib.org (accessed: 21 August 2011, from members' area).

Bloomsbury. 1997. Future, in *Bloomsbury Thematic Dictionary of Quotations [online]*. At: http://www.credoreference.com/entry/btdq/future (accessed: 22 May 2011).

Breeding, M. 2010. State of the Art in Library Discovery 2010 [online]. At: http://bit.ly/g2dCUZ (accessed: 21 August 2011).

Breeding, M. 2011. Automation Marketplace 2011: The New Frontier. *Library Journal*, 1 April [online]. At: http://bit.ly/gFCW4g (accessed: 21 August 2011).

CIBER. 2008. Information Behaviour of the Researcher of the Future [online]. At: http://www.ucl.ac.uk/infostudies/research/ciber/downloads/ (accessed: 21 August 2011).

Cornell University Library. 2010. Report of the Collection Development Executive Committee Task Force on Print Collection Usage [online]. At: http://bit.ly/fhhXXQ (accessed: 21 August 2011).

EBL. 2011. At: http://www.eblib.com/ (accessed: 1 July 2011).

EBSCO Discovery Service. 2011. At: http://www.ebscohost.com/discovery (accessed: 1 July 2011).

Edwards, H. 2010. Reinventing the Business School Library: SKOLKOVO Moscow School of Management (Online Information 2010 presentation) [online]. At: http://bit.ly/j6uYtC (accessed: 21 August 2011).

Esposito, C. 2011. The Vexed Problem of Libraries, Publishers, and E-books, in The Scholarly Kitchen: What's Hot and Cooking in Scholarly Publishing [online]. At: http://bit.ly/hhfsW8 (accessed: 21 August 2011).

Espresso Book Machine. 2011. At: http://www.ondemandbooks.com/ebm_hardware.php (accessed: 21 August 2011).

Evergreen. 2011. At: http://open-ils.org/ (accessed: 10 June 2011).

Ex Libris Aleph Integrated Library Management System. 2011. At: http://www.exlibrisgroup.com/category/Aleph (accessed: 1 June 2011).

Fortune, M. 2010. Smart Shelving in Action at the University of Cardiff – First Impressions [online]. At: http://www.mickfortune.com/Wordpress/?p=285 (accessed 21 August 2011).

Gartner. 2010. Predicts 2011: Technology and the Transformation of the Education Ecosystem [online]. At: http://bit.ly/esi11m (accessed: 1 May 2011).

Google Books. 2011. At: http://books.google.com/ (accessed: 1 May 2011).

Grigson, A., Kiely, P., Seaman, G. and Wales, T. 2010. Get Tooled Up: Xerxes at Royal Holloway, University of London. *Ariadne* 62 [online]. At: http://www.ariadne.ac.uk/issue62/grigson-et-al/ (accessed: 21 August 2011).

Holden, D. 2011. Check Out a Kindle Presentation [private correspondence].

HootSuite. 2011. At: http://hootsuite.com/ (accessed: 1 July 2011).

Knowles, E. 2009. *Oxford Dictionary of Quotations*, 7th edn. Oxford: Oxford University Press.

Koha. 2011. At: http://www.koha.org/ (accessed: 1 July 2011).

Kuali. 2011. At: http://kuali.org (accessed: 21 July 2011).

LibraryThing. 2011. At: http:/www.librarything.com (accessed: 1 August 2011).

Lionhead Studios. 2009. Project Natal demonstration [online]. At: http://bit.ly/X8jn7 (accessed: 31 July 2011).

Luther, J. and Kelly, M.C. 2011. The Next Generation of Discovery. *Library Journal*, 15 March [online]. At: http://bit.ly/gfxedy (accessed: 21 August 2011).

MediaWiki. 2011. At: http://www.mediawiki.org (accessed: 21 August 2011).

Moodle. 2011. At: http://moodle.org/ (accessed: 21 August 2011).

OCLC EZproxy. 2011. At: http://www.oclc.org/ezproxy/ (accessed: 1 June 2011).

OCLC QuestionPoint. 2011. At: http://www.questionpoint.org/ (accessed: 1 June 2011).

oMbiel Ltd. 2011. At: http://www.ombiel.com/ (accessed: 21 August 2011).

Pariser, E. 2011. The Filter Bubble [online]. At: http://www.thefilterbubble.com (accessed: 21 August 2011).

Priestner, A. and Tilley, E. 2010. Boutique Libraries at your Service. *Library & Information Update*, 9(6), 36–9.

Research Information Network (RIN). 2010. If You Build it, Will They Come? How Researchers Perceive and Use Web 2.0: A Report Funded by the Research Information Network (RIN) [online]. At: http://www.rin.ac.uk/our-work/communicating-and-disseminating-research/use-and-relevance-web-20-researchers (accessed: 10 March 2012).

Robertson, P. and Wales, T. 2008. Captivating Open University Students with Online Literature Search Tutorials Created Using Screen Capture Software. *Program*, 42(4), 365–81 [online]. At: http://oro.open.ac.uk/12218/1/wales08rev2.pdf (accessed: 1 August 2011).

Royal Holloway LibrarySearch. 2011. At: http://librarysearch.rhul.ac.uk/ (accessed: 21 August 2011).

SCONUL. 2011. SCONUL Shared Services Project [online). At: http://helibtech.com/SCONUL_Shared_Services (accessed: 21 August 2011).

Serials Solutions Summon. 2011. At: http://www.serialsolutions.com/summon/ (accessed: 21 August 2011).

Smith, G., Street, K. and Wales, T. 2007. An Online Library Service for Open University MBA Alumni – Challenges and Opportunities. *Journal of Librarianship and Information Science*, 39(3), 162–76.

TwInbox. 2011. At: http://www.techhit.com/TwInbox/ (accessed: 23 July 2011).

Twitter. 2011. At: http://www.twitter.com/ (accessed: 21 August 2011).

VuFind. 2011. At: http://www.vufind.org (accessed: 23 July 2011).

Wikipedia. 2011. At: http://en.wikipedia.org/ (accessed: 21 August 2011).

CHAPTER 5

MAXIMISING VALUE, ENHANCING LEARNING: BOUTIQUE TEACHING AND TRAINING
CHRIS POWIS

INTRODUCTION: TEACHING IN LIBRARIES

Much has been written about the role of librarians as teachers and it is not the intention of this chapter to repeat those discussions and rehearse the same arguments. That part of the professional identity of a librarian is a teacher, trainer or, at least, a facilitator of learning is widely established. Although this is particularly manifested in subject librarians, who work alongside academic colleagues to integrate information skills or digital literacy within academic disciplines, it applies to librarians working in all sectors. It is, however, pertinent to examine what is meant by teaching and training in a library context before examining how the boutique model can be applied to this activity.

The image of teaching that most will identify with is that of a teacher standing in front of a room of learners. This is still certainly a common scenario for library and information professionals as it is relatively cost effective in terms of the numbers that can be taught and matches the expectations and experience of learners and of those arranging for the teaching. It is also a comforting model for librarians who can prepare for and deliver teaching within a framework that they understand and can usually control. Librarians, especially those in schools, colleges and universities, can therefore be found delivering lectures, workshops and seminars in much the same way as their academic colleagues. These methods are also the default mode of delivery used by librarians in all sectors for staff development.

But this is not the only way in which librarians can or should deliver their teaching or training and it is absolutely not the only, or indeed most common, way that learning will take place. Squires (1994: 14) defines learning as being an interaction with people, information, events and experiences 'including but not confined to teaching/training.' This definition is key to understanding the role of librarians in teaching and learning. Interactions with information happen all the time in libraries – opening a book, clicking on a web page or even reading a poster can be part of a learning experience. Learning can take place over an information desk or through a conversation with a library user. Peer learning is ubiquitous in libraries as people with common interests share knowledge in formal or informal settings, often without the intervention of a librarian but within an environment designed and managed by library staff. Librarians are still working as teachers or trainers when designing online learning activities or even their departmental or service web pages. They are teaching or training when they write leaflets or guides, when they tour people around or create self-guided tours, workbooks or trails. The common factor in all of these activities is that they require the librarian to understand learning and their learners. This applies whether or not the people they work with would identify themselves as learners.

This is where the boutique model has a clear resonance to teaching and learning in libraries. At the heart of the model lies a desire to deliver services and experiences that meet individual customer, or here learner, expectations, needs and desires. Whatever the context of the learning, and whatever the delivery method, the learner must be at the heart of the learning experience. Designing the teaching, training and learning around the learner will mean a more satisfying and fulfilling experience for both learner and teacher/librarian, but it can also mean a loss, real or perceived, of control in the teacher–learner relationship. It will certainly mean a questioning of delivery methods and perhaps a shift in emphasis away from classroom delivery to more learning experiences where the focus of teaching and learning is not a formal classroom situation but rather interaction with carefully designed learning environments (physical and virtual) accessing support as needed.

This may require a radical shift in our understanding of what makes an effective learning opportunity. Sugata Mitra's 'Hole in the Wall' experiment in 'Minimally Invasive Education' is a great, and sobering, example for those librarians working on 'how to' guides, planning lectures or struggling to run voluntary workshops. It offers a completely differently paradigm of how to create effective learning opportunities. In 1999 a computer was placed in a kiosk created within a wall in a slum at Delhi and children were allowed to use it freely. The 'Hole in the Wall' (HIW) experiment aimed at proving that young people could be taught by computers very easily without any formal training. The experiment has since been repeated in other parts of India and in other countries. This work demonstrated that groups of children, irrespective of who or where they are, can learn to use computers and the internet on their own using public computers in open spaces such as roads and playgrounds. Even more powerfully, the children not only worked out how to use it themselves but shared that knowledge without intervention from a teacher or trainer (Hole-in-the-Wall Education Ltd 2011).

The mass inductions and endlessly repeated largely generic information skills workshops that have characterised much of the further and higher education teaching landscape for librarians over the last 30 years are good examples of a 'fast food' style of delivery – the antithesis of boutique. The growth in student numbers over the same period, and the concurrent success of librarians in convincing their academic colleagues of the importance of information skills, has meant that sheer economies of scale have driven many librarians to delivery methods that seem to compromise the personalised and highly tailored offerings of a boutique approach. However, a closer look at the characteristics of the components of the model shows a more nuanced and encouraging picture.

A LEARNER FOCUS

Customer or learner focus is central to the idea of the boutique library. This is achieved through understanding the learner needs and targeting the teaching and training, and the services that back up the teaching, to those needs. The method of delivery is not as important as the ethos of the service. Lectures and workshops can be learner focused if librarians take time to work with the students and other parties to make examples and case studies relevant. Strategies to enhance liaison with stakeholders will be covered in more detail later in the chapter, but it is important to stress that, however good a teaching session, however well prepared and delivered, however targeted and pertinent and however sound the learning materials are, it will all fail the learner-focused test if the services offered elsewhere in the library (virtual or actual) are not also designed with the learner in mind. These should include appropriate and accessible learning resources, well-designed websites, help pages and other guide material, well-trained staff on help points or staffing virtual services, and well-laid-out and intuitive environments. These will provide the tools for the learners to actually put into practice the skills learnt during the teaching and training.

Highly tailored teaching does not need to be confined to one-to-one engagements with learners although these should be a part of any library's service offering. By using topics gleaned from the learners during demonstrations or a Q&A session, and by building in time during workshops for the learners to explore using their own examples, a generic teaching session on, for example, evaluating information can seem to be tailored to the individual's needs. In part this is an illusion, just as a boutique hotel does not really cater exclusively to the individual but offers a suite of things that match what that customer wants from a hotel experience. The tailored teaching session is essentially a generic class with some individualised inputs, but it will allow the user to take from it something memorable and personal to their learning needs.

Tailoring the teaching to an individual learner is also, inevitably, linked to understanding the context within which the learner is working. Librarians are often involved in the teaching of referencing, for example, and although it might be interesting to explore the nature of referencing by looking across different referencing systems it would make little sense to do so with learners who are only concerned with 'getting it right' using the organisation's or subject's favoured system. Tailoring the teaching to individual learners is probably best achieved through integrating the information skills elements into their wider learning framework – for example, the course, module or subject being followed. Typically, in education this would mean teaching on timetabled slots rather than optional sessions, or team teaching alongside academic colleagues to present a seamless front between subject and information skills. True integration is difficult to achieve and can often be undone through careless branding of the sessions. A boutique experience needs to speak to the individual and the title, and particularly the learning outcomes of any teaching event need to appeal to a particular learning need or desire. A generic session (a drop-in or something titled 'Library Workshop' or similar) will only rarely do this.

INNOVATION IN TEACHING

The marketing efforts of boutique hotels emphasise uniqueness, usually through the quirky or themed decor and service. This is clearly more difficult to achieve when teaching information skills. However, to be properly boutique our teaching needs to offer something fresh to the learner. This means that it does not have to be unique per se but just fresh to their experience of learning and can often be achieved through delivering the unexpected or simply being the first to do something in your institution. This can vary between the completely unexpected, for example the use of music and audience participation during the Cephalonian induction method (Morgan and Davies 2004: 4–8), or may be as simple as a change in seating plan or the use of gaming techniques in an online teaching package. Try introducing competition into your sessions (at Northampton we have used a pub quiz format to teach referencing) or simply vary the 'usual' format of your teaching.

Much of our teaching follows a very safe format of introduction, demonstration, practical and conclusion. As a structure, it is reliable and effective, especially in a one-off teaching session, but it is also a format that learners will probably have experienced before in their education. Thinking about other structures for the session design can make your standard content seem novel and fresh. For example, instead of demonstrating good searching techniques and then letting the learners try them out, why not start with a practical first followed by an analysis of the results? This can start a personalised discussion about how to improve (and assess) the quality of your results. It will inject interest, create opportunities for debate and reflection, and seem different, with content unique to that specific class. It is, of course, based on the classical Socratic method!

Freshness can be injected into your teaching through early adoption of new techniques and/or tools within your organisation. These have included (in the 1990s) use of CD-ROMs and the web, and more recently may comprise Web 2.0

technology, handheld voting devices, integrating multimedia or whatever may be the latest teaching tools. Their use will seem different and innovative, even unique in context, to the user. This does require constant refreshing of your teaching, but remember that is a characteristic of good teachers anyway.

Libraries are often seen by their users as conservative places and in some ways this conservatism is a positive force. Defenders of libraries (for example, Flood 2008) will often cite the need for an oasis of quiet in a busy world as a reason for saving public libraries and there are powerful arguments for retaining core values of librarianship in the age of unfettered and unmediated information via an increasingly commercialised web. However, libraries are also often trendsetters in the application of technology and in understanding how to shape learning opportunities within their parent organisations. So they will usually have been among the first to develop a significant web presence, invest substantially in a huge array of digital resources, use Web 2.0 and multimedia for teaching, introduce social learning spaces and have innovative IT-rich teaching spaces (Northampton's T-Pod, Warwick's Teaching Grid, and so on), and this spirit of adventure and novelty in teaching is very much part of the boutique model.

THE ROLE OF THE SUBJECT LIBRARIAN

The role of the subject librarian is a crucial one in creating and delivering boutique teaching and learning in academic libraries. Most boutique hotels will offer a distinctly 'expert' experience. Staff will be especially knowledgeable about the local area or about the theme of the hotel. Translating this approach into information skills teaching and training requires a profound knowledge of the information landscape in particular subjects and the contexts in which the information will be used. It does not require a deep knowledge of the subject itself as that is the province of the academic, but it needs to go into more depth than a generic grasp of information skills. This is where subject librarians or academic liaison librarians should really make a difference – as long as they are competent and effective – for they should understand not only the structure of knowledge in the subjects they work with, but also have a nuanced understanding of what that means in application for their stakeholders. So, for example, a business librarian should know key information resources for that subject but also understand the comparative value placed on their use within the curriculum at that institution.

This can be challenging for library and information professionals as it means that resource solutions cannot always be purchased 'off-the-peg' to be used until they wear out but need to be selected carefully, customised as appropriate, and reviewed on a regular basis. It means that those involved in working with stakeholders within an organisation need to be proactive in identifying ways of supporting the curriculum and focusing on bringing value into their interactions with learners and faculty.

It is also important that subject librarians, and the rest of the library staff, have autonomy over their teaching. They will need to be able to tailor their delivery methods and content to the needs of each group or even to the level of the individual, to maximise its effectiveness. Centralised and generic approaches can be appealing to managers, ensuring standardisation and achieving value for money through economies of scale. It also increases management control and ensures conformance to standards. Yet from a pedagogic perspective this level of control is deeply suspect since it fails to appreciate the complexity of disciplines, differences in information behaviour, and diversity within organisations. A distributed model of provision means that teaching can be targeted and learner focused as it will draw on what is known about those individuals, subjects and groups.

A high degree of autonomy in the design and delivery of teaching and training will also allow the teachers to react quickly and appropriately to changing circumstances. Teaching is prey to many variables (Squires 1994: 57) and teachers must be able to respond to those variables. Group and individual dynamics, social and organisational settings, and the physical environment may all affect the teaching session and/or the learning. A generic teaching session delivered by librarians who are perhaps divorced from the learner context will be difficult to amend, moderate or refocus properly if the teacher does not have the autonomy to change content and delivery. This requires an understanding of pedagogy and good presentational skills, but it will also work much more effectively if it is combined with the good subject librarian's knowledge of learner and context.

THE LEARNING ENVIRONMENT

Most boutique services will place great emphasis on the setting or environment. Hotels will be located in converted historic houses or use decor and space to create a very different environment to the uniformity of the generic chains. They will often stress their convenience for local attractions. Boutique teaching and training should take the same consideration over the environment. As a starting point it is important to consider carefully the design and layout of the learning spaces. Attractive and well-laid-out spaces enhance the quality of learning opportunities. The accommodation you use will shape expectations – whether it seems like a valued and cared-for space, for example, if it is designed to look cutting edge (in the type of furniture used or colours) – and it will shape what you can do in terms of the kind of technology available and the flexibility in layout.

Information skills teaching will usually be done in specialist library training rooms, often an IT laboratory. These are convenient and usually controlled by the library rather than central timetabling or another part of the organisation. This makes for a safe environment in which to teach: one that is controllable and near to other resources. However, it is often not particularly convenient for the learner who may have to make a special trip into the library for that teaching session alone. When planning a boutique teaching experience the teacher should see to match the environment to both the appropriate delivery model and to the location. Many academic libraries already take the teaching to the student by teaching in their usual classrooms or labs rather than in the library. Integration of online information skills teaching into virtual learning environments (VLEs) (also called learning management systems) means that the teaching goes to the learner rather than expecting the learner to come to the teaching. This reinforces integration with the learning context and gives more opportunity to personalise the experience.

ADDING VALUE, ENHANCING LEARNING

A boutique experience should provide added value to what may be perceived to be a standard service. In a hotel this could be a pillow menu for the beds or a bespoke breakfast in your room rather than a preset buffet. For boutique teaching and training in a library this contribution is more about enhancing the overall learning experience for the institution in a seamless and integrated way. Librarians could already argue that this is achieved through embedded information skills teaching, but it needs to be underpinned by more fundamental customisation. It is unlikely that a student would fail a course if he or she did not have a library session, as reading the books on the reading list (or the key extracts scanned into the VLE, perhaps) and attending the lectures would probably be enough to pass. However, information skills teaching must enhance student learning opportunities, complementing and extending other curriculum opportunities so that learners will develop more effective learning and research habits, locating, reading, evaluating and referencing more and better sources and in other terms adding value to their overall experience of that course.

Added value should also be a theme within the teaching session itself. Personalising the teaching so that the learner can work on his or her own problems within a framework of general information skills will mean that they take more from the session than they would perhaps expect. Pedagogically, by using meaningful problems, the learning is always likely to be more effective. Following up a session with advice on a Twitter feed, Facebook site or blog linked to a specific problem or assessment extends the teaching conversation, creating a golden thread of learning opportunities, and offers support and development without a requirement to attend a follow-up event.

THE TEACHING TEAM

Boutique teaching and training clearly does happen in libraries already. Conveniently located, learner-focused, subject-specific teaching offering added value to the learners is probably the norm across the education sector. However, it often happens in isolation from other key stakeholders and this integration with the wider learning environment is something that librarians need to address if they are to fully engage with the model. Any teaching and training delivery requires the support of a team of people to be truly effective. Some may only be involved in the planning stage, others only if things go wrong, but our working relationships with them are critical to the success of the teaching.

When planning for teaching the teacher should identify all those needed to make it succeed and establish a teaching team. This is meant in a loose sense as the collaborators may not need to meet as such, or even interact with anyone other than the teacher, but an understanding of the different roles and expectations of those involved is important. If it is part of a wider learning programme then the other teachers or trainers should be included to help in the formulation of the learning outcomes and, critically, in providing and understanding learner needs and expectations. Without the latter it will be difficult to provide a boutique, learner-focused experience.

IT or media support is probably required for most information skills teaching, from the initial setting up and configuration of the equipment and for troubleshooting. This relationship will not be required every time, but if the IT or media people do not see themselves as having a stake in the teaching then it could mean delay and confusion for the teacher and learner when things do go wrong.

Learners, too, should be viewed as part of the teaching team, for their input to the teacher–learner relationship is crucial to its success. The best teaching cannot be one way and the learner too must see that he or she has a stake in it. Effective teaching and learning can only happen through mutual consent. Learning is not a simple transaction involving one person telling another something. The learner needs to process that learning and place it into his or her own context. This requires active engagement rather than passive reception in order to turn information into knowledge.

At the heart of all of these relationships lies mutual respect. The academics or other teachers need to acknowledge the professionalism of the librarians in their teaching role. The IT and media technicians need to appreciate the librarian's knowledge of technical applications and especially of how learners interact with computers. Learners need to value the knowledge and authority of librarians in a teaching context. Librarians need to take heed of all of their partners and to work on their relationships with them.

We are a collaborative profession and we can usually be relied upon to treat people with respect and courtesy. However, take a moment to think about your relationship with academics or teachers, with IT and media technicians or with learners. Specifically think of one or two adjectives that describe each of those groups (as groups and not individuals). When this exercise has been run with librarians, words like *arrogant, patronising* and *dismissive* are used to describe academics and technicians. *Rude, disinterested* and *ignorant* are applied to learners. Positive words are also used, but they tend to be easily outnumbered by the negative. Now think also what words would be used if the position was reversed. *Authoritarian, obstructive, know-it-all* alongside *caring* and *helpful*, perhaps?

Clearly this is a trite exercise, but it uncovers an uncomfortable truth. It is easy to look for someone to blame when things do not go as well as planned. 'If only they would/had ...' is an easy way to explain away anything from latecomers to failing equipment, from badly suited teaching rooms to firewall problems. It is easy because it is probably true. You may have planned your teaching meticulously, have created elegant and effective online materials, and have worked on innovative and engaging practical exercises only to see them fail due to circumstances outside your control. Events will, of course, sometimes conspire to inconvenience or interfere with the success of your teaching. However, in most cases working with colleagues in the wider teaching team will be able to neutralise or at least mitigate their effects.

Working closely with academic colleagues will help with the marketing of your teaching so that it is attended by learners who know already what the learning outcomes are and how it fits into their wider learning. Group dynamics and individuals who may disrupt or enhance the learning can be identified beforehand. Working with IT and media colleagues, especially on creating and maintaining mutually respectful personal relationships, will be fruitful in ensuring that the technical element of your teaching will run smoothly. Working on your relationships with timetabling or estates departments may help you to secure favourable and appropriate accommodation for your teaching. Treating learners as a vital part of the learning experience, rather than as vessels to be filled with information skills, will enhance the learning experience for them and for you.

The underlying assumptions and stereotypes that are uncovered by the word association exercise mentioned above will not in themselves undermine relationships between the key constituents of the teaching team. But they are indicative of a reluctance to engage fully with the idea of professional colleagues and learners being co-producers of the teaching and learning experience. They are part of the baggage that we all carry based on personal and organisational experience, but they need to be shed if we are to progress with developing reliably learner-focused and effective teaching.

CASE STUDY: FORMING A TEACHING TEAM: CREATING ALIGNED INTERACTIVE EDUCATIONAL RESOURCE OPPORTUNITIES (CAIeRO) AT THE UNIVERSITY OF NORTHAMPTON

Librarians and other professional support are usually left out of the planning for university courses. They may be sent a reading list or be invited to a validation event, but the real planning and design of the course will already have taken place by then. At the University of Northampton subject librarians were nominally part of course planning through a requirement for consultation as part of the pre-validation planning, but this was often little more than a tick-box exercise. At module level there was even less consultation, with the sending through of a reading list often the first notification that a new module had been created. The CAIeRO planning methodology developed by the School of Health has changed this by bringing academics, learning technologists, librarians and others together for intensive two-day planning workshops to develop new online courses or modules. The first day concentrates on learning and teaching with aims and outcomes developed and questioned and a module/course plan developed. Day two concentrates on resources and finishes with independent colleagues providing feedback. Work then continues outside the CAIeRO meetings until the team is convened for a final evaluation before formal validation.

The process involves a range of academic and professional staff plus students working as equals within a teaching team. Participants start with the learning outcomes for the course and then map delivery, resources and support onto them to create a holistic and rounded learning experience that uses, but is not driven by, learning technology. Learning objects are planned, and work on them begun, over the course of the workshop, but existing educational resources are also sourced and the input of the librarians is usually key at this point, not only advising on where to locate such material but also on its potential use and exploitation. Library staff are expected to contribute fully to discussions of pedagogy and the use of learning technology as well as inputting on their 'specialism'. They are full members of the development team.

The result has been highly integrated modules working with specifically designed or sourced resources from the start. Librarians are not surprised by new courses or modules and are able to better support students as they learn. The professional input of all partners is recognised and valued and that mutual respect continues into the actual delivery of the teaching, creating a true teaching team and enhancing the learning experience for the learners.

KNOWING YOUR LEARNERS

Making assumptions about the participants in the learning and teaching experience is not limited to judgments on their personal or professional personalities. It is also dangerous to jump to conclusions about what your learners need and want from information skills teaching. All teaching, but perhaps especially boutique teaching, needs to meet the learners' needs. If assumptions are made about those needs without an audit of some sort then there is a real danger that the level and content will be wrong for those learners. There can be a tendency, often based on bitter experience, to underestimate the level of information skills among your learners. This may lead to a lowering of expectations on your part and consequently pitching your teaching at a very low level. This is a dangerous pitfall. To use a simple example: just because new students may not know the proper terms for 'borrowing' (rather than 'renting' a book) may not be an indicator that they have no desire to engage with its content. They may in fact have an earnest desire to learn, but lack the specialist vocabulary required in their new educational environment. But be careful, for sometimes the opposite is also true in that it can be easy to assume that your learners know more than they do, especially if you have taught them previously. You need to be realistic in your assessment of what learners have taken away from any session. A helpful starting point is to assume that your learners will have taken away one or two key points but that the details and fancy bits of your session may not be remembered. After all, most learners are pragmatists and will remember what will make a difference to their work, rather than the model or best approach. Real-life searching and research is a messy and haphazard process outside the information skills session. An added complication can be working with very diverse groups containing both the experienced and novice in the same set. Unless handled carefully by the teacher, this mixture of abilities can leave both groups dissatisfied as one does not learn anything new, while the other does not have an opportunity to learn the basics.

Lazy preconceptions about learners are common, especially in higher education. Assumptions that nurses are computer-phobic or historians are only interested in paper sources can subtly influence teaching styles and content. Mature learners are often seen as needing more help with IT than younger learners. Planning for the teaching of international students may be influenced by national or ethnic stereotypes that have no basis in fact. These prejudices are profoundly unhelpful and will undermine your teaching.

Auditing the learners is therefore critical to the success of your teaching, and this should apply to individual learners as well as to groups. The logistics of teaching, especially in the sort of service teaching for others in which librarians typically engage, often mean that discovering more about your learners is difficult. Librarians rarely have the opportunity to form the longer-term teaching relationships that can provide the intelligence needed, but this should not mean that an audit of learners is ignored. Without properly understanding the learners, the boutique approach cannot fully succeed.

Use the experience of colleagues, academics or teachers as well as fellow librarians to identify the level and experience of the group as well as any potential problems with them as a group or with individuals within it. This is not always possible, though, as the learners may be new to your institution or others unwilling to pass judgments on them in an information skills context. If this is the case then the teacher will be forced back on their own resources.

Self assessments undertaken pre-teaching or early on in a session are useful but should not be relied upon to uncover the full extent of an individual's information literacy. Learners will often under- or overestimate their abilities and may also confuse what is meant by information skills or information literacy. Many conflate information skills with the technical ability to manipulate software packages so that understanding how to use Google or a bibliographic database is seen as being highly information literate whereas the key skills of evaluation and manipulation of information are ignored. For pre-teaching assessments to work, the language used needs to be unambiguous and specific. Simple testing at an early point in the teaching is a better gauge of level, but it is probably best done subtly rather than explicitly. Setting the group or individual a task such as finding information on a relevant topic in a particular database and then reporting back to the group under the auspices of evaluating the database will provide a quick assessment of skill levels.

Finding out what the learners are hoping to get from the teaching can also be achieved easily by asking them. Set out your aims and learning outcomes explicitly at the start and ask for comments. Always act on the comments, though, as continuing with redundant or irrelevant outcomes will only disillusion and disengage learners from your teaching. An even simpler strategy is to talk to learners as they arrive for the teaching. This is particularly effective in understanding the subject needs of learners (and you can gauge their technical knowledge too), but it does require the teacher to be flexible in the examples that they then use. Those new to teaching will often prefer to have prearranged examples of information search strategies, but these rarely match the lived experience of the learners and should be avoided if the teaching is to be targeted at the real needs of specific learners. The success of the boutique model relies on meeting the real and perceived needs of the learners, auditing these needs and engaging in an active teaching dialogue with them.

FLEXIBLE APPROACHES TO TEACHING

Flexibility in response to the audit means the teacher must do more than simply avoid prepared examples. The boutique approach requires that the teacher is capable of changing a teaching session if the learners are not responding or if it is clear that learner needs are not being met. All teachers should have the capability to add or remove learning outcomes from their teaching without compromising the overall aim. This is easier online where routes can be built into the learning experience depending on success at previous exercises or a learner-led self-assessment of needs. In a teaching session this requires planning rather than the rigid adherence to plans. Planning should take into account the possibility that the learners will be more or less experienced, knowledgeable or skilled and have strategies to cope with these possibilities. Plans, on the other hand, will inevitably be derailed by external circumstances.

Flexibility in planning should be reflected in flexibility in the nature of the teaching intervention. Librarians are often wary of imposing their knowledge and understanding of how learners interact with information onto accepted teaching patterns. This can lead to others using the library skills session as a crèche, hoping that they will be entertained, amused and informed for an hour but not engaging themselves with the learning outcomes beyond a vague wish that the learners should find out about the databases/e-books/journals/referencing, and so on. This will often mean that the main part of the learning experience feels disconnected from information skills. It also usually means that the librarian will be given a single session of an hour as this is either the usual length of the teaching session or often all that can be spared from the wider course or programme.

However, the orthodoxy of the single, or at best couple, of information skills sessions should be challenged. Online learning does give opportunities for self-paced learning that can take place where and when the learner needs it, but it is in the classroom where the orthodox model should be challenged most. It may be that a traditional one-hour session fulfils what is needed, especially when built around a particular piece of work that needs a particular skill set. However, it may be that smaller-scale but more targeted teaching interventions will be more effective in integrating information skills into the wider learning landscape (Lumsden, Mcbryde Wilding and Rose 2010). The adoption of this more scaffolded approach to teaching means that support is given at more appropriate points for the learners. Ten minutes at the start of a number of lectures over the course of the learning or the insertion of an online learning object into a VLE may well have a greater effect than a whole hour of information skills if that hour is badly timed for the learners.

Negotiating skills are crucial to the success of this model. Most academics or teachers will want to maintain the normal structure, of course, and prefer to use one of the existing timetabled slots for information skills. This aids planning and means that the learners remain comfortable. It also, on first glance, demonstrates the importance of information skills and superficially embeds it into the mainstream of the learning. However, adopting a model that uses shorter slots within existing lectures or workshops takes time from the subject of the day unless it is carefully planned and seamlessly delivered. Academics or teachers can deliver the information skills element themselves, usually with support from librarians in the form of materials, but an intervention from the librarian is equally valid. Negotiating that slot within a session requires tact, imagination and the ability to work with academics and teachers in their sphere. An understanding of the content and language of pedagogy is essential if the librarian is to convince others of their case. To provide a more concrete example of a very short intervention, giving a very short talk to students as they start to research their first essay can be extremely powerful. Just using an essay title as a springboard for a search on Google compared to the library catalogue and electronic journals services can demonstrate the power of keywords and get a whole group to evaluate and contrast the variety of sources and their relevance, quality and currency. This simple intervention, modelling an effective search, will spur easier discovery and critical evaluation. It is also important to remember that *finding* is not the same as understanding, so demonstrating how to find relevant material is not spoonfeeding your learners.

The politics of teaching should not be underestimated here. It may be organisationally difficult to convince management or academics that what are now often called professional services staff can operate explicitly as teachers. Librarians should not compromise on their input to the learning process, though. Part of the professional identity of a librarian is as a teacher and as teachers they should contribute to the wider pedagogical debate in their organisation and outside it. Political skills are certainly part of the subject librarian's everyday toolkit, but they may be reticent to use them in this context. Hence the continuation of one-hour teaching sessions at the start of the academic year that add little to the learner experience short of a usually interesting and enjoyable time on the web.

There is clearly a problem of scale in most academic institutions. It would be naive not to recognise that if the majority of students are to be seen in a year then the default of the one-hour session is possibly the only way, given the numbers of students. There is little flexibility possible in already-crowded timetables. However, the mass processing of learners is the antithesis of the boutique, personalised model advocated in this book. By using online learning objects, shorter interventions within existing teaching, and appropriate and cost-effective follow-up activities (see below) it is possible to target the learners more effectively and achieve a more personalised learning experience.

It is perhaps worth exploring the notion of integration a little more. True integration of information skills within a wider learning experience requires the information skills element to be seamless and implicit in the rest of the learning. It cannot be said to be *fully* integrated if it sits as a separate element, however well taught and however responsive to learner needs. A complete boutique experience requires something different from the norm, but the elements of it should not seem different from the rest of the boutique experience. So the information skills elements of a course should seem to be a natural part of the whole rather than something bolted on. To achieve this objective, the librarian may need to cede some control to teaching partners and either allow them to deliver the information skills objectives themselves or to team teach. This may feel uncomfortable at first, but achieving the learning outcomes should be the goal, not maintaining personal power in the teaching relationship.

FEEDBACK FROM YOUR LEARNERS

Personalised teaching needs the teacher to gather and act on feedback in a timely manner. This does not necessarily mean handing out feedback sheets at the end of a session because although they may have a place in developing your teaching for others they will not benefit the teaching that has just occurred. Use simple methods like Race's (1999) 'Stop, Start, Continue' where simple qualitative data can be collected via post-it notes during the session, and act on the feedback given under those headings. Use the body language of your learners to check whether the whole group is looking bored, demotivated or engaged and enthusiastic, and amend your teaching accordingly. Responding quickly to learner feedback allows the teacher to match the teaching to learner needs and to recognise when they are or when they are not achieving this. By continuing to deliver teaching when it is patently not meeting these needs, or waiting until after it is too late to do anything about it, could mean that the rest of the boutique model fails as learners disengage with the library as a legitimate and useful part of their learning experience.

LEARNING SPACES

Boutique library spaces are covered elsewhere in this book, but for boutique teaching and training to work it needs appropriate teaching and learning spaces. Some of the elements of a boutique space will clearly apply to a teaching space: it should be close to the learner; it should cater for the user or learner; it should be intimate and/or niche. In addition, there can be an emotional attachment of the teaching space to the idea of learning.

Locating the 'library' teaching space close to the learners can be interpreted in two ways. It could be argued that by having a teaching room or computer lab within the library space the learners will understand the connection between what the librarian is teaching them and the resources that they will need to use. The library is also somewhere that all, or at least most, learners will visit at some point, so it makes sense to locate teaching rooms there. This is a powerful argument and lies behind much of the information or learning commons developments in educational institutions. It consolidates the idea of the library as being the core building for learning by also placing teaching there and reinforces the importance of information skills to the wider learning experience.

However, it could also be interpreted as creating a separation between the usual learning and teaching experience, which typically takes place in a classroom in a teaching block, and information skills. It could be argued that taking the information skills teaching closer to the learners means forgoing library teaching spaces and delivering information skills in teaching rooms and labs in teaching blocks. Whichever the librarian decides on will depend on organisational opportunity, appropriateness of resource and the nature of the teaching rooms available.

That the teaching rooms should cater for the learners is perhaps obvious. If a particular piece of software is necessary for the teaching, if a particular layout of furniture or a configuration of computers is required, then the teaching rooms should provide it. Librarians may have influence on these things or they may have to work with preset design and configuration, but they should at least teach to the spaces that they have in place. Attempting to deliver teaching that requires a particular set of resources in spaces that do not contain them or are equipped with furniture and resources that are not flexible enough to facilitate the activities that are planned for, will inevitably lead to a less-than-satisfactory outcome. Flexible planning and an audit of the facilities and resources will overcome environmental issues but may also require the librarian to change their learning outcomes or methods very quickly during the teaching.

Intimate or niche teaching spaces will allow librarians to personalise their teaching in ways that the anonymous lecture theatre or computer lab cannot. Think about using spaces that are designed for other purposes as possible venues for information skills teaching. School lessons taken outside are often happy memories many years after they took place, and the same effect could be applied to information skills through the use of different spaces. Use more intimate spaces within the library itself rather than the training room, or take laptops outside the library. Think innovatively about space and use the technology available, for example portable smartboards, projectors, tablets, smartphones, and so on, to create teaching spaces out of other areas.

Although many online learning environments offer uniform experiences, often deliberately to combat possible confusion as learners move between modules, there is still usually scope for learners to customise screens, add RSS feeds or other Web 2.0 applications, and otherwise personalise the experience. This should be encouraged to enhance a feeling of ownership of the learning by the learner. Learning objects should be designed to allow customisation, including physical objects such as handouts. Allowing space to make notes on these is simple to achieve and changes the nature of the object from a passive to a dynamic learning tool. Most teachers do this already but do not necessarily include the same facility in an online version, which they often convert to a pdf thus making it difficult to change. There can be a fear that learners will amend and change the text thus making it less useful, but by allowing them to delete or add text to make it more meaningful to them teachers are encouraging the creation of knowledge rather than the simple receipt of information.

The personalisation of a learning environment should not necessarily be confined to resources. Allow learners to have some input into the design of the teaching room by using flexible furniture and equipment. Using laptops instead of fixed PCs does risk reliability as wireless access is usually more fragile, but it does make group work much easier. Let groups form around the resources that they need to use rather than bringing the resources to a group, and offer choices of furniture configuration if the room allows. This does mean a loss of control but will repay through a greater learner involvement.

Libraries can have a real emotional resonance for a learner. Bourdieu and St Martin (1994) discovered learners in Lille University library who hoped that simply being in the building would encourage learning. This is a powerful platform to build upon, but the conversion of this sense that libraries equal learning will need to be translated into a similar feeling that librarians are involved in teaching. The two feelings are not automatically linked and it is for the librarian/teacher to make the connection. Although classrooms will usually equate with teaching, this can mean a passive feeling that teaching is something done to the learner. Using the library, a place of learning, innovatively may give the librarian a useful emotional basis for their teaching.

THE ROLE OF THE CENTRE

Boutique teaching requires significant levels of autonomy for the librarian/teachers. They need to be able to plan, deliver and assess based on the needs of their learners rather than the requirements of a centralised authority. This autonomy allows the teacher to match their content very closely to the needs of the learners and to have the flexibility to respond quickly to changing circumstances: environmental, personal and organisational. Although the idea of being able to take an 'off-the-shelf' solution to any aspect of teaching is an attractive prospect, it cannot ever deliver the personalised learning experience of the boutique model.

However, there is still a need for some central input for the teaching to occur. Content and delivery may be controlled by the teacher, but without a robust infrastructure the factors outside those areas will collapse into chaos. The IT and environmental infrastructure, staffing structures and their management, training and development all operate better under central control and if managed well will unobtrusively allow the librarian/teachers to be free to teach.

Teachers should be able to control their teaching and learning environment. The physical environment of the classroom, library teaching room or IT suite should be flexible enough for them to change and control the room. They should be able to request and get appropriate levels of access and support for the IT they need. However, it is only through central control that teaching rooms can be maintained, equipped and managed. Few teachers would want to be involved in the equipping of their teaching rooms beyond the desire to be involved in decisions regarding the type of facilities. Management of those facilities should reside centrally, as should timetabling and maintenance and support.

Staffing structures should reflect the need to work in teaching teams. These teams should include the necessary administrative support and be flexible enough for team teaching, peer review and reflection to take place. Too much local authority can result in teaching silos whereas a flexible but interconnected staff structure can deliver plentiful opportunity for the sharing of good practice, support mechanisms for new and inexperienced staff, and support when the political agenda requires it. The management system should encourage innovation and tolerate failure if it is used to develop future strategies. The freedom to take risks and to follow the learner rather than precedent or peers needs to be supported by sympathetic and flexible managers. Fear of the consequences of failure will stifle the boutique model as it is always safer to deliver a standardised version. Pretested examples, shared slides and generic learning outcomes will all work in that they will sustain a workshop or lecture. However, they will not enable personalisation of learning that turns the mechanistic understanding of which databases are useful or the basic rules of the Harvard referencing system into an understanding of the information landscape in a particular subject or why referencing is required at all.

Training and development for teaching is also best delivered centrally. Courses leading to qualification such as the postgraduate diplomas or certificates in teaching in higher education run in virtually all UK universities clearly need central coordination and management to meet quality standards. But there is also much merit in other centrally coordinated staff development that brings together teachers from across the organisation to learn and to discuss pedagogy. Learning and teaching away days, conferences or 'show and tell' events will all benefit from central organisation that can encourage sharing across disciplines and include library papers alongside academic input.

AFTER THE SESSION

The teaching session should not be the end of the relationship with the learners. Librarians will often see the learners again informally as they use the services and resources, but there should be other, more structured opportunities to work with them. This will reinforce key elements of personalised learning, especially the highly tailored and learner-focused nature of the boutique model.

Extending the relationship beyond the teaching session can begin with the provision of materials to reinforce the learning and to encourage learners to develop their own understanding of information skills. Handouts, online links to further resources, exercises, games and examples to reinforce learning should all be considered at the planning stage. Away from the directed learning offered by these resources should be a framework of support including phone or online (virtual librarian) help and the availability of tutorial or other one-to-one support. This is labour intensive to deliver but means that learners can access support at the point of their need, and is particularly useful when the timing of library teaching is dictated by outside circumstance. One-to-one follow-up opportunities for learners is also helpful to those doing personal research such as a dissertation, as learners can often fail to see immediately how to apply the generic information skills covered in a teaching session to their own research topic. A tutorial or drop-in can personalise the learning in a way that a workshop or lecture cannot hope to achieve.

The teaching team is important in following up the teaching. Robust IT support is needed to facilitate the use of information resources. Academics and library colleagues will need to understand what you have covered with learners so that they too can support them. Learners should be encouraged to offer peer support with access to materials and knowledge of the resources available. Those relationships forged to deliver teaching sessions are just as important in the delivery of follow-up support.

CONCLUSION

The boutique model can be applied to teaching and training. Librarians already strive to offer teaching in information skills that is learner focused, relevant and tailored to their needs. Many operate with a degree of autonomy and are able to utilise the latest technology to create exciting, accessible and innovative teaching. They work closely with colleagues, inside and outside the library, to create real teaching teams. Most of all they care about the learners, and it is this that lies at the heart of the boutique model. The desire to deliver something that meets the needs of individual learners, and that values them as individuals, is what drives the model, and librarians have long seen this as a core professional value. In that they are well placed to implement boutique learning experiences.

TOP TIPS

- Do not judge people based on previous unfortunate experiences and do not make assumptions about other professions or your users: treat people as you would wish to be treated by them.
- Take time to audit your learners: minutes spent finding out about their real information needs will repay you tenfold.
- Be flexible: in planning, delivery, the teaching environment and in offering follow-up to your teaching.
- Innovate: this does not mean that you need to shock, but do think about doing things differently as this will shake learners out of their preconceived ideas about librarians.
- Work together: boutique teaching cannot work without support and a solid infrastructure.

REFERENCES

Bourdieu, P. and Saint Martin, M. de. 1994. The Users of Lille University Library, in Bourdieu, P., Passeron, J. and Saint Martin, M. de (eds), *Academic Discourse*. Cambridge: Polity Press, 122–33.

Flood, A. 2008. Poet Laureate Speaks Out Against Library Closures. *The Guardian*, 19 December [online]. At: www.guardian.co.uk/books/2008/dec/19/andrew-motion-library-closures?INTCMP=SRCH (accessed: 30 August 2011).

Hole-in-the-Wall Education Ltd. 2011. Hole in the Wall: Lighting the Spark of Learning [online]. At: http://hole-in-the-wall.com (accessed: 30 August 2011).

Lumsden, E., Mcbryde Wilding, H. and Rose, H. 2010. Collaborative Practice in Enhancing the First Year Experience in Higher Education. *Enhancing the Learner Experience in Higher Education* 2(1), 12–24 [online]. At: http://journals.northampton.ac.uk/index.php/elehe/issue/view/2   (accessed: 30 August 2011).

Morgan, N. and Davies, L. 2004. Innovative Induction: Introducing the Cephalonian Method. *SCONUL Focus*, 32, 4–8.

Race, P. (ed.) 1999. *2000 Tips for Lecturers*. London: Kogan Page.

Squires, G. 1994. *A New Model of Teaching and Training*. Hull: University of Hull.

CHAPTER 6

DIGITAL LITERACY SUPPORT FOR RESEARCHERS: THE PERSONALISED APPROACH
JANE SECKER

INTRODUCTION

> *The illiterate of the 21st Century will not be those who cannot read and write,*
> *but those who cannot learn, unlearn, and relearn. (Alvin Toffler 1971: 414)*

Supporting researchers in the digital age is a challenging, rewarding and expanding area of work for academic libraries and related support services in higher education. Over the past ten years there has been a huge growth in research support services offered in higher education. The range and types of activities that these services now include has expanded considerably since the Roberts Review of 2002 and the consequent funding that was made available to higher education institutions. Research Councils UK (RCUK) committed £20 million annually for the period 2008–2011 to the development of transferable skills for researchers. The growth in support services led to a number of recent publications in the librarianship field documenting these initiatives and highlighting good practice (for example, Webb, Gannon-Leary and Bent 2007, Allan 2009). In addition there have been a number of important studies commissioned and undertaken by organisations such as the Research Information Network (RIN). While current government priorities are for research funding in Science Technology Education and Medicine (STEM), all universities recognise the value of providing professional development opportunities for their researchers.

One thing is clear, however: researchers are not a homogenous group; they are made up of distinct groups who fall under this umbrella term. Given the diversity of researchers both in terms of the disciplines in which they work and the levels at which they work, the nature of the support that can be offered fits better with the boutique approach. Support for researchers can be approached quite differently to other categories of users in a university, such as undergraduate students. While undergraduates are also not homogenous, they are generally greater in number and so if only for practical reasons the ability to tailor and customise services for students is more difficult. Researchers, however, even in research-intensive universities, almost always exist in smaller numbers than undergraduates. In addition their needs are more specialist and consequently the support and services that libraries provide are far more suited to the boutique approach. If undergraduates are the 'bread and butter' work of the librarian, researchers are the speciality pastries!

This chapter will outline some of the key issues to consider when planning or improving the support that an academic institution provides for its researchers. It will start by considering the work of researchers, to examine the different groups that exist within universities and understand the 'researcher lifecycle'. This lifecycle starts with research that might be undertaken at undergraduate and masters level, moving on to PhD level, to postdoctoral level, and finally to the later-stage researcher who might be a senior professor or a research fellow. At each of the different stages, not only the needs of the researcher, but also their attitude towards those who are offering support to them, will change. At each stage it is essential to understand the prior knowledge and experience of the individual researcher, but also to ascertain something of their specific area of research interest, not just the academic department they are based within. In addition to the level of the researcher, the process of undertaking research is a lifecycle and one where needs will vary. At the initial stage in any research process researchers will often be looking to identify previous studies in their field, whereas later on they will be generating theories and finally looking for ways to check the quality of their data and then publish their work. One size does certainly not fit all when providing support to researchers, and the need to personalise, adapt and tailor services is essential in order to be successful. Even within the same institution, the interests and expertise of researchers, whether they are a physicist, a historian or a lawyer, will vary enormously. It is important to know which particular aspect, for example, of a law a researcher is interested in, or the theoretical background or philosophy that underpins their work.

The chapter is largely based on the author's experience of supporting researchers in the social sciences; however, there is no reason to suggest that researchers in the humanities or in the sciences are any different, even if the funding models will vary. Therefore, much of what is written should hopefully be of relevance to those supporting all types of researchers at higher education level. Most importantly this chapter suggests that getting to know researchers personally will help you understand their needs, so building networks and contacts within academic departments is extremely important. In addition, if you can, actually spend some time being a researcher as it will also help you to understand the research process and empathise with this group. For example, attending training courses alongside researchers can be a helpful way of learning what researchers really do and what their needs might be. One of the biggest challenges to librarians and other support staff seems to be their reluctance to interact with researchers in their own environment. Librarians must leave the library, IT trainers move away from the computer training room. Sometimes a researcher will only tell you what they really want or need over a coffee, or during the lunch break of a training course, not when you are sitting at the enquiry desk or gathering feedback from an online survey. It is important to find out what help and support researchers really need, rather than making assumptions about what you think they need, or what services your library has traditionally offered. It is also important for groups of support staff to work together collaboratively, to run training sessions and ensure the support provided in their institution is as joined up and seamless as possible.

RESEARCH INFORMATION NETWORK (RIN) AND VITAE RESEARCH AND THE BOUTIQUE APPROACH

The chapter will start by drawing on some of the literature in this area, including recent research commissioned and undertaken by RIN and Vitae. Both these organisations are valuable sources of training and advice for researchers and for the research support community. However, this section will specifically concentrate on themes from their recent research that support the personalised model of research support. RIN was set up back in 2004 and is a policy unit funded by the UK higher education funding councils, the seven research councils and the three national libraries.

Its aims are to

- 'Enhance and broaden understanding of how researchers in the UK create and use information resources and services of all kinds'.
- 'Support the development of effective policies and practices for researchers, institutions, funders, information professionals and everyone who is involved in the information landscape' (RIN 2011a).

Since its establishment, RIN has commissioned a range of valuable studies aimed at the broad range of individuals and organisations that provide services and support for the research community. However, RIN has been particularly successful at engaging with the library community. It has established a number of working groups that have developed policy and guidance for the research support community, but librarians in particular have participated in and welcomed its work.

Another important organisation is Vitae, which is primarily tasked with championing the personal, professional and career development of doctoral researchers and research staff in higher education institutions and research institutes. It is funded through the Research Careers and Diversity Unit of the Research Councils and CRAC: The Career Development Organisation. Vitae runs national events such as conferences, providing support at the policy level for institutions and engaging with stakeholders, including researchers, employers and research supervisors and managers. It also has eight regional hubs that offer training and support to postgraduate researchers, encouraging collaboration between institutions and the sharing of good practice. With this in mind it maintains a database of good practice, which includes examples of high-quality courses and initiatives run in higher education institutions to support researchers (Vitae 2011a). A quick browse through this database reveals a wealth of examples that echo boutique principles. One example is the University of York's Engagement, Impact and Influence Programme, which in addition to the four workshops for PhD students includes coaching and one-to-one support (Vitae 2011b). Other courses and initiatives are clearly aimed at researchers either in specific disciplines or at key stages in their career.

Both RIN and Vitae commission and undertake research themselves. For example, the joint RIN and OCLC Research Study undertaken in 2010 on research support services (RIN 2010) had a number of significant findings for higher education. The work also supports the boutique approach, for instance in suggesting:

- Institutions should review their training provision and the configuration of support services to develop shared services but also look to provide customised support.
- Researchers need specialist training and guidance on copyright, IPR and licensing issues.

The study suggested that, despite the significant growth of services in this area, researcher's needs were still not fully being met. RIN have published a number of other relevant studies, for example on the use of social media by researchers (RIN 2011b) and the value of libraries (RIN 2011c). In both reports it is clear that the needs of researchers are highly specific and that a generic approach to support services is only going to be of limited success. For example, the Value of Libraries Study found that researchers highly rated the personal contact and expertise of subject liaison libraries (RIN 2011c: 43). PhD students, in particular, valued having a named contact in the library to help prevent feelings of isolation. In one institution desktop visits were very popular with research staff and the report described the importance of 'proactive' librarians.

It is common in academic libraries to have subject librarians, sometimes called liaison librarians or academic support librarians, who act as a first port of call for academic staff in a department. Many will also provide training for students, staff and researchers, and they may be available for one-to-one consultations. Learning support staff similarly may have dedicated responsibility for specific departments across a university. However, support staff can soon become stretched for time if large numbers of researchers call on them for one-to-one help and advice. This can also compete with their other responsibilities to provide classes for students, which has led some institutions to appoint a dedicated research support post in the library to focus on the needs of this group. However, the problem remains that providing large numbers of individual consultations may seem less effective and less scalable than offering a more generic programme of support. It also becomes extremely important to capture the value of the one-to-one interactions, which may be statistically less significant than large numbers of students attending a training class, but overall far more rewarding for the individuals concerned.

THE RESEARCH AND RESEARCHER LIFECYCLE

When discussing researchers it is clear that the term can be used to describe a wide range of different types of individuals undertaking research at different stages of their career. While undergraduate and masters students often do not perceive themselves as 'researchers', almost all degree programmes include an element of independent work that a student is required to undertake, such as an extended essay or dissertation. When we think of researchers we might traditionally associate this with doctoral students or postdoctoral research staff, but in almost all higher education institutions research is carried out at many different levels, by students, research students, lecturers and senior research fellows.

The 'research lifecycle' has been categorised into seven ages by Bent, Webb and Gannon-Leary (2007: 81–99), which includes:

- masters students
- doctoral students
- contract researchers
- early career researchers
- established academic staff
- senior researchers
- experts.

When considering the seven groups listed above, what is clear is that the needs of early career researchers such as doctoral students will be very different to senior research fellows. The knowledge, experience and skills of the different groups will also vary enormously, with senior researchers often being highly specialised in their interests but also fairly confident about their abilities and less likely to see the need to attend a training session. It is important to consider the help and support available to all these groups of researchers in your institution. It is also vital that any services and support are marketed effectively to the different groups. For example, new researchers are often very keen to find out about electronic resources and tools that can help them, such as when they are first undertaking a detailed literature search. Meanwhile senior researchers often have well-established networks and methods for keeping up to date in their field. They may not, however, have kept up with changes to services they use, or be using the most appropriate tools to support their work. Offering training courses across the board to researchers in your institution may not take into account the different needs within the group. However, the flexibility and personalised nature of the components of the boutique approach mean that services can be adapted and targeted at a specialist audience.

In addition to the researcher lifecycle, the research process itself is often described as an iterative cyclical process. The RIN study on the value of social media for researchers (RIN 2011b: 15) encapsulates the research cycle succinctly, describing it as having four stages:

1. identification of knowledge (literature review, and so on).
2. creation of knowledge (the actual research process).
3. quality assurance of knowledge (for example, peer review).
4. dissemination of knowledge (publication, presentation at conferences, and so on).

All four are underpinned by social interaction and collaboration, and the RIN study considers the role of social media at each of these different stages. However, understanding this cycle can also be helpful when framing services and support for the research community. There are specific points in this cycle when input from library and learning support staff might be more helpful (for example at stages 1 and 4) and times when researchers may prefer to work alone or with their colleagues. The next section will examine in more detail how boutique principles work in one higher education institution to provide support for varying groups of researchers at different points in their careers, but also at different stages of the research process.

INTRODUCTION TO DIGITAL LITERACY PROGRAMME IN CLT AT LSE

There are many different ways that institutions provide support to researchers; however, drawing on my own experiences at the London School of Economics and Political Science (LSE) provides a useful example of a method that echoes many of the characteristics of the boutique approach. There are a wide range of research support services offered across LSE, from several different departments including the library, Centre for Learning Technology (CLT), Teaching and Learning Centre, and Research Office. This chapter will focus on the support offered by CLT. Elsewhere in this book a case study is provided by colleagues in the library to illustrate other services they provide to researchers. However, in CLT the move towards providing boutique services has evolved over the last five years and seems to offer a useful way of defining the specialist support on offer. Throughout this section of the chapter references will be made to the key characteristics of the boutique library component model.

Background and Context

At LSE, CLT was established in 2001 to support teaching and administrative staff in the effective use of technology in their teaching. LSE uses the virtual learning environment Moodle to provide blended learning support for campus-based students, including some online activities and access to resources. The small team of eight staff primarily offers training and support to staff at LSE to enable them to use technology effectively in teaching. However, at LSE PhD students increasingly act as 'Moodle editors' working alongside an academic colleague to edit the online course and so training and support is also offered to this group. CLT has responsibility for providing wider support for staff and researchers in what are termed 'digital literacy' skills. A programme of digital literacy classes was launched to stimulate an interest in e-learning and partly in response to the growing recognition that staff and researchers had limited knowledge of the potential that new technologies could offer them. The team was also aware that, if staff did not have the required skills or understanding about technologies to support their research, they would be less likely to use these tools in teaching. So part of the reason for offering this programme was a desire to be trend setting and reactive to a perceived need.

LSE use the following definition of digital literacy: 'the skills, knowledge and understanding that enables critical, creative, discerning and safe practices when engaging with digital technologies in all areas of life' (FutureLab 2010: 19). As LSE is a research-intensive university, staff in CLT are also aware that research activities are hugely important to the academic staff and the institution as a whole. In the 2008 Research Assessment Exercise, LSE had the highest percentage of world-leading research of any university in the UK and topped or came close to the top of a number of other rankings of research excellence. Ninety per cent of staff were returned as research active and there are around 20 research centres, many of which are world renowned. Therefore, while the role of CLT is primarily to support staff in their use of technology for teaching, providing staff with support for their research is crucial. Research and teaching are closely intertwined and the skills, technologies and tools that help staff become better teachers often help support their research activities. Consequently, CLT felt it was uniquely placed to offer research support in the area of digital literacy.

Digital Literacy and Boutique Services

Support for staff is offered in a variety of ways in CLT, including providing advice and guidance on the department website, and dealing with high numbers of queries via email but also over the telephone and in person. A mixture of one-to-one appointments and more formal dedicated training sessions is offered to staff throughout the year. Training in how to use Moodle is by far the most popular course on offer; however, the team has always offered a range of specialist workshops for staff as part of the academic staff development programme. Attendance at formal workshop sessions has been variable and individual consultations have remained popular with staff who favour the personalised nature of such an appointment and the ability to schedule a meeting to suit their busy lives. Appointments are usually in the CLT office, but visits to staff in their department are not uncommon. The work of CLT has many of the characteristics of the boutique approach at its heart, including:

- offering highly tailored support and a personalised approach to services.
- being trendsetting and reactive to requests for new services.
- being customer focused and offering support at a convenient time and location for staff.
- additionally, a high degree of autonomy among the team, who can focus on areas of interest to them, respond to enquiries from staff, and provide support for staff with a specific discipline focus.

The Digital Literacy Programme originated in 2005/2006 with the launch of several classes for new staff on how to find and use electronic resources, how to find and use images and digital media in teaching, and how to use reference management software. A key aspect of these classes is they are all held in computer classrooms so require attendees to participate in a series of hands-on activities. They are also typically offered at a time convenient for staff, such as lunchtime or on Wednesday afternoons when teaching is kept to a minimum. As technology has evolved, in particular with the growth of social media, new classes have been developed to cover many of the Web 2.0 tools and services such as blogs and social media. In fact each year new classes have been developed and existing classes have been updated. Some of the classes on offer in 2010/11 included:

- Keeping Up To Date: this features using alerting services from key bibliographic databases, identifying RSS feeds, and using a reader to keep up to date with blogs and other websites using this technology.
- Managing Your Internet Resources: this shows staff how to use social bookmarking tools such as Delicious and Diigo – these are useful for teaching, but particularly useful for researchers.
- Blogging For Beginners: this covers how to set up a blog using WordPress software, in addition to tips for getting started with customising your blog and writing your first post.
- Collaborative Writing Tools: this includes using wikis and Google docs and is particularly aimed at researchers who might need to share documents with staff based at other institutions.
- Introduction to Twitter: this covers using Twitter for professional purposes and academic networking and to keep up to date with research interests.

One of the new classes launched in 2010 was a course on managing your web presence. This had proved popular as a half-day workshop, but numbers were low due to the time commitment required. Therefore the class was adapted to create an hour-and-a-half-long digital literacy class and has proved popular over the past year. The team obtains feedback on the programme in its annual staff survey and has responded to requests for new areas of support, for example launching a class in 2011/12 on managing information using tools such as Zotero and Mendeley. However, the programme arguably has another valuable role in highlighting the broader remit of the Centre for Learning Technology. The team is aware that some staff at LSE perceive CLT as the department that supports Moodle. By offering the Digital Literacy Programme, it highlights a broader range of expertise in the team; and there is some evidence that this leads to a greater range of enquiries from staff and PhD students.

Trendsetting and Reacting to Change

An important part of the boutique approach is the flexibility of service provision and the ability to react to new developments and trends. Research support services offered in CLT arguably fit this model well as the department deals with the ever-changing nature of technology-enhanced learning. This means the team has adapted its services and has developed a range of initiatives in collaboration with other departments at LSE. So, for example, the six-week information literacy programme offered to PhD students (Secker and Macrae-Gibson 2011) was developed by CLT and LSE Library. It partly drew on the experiences of the Digital Literacy Programme, incorporating aspects of some of the classes. Additionally, the provision of personalised support for PhD students lies at the heart of this programme. So, for example, students are asked to complete a pre-course questionnaire and are provided with specialist help and advice based on the nature of their thesis or research area. They are also put in contact with their academic support librarian to allow the support to continue once they have completed the course.

Other courses that have been developed echoing boutique principles include a course on the effective use of PowerPoint that was developed by CLT and the IT training team. This course is a half-day workshop that includes aspects of pedagogy, IT training and effective presentation skills. Some courses have developed in response to requests for training and support in a specific area. For example, a popular course on preparing poster presentations now runs several times per year and usually is attended by early career researchers such as doctoral students. The course was first developed to support an internal one-day conference for PhD students, where it was decided to include a poster exhibition. Students were invited to submit posters for a competition to showcase their research and to give them the experience of presenting in this format. Increasingly poster presentations feature at academic conferences and PhD students often find this a relatively easy way of getting recognition and feedback on their research findings. It can also be a less intimidating way of presenting at a conference for a novice. The Centre for Learning Technology itself had some experience of preparing posters from attending and presenting in this format at academic conferences. Therefore several members of staff agreed to prepare some materials to support the poster exhibition. A set of resources is available on the CLT website (LSE 2011); however, in addition, the staff now run a short workshop on poster presentations, which has proved consistently popular. Finally, the most recent initiative has been the scheduling of joint 'software surgeries' offered to staff at a set lunchtime each week in Autumn Term 2011. Representatives from a range of support services are on hand to answer queries. They can also usefully cross-refer issues that straddle service areas, for example both an IT and library query. To date, the feedback has been extremely popular as staff can visit the surgery without booking to get personalised support and training.

Personalised, Subject-specific and Customer-focused Services

The range of workshops offered by CLT leads to a steady number of enquiries from researchers who are seeking specialist advice or support. In some instances staff are referred to another department that may already offer a training course or be better suited to dealing with their request. However, where the enquiry falls into the remit of CLT, these enquiries are usually followed up through one-to-one consultations, which can really focus on the specific needs of the individual or the group of researchers. Some of the recent one-to-one sessions that have been arranged include:

- Consultation with a project team over the best social citation or social bookmarking tool to use in their project, which involved staff from universities in several different countries. This led to several meetings and providing written advice about a comparison of three social citation tools: Mendeley, Zotero and CiteULike.
- Consultation with a project director about which tools to employ to best support their team in communicating with each other, sharing resources, and managing their project effectively using appropriate technologies. This involved an investigation of various academic networking and project management tools. The team eventually decided to subscribe to a project management tool.
- Following on from attendance at a Facebook workshop, several *one-to-one* consultations with administrative staff have taken place over the setup of Facebook pages to support incoming students on specific courses at LSE.

The Centre for Learning Technology web pages on digital and information literacy now include information about the one-to-one consultation service. It is also important that the team has a clear understanding both of its own remit and of the expertise available elsewhere at LSE, and refers enquiries outside its remit to the appropriate department. A cross-department forum set up at LSE several years ago, known as the Training and Development Group, helps to ensure there is good communication between all training and support departments. This group meets once per month and membership is open to all those offering training (whether to staff or students) across LSE. The existence of a shared Training and Development System to advertise courses on offer across LSE has also helped communication and collaboration between the different departments. This system allows students and staff to browse all the courses available to them and to manage their bookings for training sessions.

Other Support for Researchers

The programme run at LSE in the Centre for Learning Technology is primarily delivered by learning technologists who focus on using a range of new technologies to support research activity. However, as in most institutions the support that is offered to researchers is far broader than the Digital Literacy Programme. In some institutions a graduate school or research office may coordinate a wider programme of training that is offered by a number of different units. Roberts funding has been used in many institutions since 2002 to fund the support of PhD students specifically. More recently, a number of institutions have bid for and been awarded funding from the funding councils, such as ESRC to set up doctoral training centres. LSE has been fortunate enough to be recently appointed as an ESRC doctoral training centre. This will lead to a greater level of collaboration between training providers and may lead to further development in research support provision. However, in summary, other types of support offered to researchers at higher education level include:

* High-level information literacy/information skills support for PhD students and researchers. Sessions usually focus on finding, using and managing specialist sources such as archival materials and data sources. At LSE a six-week course is offered to PhD students; however, researchers can attend any classes in the information skills programme, some of which are more suitable for researchers. They also have support provided online through Moodle in a course called 'Researcher's Companion to Moodle'. Finally they are encouraged to book a *one-to-one* consultation with their liaison librarian, who can run specialist training for individuals or groups of researchers on request.
* Bibliographic/bibliometric support, which can help researchers demonstrate their research impact. This has proved useful in preparing for the Research Assessment Exercise (RAE)/Research Excellence Framework (REF). Institutional repositories to manage research output are an important way that academic libraries provide support for researchers. Increasingly librarians are running sessions on citation analysis and other bibliometric

techniques that can all help demonstrate the impact of research.

- Research skills and methods training in both qualitative and quantitative techniques. In many institutions this may be offered within academic departments as research methods are often discipline specific. LSE has a methodology institute that offers a range of workshops in both qualitative and quantitative research methods. In other institutions these courses may be coordinated by a graduate school or at a faculty or departmental level. In many instances this will also include IT training in specialist software including qualitative and quantitative packages such as SPSS, NVivo and Stata.
- Careers advice and personal development sessions. Careers services often cater for PhD students and researchers. Increasingly PhD students are keen to demonstrate the transferability of research skills outside academia and many may be looking to find work in other sectors. LSE employs a specific careers adviser to support PhD students.

As mentioned earlier, the Training and Development Group has helped to improve communication between the different training providers at LSE. In addition to this group, a research support group has also been established, which looks in particular at the needs of PhD students across LSE. As well as being a group for staff who support researchers, it is supported by a number of PhD students acting as representatives for their peers.

Research Support and the Boutique Approach

When the Digital Literacy Programme was launched in 2005, one of its underlying motivations was the need to cope with growing demands on staff time for one-to-one consultations. In the early years of the CLT all training was offered on a one-to-one basis, including support for using the VLE. This meant that staff received a highly personalised training session to set up their e-learning course, which focused on their specific needs. However, the decision to use the VLE was entirely optional and the numbers of courses using technology was relatively small. When the team were planning the move to a new VLE in 2007 it became clear this transition could not be supported through one-to-one training. Group training had the advantage of reaching larger numbers of staff and was also a more time-efficient way of using learning technologists' time. However, it has always been recognised that training in a group does not always meet the specific needs of a teacher or a researcher.

The combination of providing group training sessions with the ability of staff to book individual consultations as a follow-up has been working effectively for four years now at LSE. The training programmes act as a showcase for the range of support that is offered by the team, beyond simply training for Moodle or other learning technologies. However, the model does rely on only a relatively small number of staff taking up the offer of a follow-on one-to-one session. Clearly with over 2,000 staff at LSE, it would not be feasible for the eight members of staff in CLT to offer everyone this intensive style of session. The team also needs to be clear about which areas are within its remit and when to refer staff to other colleagues, for example in IT training, the library, or the Teaching and Learning Centre. However, the library also offers research consultations to staff, and IT training has a similar model of allowing staff to request up to three personalised sessions per year. The close working relationship between the departments hopefully minimises the possibility of duplication as far as possible.

Higher education institutions would rarely contemplate charging their own staff for the range of research support services that they offer. However, in the future as funding models in higher education are changing this might be something institutions will consider. It is also important to cost the time spent by research support staff in external project proposals. For example, when external project funding is being sought, it is important that the expertise and any additional resources are factored into the research proposal. As many research projects now increasingly work on full economic costings, with associated charges for estates (covering heating, lighting, office space), so the associated costs of research support services should also be included. In some instances a research project may require the purchase of additional bibliographic databases or software, but if staff expertise in support departments is also used, then this should surely be costed as well. It is therefore essential that a good working relationship with the Research Office is established, to ensure that the proper contribution of support staff to externally funded projects is taken into consideration.

INTRODUCTION TO THE RDF AS A FRAMEWORK TO PROVIDING TARGETED SUPPORT

Research support provision in higher education has been guided by RCUK and bodies such as Vitae. The launch of new guidance in 2011 in the form of the Researcher Development Framework (RDF) and Researcher Development Statement (RDS) comprises a helpful document for institutions seeking to target the support they provide for researchers. The RDF and RDS replaced the 2001 Joint Skills Statement (JSS) that had been developed collaboratively by the research councils to describe the skills a doctoral student would be expected to have by the time they had completed their degree. The RDF, however, covers a longer period of a researcher's career, is broader, and has been described as

> *a tool for planning, promoting and supporting the personal, professional and career development of researchers in higher education. It describes the knowledge, skills, behaviours and personal qualities of researchers and encourages them to aspire to excellence through achieving higher levels of development. (Vitae 2011c)*

The framework is designed for two audiences: researchers themselves, and managers, supervisors, research support staff and institutions as a whole for planning their support for researchers more strategically. There is a range of resources for researchers on the RDF website, for example they can download a professional development planner (Vitae 2011d) to help plan the support and training they might need. However, in the context of this chapter, the RDF is a valuable way of auditing current research support services within an institution and could be a way to identify areas for more personalised services.

The RDF describes four areas of knowledge, skills, behaviours and personal qualities of researchers across their career. The framework is divided into four domains and three sub-domains, as follows:

- Domain A: Knowledge and intellectual abilities
    a.   A1 Knowledge base
    b.   A2 Cognitive abilities
    c.   A3 Creativity
- Domain B: Personal effectiveness
    a.   B1 Personal qualities
    b.   B2 Self-management
    c.   B3 Professional and career development
- Domain C: Research governance and organisation
    a.   C1 Professional conduct
    b.   C2 Research management
    c.   C3 Finance, Funding and Resources
- Domain D: Engagement, influence and impact
    a.   D1 Working with others
    b.   D2 Communication and dissemination
    c.   D3 Engagement and impact.

A visual representation of the framework is reproduced in Figure 6.1.

Within each domain each of the three sub-domains is further broken down into 63 'descriptors'. The framework was produced empirically using interviews with researchers who described the characteristics of excellent researchers. For example, section A1 (Knowledge base) includes descriptors in the following areas:

- subject knowledge
- research methods: theoretical knowledge
- research methods: practical application
- information seeking
- information literacy and management
- languages
- academic literacy and numeracy.

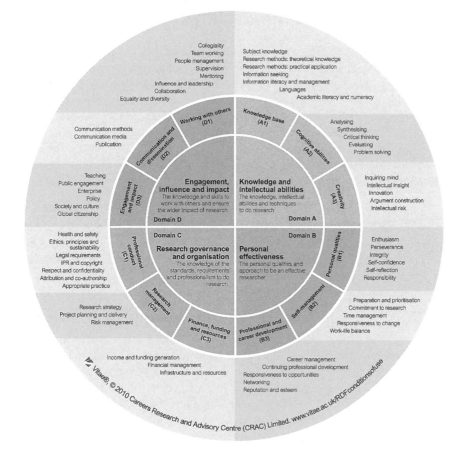

Figure 6.1   Vitae Researcher Development Framework (Vitae 2011)

The RDF is a comprehensive framework of researcher development, and within an institution different departments will provide specific research support services. Libraries and librarians will naturally tend to focus on specific activities around developing researchers' information literacy skills. Meanwhile, a graduate school or academic development unit will focus on other aspects of the framework, such as knowledge about different research methods or developing academic literacy. Ideally, all research support staff should use the RDF to audit provision across their institution. However, Vitae is aware that specific parts of the RDF are more relevant to certain groups of staff. It is therefore in the process of developing lenses that focus on aspects of the framework to demonstrate how they apply in different contexts. Helpfully for the library profession, one of these lenses focuses on information literacy, and it was due for release in 2012.

USING THE RDF WITH THE BOUTIQUE APPROACH

The RDF can be used in a variety of ways by those delivering research support services in libraries and related departments. The framework can be used as a way of auditing research support provision within a specific department to identify related support services and opportunities for collaboration. It can also be used to highlight any opportunities to build on existing training or to identify gaps in provision. The Researcher Development Statement can support and inform future training and development strategy within research degrees. Following the audit process the RDF could highlight areas where specialised or boutique research support services could be developed.

It would be helpful for a group of researchers and those supporting them to undertake an audit of support jointly to map out the provision that is available across the institution. This will be a practical way to avoid any assumptions and misunderstandings about what each department is offering. For example, librarians are typically seen as being able to offer help around finding resources and literature searching. However, other training providers do not always recognise their ability to help researchers evaluate and manage information. In some areas it may be helpful for research support staff to team up to offer joint training or guidance. For example, at LSE at undergraduate and masters level it has proved useful for library staff to work with educational developers to run a session on avoiding plagiarism. The grouping of descriptions under the four domains may offer other opportunities to see synergies between different areas of skills development, which may traditionally be offered by separate units. For example, the descriptor D2 (Communication and dissemination) includes activities around communication methods, communication media and publication. Courses and guidance in this area might be developed by a combination of librarians, supervisors, IT staff and learning technologists to cover not only traditional publishing in journals but also the use of new media such as blogs and issues such as open access.

Once the audit has been undertaken, how to provide support and guidance can be reviewed. Generic training courses could be one way of providing researchers with the knowledge and behaviour outlined above, but researchers need support appropriate to their level and discipline, which means a course might not always be cost effective or feasible. For example, descriptor C1 (Professional conduct) says researchers should have knowledge of health and safety, ethics, legal requirements, IPR, copyright, and confidentiality issues, among others. Many of these areas are ones in which all researchers will need specific guidance, and so a training or information session would be appropriate. However, descriptor B3 (Professional and career development) covers career management, continuing professional development, responsiveness to opportunities, networking, and reputation and esteem. It is much more difficult to envisage generic courses that would work in this area and it may be more appropriate to provide one-to-one guidance.

The RDF also encourages researchers to evaluate and plan their own career development, which suggests a high level of personalised services. If researchers are encouraged to use the professional development planner, it could provide a way of flagging up both generic training on offer and more specialised support.

CONCLUSION

Researchers like students will not always know who can help them in their own institution. Therefore it is vital that research services are targeted appropriately and that research support staff work together collaboratively to promote their services effectively. The ideal scenario is one where a researcher will use a framework such as the RDF to identify their development needs. At the same time the institution will have audited their research support provision to address each of the descriptors in this framework and ensure there is a suitable programme of support in place. This approach suggests that institutions will offer a personalised model of research support that takes into account a researcher's disciplinary needs, their current skills level and their future requirements. The boutique approach can certainly help to meet the diverse needs of researchers. However, research support does need to be realistic and cost effective, so services will need to be planned appropriately taking into account the staff available to provide the support and the numbers of researchers within the institution.

While attempts are being made at LSE to encourage collaboration and shared knowledge and understanding, through groups such as the Training and Development Group, and the establishment of a shared training database, the situation is still not perfect. Silos of support can still exist in all institutions and it is often necessary to offer centralised research support. It is clear that service providers including libraries, IT departments, educational technology specialists, careers advisors and others need to adopt a collaborative approach to researcher development. They also need to make attempts to break down the barriers between academic staff, researchers and support staff. If they succeed in doing this, tailored and personalised services offer a way forward for developments in this field.

TOP TIPS FOR ENGAGING RESEARCHERS

While the boutique model offers much to research support services it is clearly not feasible or cost effective to provide a highly personalised model of support to meet the needs of each researcher in your institution. No institution will have the resources to provide one-to-one support for everyone. In addition there are huge benefits to bringing researchers together, even in just small groups for development activities. Research is often an inherently lonely process, and so interaction and networking is an important aspect of research support services that you offer.

However, the following list provides ten top tips for maximising the services you can provide to researchers, while not overstretching yourself or your staff:

- 'Soft' launch or pilot new boutique services perhaps with just one academic department initially to enable you to test the level of demand that there might be before committing to provide a fully functioning service.
- Do not be afraid to try out new ideas; aim to offer at least one new course or initiative each year to keep your services fresh.
- Build up a network of 'tame' researchers at different levels and in different departments who can provide you with valuable feedback for any new ideas you wish to launch.
- Spend some time carrying out research yourself to really understand the process; even if it is just a short literature review to inform your work, it will help you understand the challenges that researchers face.
- Keep records of the time spent on *one-to-one* activities and group training sessions to enable cost–benefit analysis to be carried out.
- Sometimes you need to persevere with offering services, as it may take time for word to get out about the service you are offering; this is particularly true when knowledge of your services is spread by word of mouth.
- Ask for feedback from users of boutique services to demonstrate the value you are providing, and use positive and negative feedback to inform your services.
- Collect qualitative feedback for researchers as this will tell you a lot more about what they really need than a simple survey.
- Team up with other service providers to join up the support you offer and to develop strategies for promoting your services collectively; researchers actually rarely mind who is offering the training, just that it is appropriate.
- Constantly review your marketing and promotion – are you using the appropriate channels to reach researchers and are you using the right language?

REFERENCES

Allan, B. 2009. *Supporting Research Students*. London: Facet.

Bent, M., Webb, J. and Gannon-Leary, P. 2007. Information Literacy in a Researcher's Learning Life: The Seven Ages of Research. *New Review of Information Networking*, 13(2), 81–99.

FutureLab. 2010. Digital Literacy across the Curriculum [online]. At: http://futurelab.org.uk/sites/default/files/Digital_Literacy_handbook_0.pdf (accessed: 26 March 2012).

LSE. 2011. LSE Training and Development System. At: http://training.lse.ac.uk (accessed: 14 March 2012).

Research Information Network (RIN). 2010. Research Support Services: What Services do Researchers Need and Use? [online]. At: http://www.rin.ac.uk/our-work/using-and-accessing-information-resources/research-support-services-what-services-do-resear (accessed: 24 October 2011).

Research Information Network (RIN). 2011a. Who We Are [online]. At: http://www.rin.ac.uk/about/who-we-are (accessed: 24 October 2011).

Research Information Network (RIN). 2011b. Social Media: A Guide for Researchers [online]. At: http://www.rin.ac.uk/our-work/communicating-and-disseminating-research/social-media-guide-researchers (accessed: 24 October 2011).

Research Information Network (RIN). 2011c. The Value of Libraries for Research and Researchers [online]. At: http://www.rin.ac.uk/our-work/using-and-accessing-information-resources/value-libraries-research-and-researchers (accessed: 24 October 2011).

Secker, J. and Macrae-Gibson, R. 2011. Evaluating MI512: An Information Literacy Course for PhD Students. *Library Review*, 60(2), 96–107.

Toffler, A. 1971. *Future Shock*. New York: Bantam Books.

Vitae. 2011a. Vitae Database of Practice [online]. At: http://www.vitae.ac.uk/dop (accessed: 24 October 2011).

Vitae. 2011b. Engagement, Impact and Influence Programme. [online]. At: http://www.vitae.ac.uk/dop/1277.html (accessed: 24 October 2011).

Vitae. 2011c. The Visibility of Researcher Development in UK Higher Education Institutions' Strategies [online]. At: http://www.vitae.ac.uk/policy-practice/1393-383711/The-visibility-of-researcher-development-in-UK-higher-education-institutions-strategies.html (accessed: 24 October 2011).

Vitae. 2011d. RDF Professional Development Planner [online]. At: http://www.vitae.ac.uk/researchers/291411/RDF-Professional-Development-Planner.html (accessed: 24 October 2011).

Webb, J., Gannon-Leary, P. and Bent, M. 2007. *Providing Effective Library Services for Research*. London: Facet.

SECTION 2

A VOICE IN THE WILDERNESS: PERSONALISED LIBRARY SERVICES IN A VIRTUAL ENVIRONMENT
MARGARET WESTBURY

Most librarians are to some degree virtual librarians these days. They regularly communicate and answer enquiries with users via the internet. And all are likely to have thought about how best to work with remote users in terms of doing a reference interview or offering friendly service. In the spring of 2008, however, I began working for a 100 per cent online university in the United States, which had library services but no chance ever of the librarian's meeting users face to face or regularly interacting with the university administration. The major challenge was to provide library services to a group of students who for a number of reasons (discussed below) felt disconnected from the university and each other.

My job was to provide library services to the students in an online doctoral programme for Kindergarten to Grade 12 (K-12) educational leadership. The students were passionate about reforming their schools. Most worked full time and had major family responsibilities, and many were the first to go to university from their families. The doctoral programme in education promised a doctorate in three years, but it was no degree mill: the curriculum was rigorous and demanded a lot of introspection and writing. Unlike many online universities, the students never met in person during their three years. Instead, their communication with their professors and each other happened primarily via the virtual learning environment. Unofficial communication largely was via Skype. Though the curriculum was rigorous, the school was socially quite isolating and lonely in some ways. Despite its best efforts to keep students engaged and participating, students regularly would be silent for weeks. Many also expressed feelings of isolation and alienation.

When I first started, library services were minimal. Students could email the library and were promised a response within 24 hours. Students could work with a librarian only two hours per two-month term. There was library support for their dissertation writing courses, but not for their subject-matter courses. There was no blog or wiki for regular updates and conversations. Orientations to the library were sporadic, although new students started each month. Evening library services, when students tended to need the most help, were offered by a third-party provider unconnected to the university and unaware of how to best assist with the students' topics and assignments.

With few librarians to support the students, and with the programme itself in its nascent months, this was understandable. But it was clear to me that students were not receiving library services that would help them become advanced scholars in their fields. So, during my first year, I set about to implement changes to make the library more friendly and targeted to student needs. Specifically:

- I monitored all course forums regularly, both the dissertation and subject courses. There were 40+ of these, but I managed to get into each one at least once per week and search for my name and library-related topics. I frequently posted information to help students do searches and about plagiarism, citation styles, and using EndNote. There were many assignments where students reflected on the research process, and these were perfect opportunities for me to chime in about how to find sources, write literature reviews, and use the library. I even regularly responded to postings about personal news, such as new babies, in order to help provide a friendly face to the library.
- I worked with faculty to customise the information I sent out. I often contacted the professors teaching the courses to find out how I could best support their students and I regularly sent out messages with course-specific tips and resources.
- I developed a wiki with about 25 articles with tips about how to use the library, how to cite resources, EndNote, current awareness, and writing. The wiki also linked to several online tutorials that I created.
- I made and delivered weekly webinars on using the library, citing sources, and using EndNote.
- I became the resident expert on certain topics, such as citing resources and avoiding plagiarism, and even wrote a dissertation publication manual. I became the one that everyone turned to with questions on these topics, and I would regularly proofread students' lists of references.
- I set up online office hours when I would be guaranteed to be at my computer, but I also kept Skype online and frequently instant-messaged with students via Skype during the evening hours.
- Essentially I set out to market the library and its resources at every turn I could.

Overall, it seemed from kudos sent to me and mentions that I found in the forums, that students and faculty were happy and appreciative of my help. Much of this satisfaction, it seemed, stemmed from the personal relationships I built with students and faculty. Students and faculty tended to feel isolated in the online school environment, despite the requirement to post and respond regularly in the forums. I was a friendly, non-judgemental person students seemed to feel comfortable with, just to chat with, sometimes about their personal life. I never discouraged this sort of personal interaction; it definitely helped provide a friendly face to the library, and often after having built the trust of a casual conversation, students would ask library questions.

During this time, my style as a librarian evolved. Never having worked in a 100 per cent online environment before, I was not entirely sure how to provide services. I quickly got to know the needs of the students, and one need over others stood out. They were incredibly busy people, passionate about changing the educational system, but often lacking advanced research skills. When students contacted me, they were often frustrated and desperate. Quick reference interviews – and even these are quite hard online – would reveal that they often did not know what a scholarly resource looked like or how to paraphrase properly. As a librarian I was keen to teach students how to use the library's databases, but I certainly was not beyond doing a little extra work to attach a handful of articles that looked relevant, just to get the student started. Enquiries regularly took over an hour, but the extra work paid off, as grateful students were able to see clearly what sort of databases, search terms, and resources were acceptable, and how to begin to use the plethora of electronic resources the university offered. My work really focused less on the collections per se, and more on what services I could provide to the students. The students certainly appreciated the personalised services that they got from me, and their information literacy skills clearly improved as a result.

In retrospect, the online position changed my approach to being a librarian. It made me understand that library services in a virtual environment must necessarily be personalised, or many students will be lost. I am definitely a better librarian for having had the opportunity to push myself to offer the fastest and most personalised services I could. Working 100 per cent online and trying hard to meet the needs of the students really forged my identity as a librarian who reaches out and proactively tries to provide a good and relevant service.

INTEGRATING INFORMATION SKILLS INTO THE CURRICULUM: THE NEXT STEP
VERONICA LAWRENCE

Many academic libraries remain unconvinced by suggestions that the 'Google Generation' has no need of information skills teaching (Prensky 2001; Padilla-Meléndez, Garrido-Moreno and Del Aguila-Obra 2008: 610; CIBER 2008). 'Digital natives' undoubtedly have greater facility and confidence with online environments and Web 2.0 technologies than have most 'digital immigrants'; however, there remain areas in the evolving online library environment, such as access, navigation, search strategy and the purpose and interpretation of references, that require more than intuition on its own. Holley and Oliver (2010: 698) show that a correlation exists between academic success and control over the use of technology. This necessarily includes the online library environment.

But how best to facilitate this? The trend towards personalising library services in higher education and 'valuing the unique' (Karpik 2010) has seen a move away from generic information skills teaching towards greater integration of information skills into the curriculum. Commonly, this takes the form of a timetabled session that is taught by a member of library staff, usually a subject or liaison librarian; has a practical 'hands-on' component; and is intended to introduce students to the resource finding and the evaluating skills required for a particular assessed piece of work, such as a literature review or dissertation. Often these sessions take place as part of a study skills, dissertation preparation or methods module or course.

However, are there additional ways in which librarians can personalise the acquisition of skills that may well come across to students as somewhat dry, methodical, even mechanical and divorced from the excitement that they feel when studying their academic subject? Might there be some way of making even closer connections between the acquisition of information skills and the student's subject work, of communicating information skills as part of a holistic process that is essential to the study of the student's subject?

This case study will look at two case studies that relate to work carried out at Nottingham Trent University where information skills teaching has been incorporated into subject teaching. In both cases, the teaching of information skills occupied only a small part of the session but was *needed* in order for the students to complete a subject-related task. The module/course leader was present to teach the subject-related parts of the session and to relate the skills taught by the librarian to the task that the students were required to complete as part of the session.

The first case study relates to a first-year undergraduate half-year geography module on the human geography of the United Kingdom where students went on a field excursion to Newark, Nottinghamshire, looking at the patterns and processes that have shaped the form and function of a historical market town. The week before the field excursion, students attended a session where the objectives of the field excursion were discussed and where students were expected to produce a map of the area in Newark that they would be investigating. The role of the member of academic staff present at the session was to introduce the fieldwork excursion and answer any questions about what was expected of the students during the excursion. The librarian's role was to demonstrate how students could use Digimap in order to create a detailed map of the area that they would be investigating. Both the member of academic staff and the librarian were present throughout the session to answer any questions about the task of producing the maps.

The second case study relates to a third-year undergraduate year-long history module on death and remembrance in late medieval and early modern Europe. About halfway through the year, students attended a workshop about commemoration in which they looked at examples of late medieval and early modern epitaphs and sermons. The workshop began with an introduction to the subject of epitaphs and sermons by the module leader. The librarian then demonstrated to students how to search for examples of sermons and epitaphs on Early English Books Online and Eighteenth Century Collections Online. Students then spent some time searching EEBO and ECCO in pairs and examining what they had found. The workshop concluded with a discussion led by the module leader about the nature of late medieval and early modern sermons and epitaphs based on the primary source material that the students had discovered using EEBO and ECCO.

When one considers some of the more usual forms that information skills teaching takes (sessions timed to coincide with the start of dissertation research or of a literature review assignment and geared at equipping students with the tools needed to complete this assignment), factors that affect the success of the session include: timing, authenticity, level of student motivation and perceived usefulness of the session. How do these factors relate to the case studies above?

Timing is always a major consideration when scheduling an information skills session. Providing too much information at, say, a library induction, before a student is ready to make use of that information, will result in much of its being lost. Even carefully timed information skills sessions at the start of dissertation preparation modules can sometimes feel to the person leading the session not to be as effective as it might be from a timing perspective. The dissertation hand-in date is too far in the future and the task is not sufficiently urgent to engage the entire group. Although the tasks involved in the case studies (preparing a map for a fieldwork excursion, finding early examples of epitaphs and sermons) were tiny compared to the task of preparing a dissertation, they were tasks that needed to be accomplished immediately. Student engagement with learning to use Digimap or EEBO and ECCO was necessary because the tasks could not be put off to another day. Information about the skills involved in using these databases was introduced exactly at the point of need.

Authenticity directly relates to whether students perceive the task to be 'real'. Panelli and Welch (2005: 267, 274) interviewed students about the usefulness of a methods course in preparation for fieldwork and quote one of the students as saying, 'At the time it did not seem real, so I feel not enough note was taken. Without it being put into practice and making it real, it lose[s] its purpose'. Responses suggested that students wanted the opportunity to apply their learning immediately in 'realistic formats'. In the case studies above, the authenticity of the context in which the students learned about the databases contributed to making the experience a purposeful one for them.

Student motivation and, a closely related factor, a sense of cohort identity will certainly influence how successful the librarian perceives an information skills session to have been. Motivated students will remain in the computer resource room until the end of the session to try out the databases that have been demonstrated and even make a start on finding resources for their dissertation rather than ask if they can leave as soon as the taught part of the session is over. They will be more likely to ask questions and to help one another. Interestingly, though, in the case studies, the pace of the sessions and the requisite amount to be accomplished within them was such that the sessions appeared to generate a momentum of their own, independent of individual levels of student motivation.

An offshoot of the acknowledgement that there are different styles of learning is the recognition that learning can and should be personalised. In addition to varying the way in which one teaches and assesses in order to accommodate different learning styles, the move away from generic information skills sessions to ones that focus more directly on the group that one is teaching is another form of personalisation. The case studies provide examples of ways in which transferable skills can be communicated in a highly personalised way with demonstrable relevance and 'perceived usefulness' (Padilla-Meléndez, Garrido-Moreno and Del Aguila-Obra 2008: 612).

The case studies described above are examples of what can be done to take the next step in integrating information skills into the curriculum. They are, however, not transferable, let alone prescriptive. What you do to take that next step will depend on what your students are doing. All that is required is alertness to possibilities, a little creativity, a willingness to try out new things and a close relationship with the academic departments with which you work.

THANKS

I am grateful to former colleagues at Nottingham Trent University, especially Alan Dingsdale, Kevin Gould, Clare Newstead, Angela Phelps, Trevor Pull and Amanda Smith for the opportunity to work with their students and to discuss this paper.

REFERENCES

CIBER. 2008. Information Behaviour of the Researcher of the Future: A CIBER Briefing Paper. University College London CIBER Group [online]. At: http://www.jisc.ac.uk/media/documents/programmes/reppres/gg_final_keynote_11012008.pdf (accessed: 12 April 2011).

Holley, D. and Oliver, M. 2010. Student Engagement and Blended Learning: Portraits of Risk. *Computers and Education*, 54(3), 693–700.

Karpik, L. 2010. *Valuing the Unique: The Economics of Singularities*, trans. N. Scott. Princeton, NJ: Princeton University Press.

Padilla-Meléndez, A., Garrido-Moreno, A. and Del Aguila-Obra, A.R. 2008. Factors Affecting E-Collaboration Technology Use among Management Students. *Computers and Education*, 51(2), 609–23.

Panelli, R. and Welch, R.V. 2005. Teaching Research through Field Studies: A Cumulative Opportunity for Teaching Methodology to Human Geography Undergraduates. *Journal of Geography in Higher Education*, 29(2), 255–77.

Prensky, M. 2001. Digital Natives, Digital Immigrants. *On the Horizon* 9(5) [online]. At: http://www.marcprensky.com/writing/prensky%20-%20digital%20natives,%20digital%20immigrants%20-%20part1.pdf (accessed: 12 April 2011).

ONLINE OUTREACH AND TAILORED TRAINING: THE ENGLISH FACULTY LIBRARY AT OXFORD UNIVERSITY
KERRY WEBB

INTRODUCTION

The English Faculty Library (EFL 2011) at Oxford University was first established in 1914 'to serve all those reading and teaching English at Oxford'. Almost one hundred years later we are still working to this simple remit and many of our approaches to reader services meet the boutique libraries model. However, as those we serve are members of a collegiate university, the EFL is only one of many libraries they might use during their time here.

BODLEIAN LIBRARIES OF THE UNIVERSITY OF OXFORD

The EFL is one of the Bodleian Libraries of the University of Oxford. An umbrella organisation, Oxford University Library Services (OULS) was created in 2000 to improve the user experience of Oxford's libraries and to streamline and centralise many of our services. OULS incorporated many of the departmental, faculty and research libraries (including the Bodleian Library) under one banner and saw the introduction of subject librarians to coordinate collection development across the libraries. OULS was rebranded in March 2010 as the Bodleian Libraries of the University of Oxford, with the centralisation and harmonisation of services a continuing priority. Inevitably, this more centralised and harmonised environment has led to some challenges:

- the feeling, to some extent, among individual libraries and librarians of a loss of autonomy (which can lead to frustration at times!).
- a dilution of localised financial and budgetary control.
- significant changes to localised practices and workflows – in particular with regard to systems administration and acquisitions – whereby tasks that were once achieved relatively swiftly in house have taken slightly longer in a larger, more complex arrangement. However, this has, in turn, led to

the freeing up of staff time to focus on more strategic long-term projects designed to improve our personalised services overall.

While the formation of any large organisation inevitably results in the need to change some local and more tailored working practices, without this umbrella organisation there are nevertheless many positive things, particularly with regard to information skills training, that we would not have been able to achieve as easily:

- coordinated and centralised user education programmes (in addition to those run by individual libraries) that appeal to an interdisciplinary audience
- a collaborative approach to induction for new students, ensuring they all receive an introduction to key services, as well as subject-specific resources/services
- the establishment of an information skills strategy team, with representatives from humanities, sciences, social sciences and college libraries, to develop integrated information literacy programmes and support the teaching of information skills across Oxford's libraries
- the formation of a guides for readers working party, whose remit is the oversight, quality and commissioning of printed documentation and online guides for the Bodleian Libraries.

THE ENGLISH FACULTY LIBRARY

The EFL has a small team of two part-time library assistants and five full-time staff, including the English Subject Librarian who has responsibility for collections at the EFL and the English collections at the Bodleian Library, ensuring that high-use teaching material is available on open shelves in the Bodleian Library's reading rooms rather than in closed stacks.

Tailored Training Programmes

The EFL is well placed not only for the provision of traditional lending services to our readers but also for the delivery of interactive information skills training for English students in the IT Training Room, just off the EFL's main reading room. Examples include: 'iBard: online resources for Shakespeare', 'Researching your extended essay', 'OED QED: Using online resources for FHS Paper 1' and 'OED … OIC!: Further online resources for FHS Paper 1', the latter two providing training on specialist e-resources such as online dictionaries and text analysis software for the English Language examination paper.

We carefully tailor our training programme to be delivered at point of need, so we monitor the syllabus, exam timetables and submission dates for coursework, so that we can provide subject-specific support at key times. In addition to this we offer an evening class for students studying the English Literature Foundation course provided by the university's Continuing Education Department at the start of their studies, introducing them to e-resources for English – crucial tools for those studying 'off campus' most of the time; again, customising our training programme to meet the needs of our readers. In all these initiatives, we are mindful to ask our students for feedback on the timing of training sessions and act on this accordingly. Sessions are well attended and have enabled us to promote not only our subject-specific e-resources and library services but also our team's subject knowledge so that readers feel confident about approaching library staff with their research needs.

Sharing Good Practice

While the EFL staff seek to provide specialist 'personalised' services to its particular group of users, they also participate in the wider activities of the Bodleian Libraries. The benefits of this to the EFL are most apparent in the sharing of good practice through collaboration with colleagues across the university's libraries. Faculty and departmental libraries are able not only to benchmark their services but also to learn from one another, repurposing existing resources for their own libraries, thus saving time, energy and resources.

Many of the new approaches individual libraries are taking in information skills training would not have been possible without central funding from the Bodleian Libraries for site licences and staff training programmes, and so on. It is unlikely that an individual library would have been able to budget for site licenses or specialist software but, collectively, these have been negotiated and purchased. One good example of this has been the purchase of a licence to use the Springshare (2011) software, LibGuides, which has enabled libraries to produce not only general guides to centralised library services but also subject-specific guides (Oxford LibGuides 2011a, b, c). While this was a central initiative (originating from the Guides for Readers Working Party) taken in part to avoid the large costs involved in centrally produced printed guides that quickly become out of date, it was primarily implemented to meet one of the Bodleian Libraries' strategic objectives 'to communicate effectively with our users through a variety of channels.'

The Working Party's intention was to develop a suite of subject-specific online guides for the start of the 2010/11 academic year, through the training of library staff during the summer on the use of the Springshare software. While there were some initial reservations about the provision of online guides over the more traditional printed guides, the group felt that this format would 'deliver substantial improvements', with the ability to create direct links to online resources, embed multimedia content (such as online tutorials), allow for quick and easy editing and updating of guides (future-proofing printed guides was seen as a constant and unsolvable problem), and again, in this culture of collaboration, to enable the reuse and sharing of information between Oxford librarians. The EFL was involved in the pilot project for the introduction of LibGuides across Oxford, with the EFL becoming an early adopter of this new generation of online guides.

EFL Libguides

The EFL has always been proactive in the production of printed guides for readers, using its own 'house style' to brand these. Guides were produced to address common reader enquiries (encountered either at our Issue Desk or via our enquiries email address) as well as promoting the subject-specific resources and services that the library provides. Delivering a suite of online guides for English in an age where mobile technologies are increasingly the platform of choice for those seeking information seemed like an unmissable opportunity to further promote our personalised services to those studying and teaching English at Oxford. Several of our existing printed guides were 'converted' to the new format, which enabled us to embed live links, widgets and search applications to specific resources as well as the university's online library catalogue. We also generated 'QR Codes', which have been added to library posters, providing links to relevant guides at appropriate points around the library. In addition to this, an online 'portal' was created so that all our guides could be accessed from one URL; within this portal we have also included links to guides for centralised services, such as photocopying and printing, using the online catalogue, and so on. Furthermore, we are working on a suite of guides specifically for topics covered by the Final Honours School exam papers taken by undergraduates. Those already published have been well received. Further guides will be added in the future to provide information for postgraduates (research and taught students), and for courses convened in other faculties that include elements of English Literature and Language teaching, such as the MSt in Women's Studies.

An online survey was recently conducted asking members of the English faculty how we could improve the guides. One student said, 'Make sure more people know about them! They're great!', which suggests that, although further work is required to promote them, the initial signs are good. Just as we provide customised training programmes we have also created guides directly relevant to the English syllabus, such as 'English Language: a short guide to online resources', 'Old Norse-Icelandic language and literature at the EFL' and 'Shakespeare: a short guide to online resources'. Lecturers teaching specific topics have been approached for their comments on new/revised guides and in turn they have agreed to promote them to their tutorial groups; faculty endorsement is almost always the best way of promoting new resources to the students.

In August 2011 we also published a new LibGuide specifically targeting 'A' Level candidates starting their English Language & Literature studies at Oxford the following October. It is intended to bridge the gap between school and university, demystifying the use and range of library resources available to them at Oxford so that they will feel a bit more prepared when it comes to using them for their studies. Published online two days before the 'A' Level results came out, the guide has received over 900 'hits' between then and the start of the student's first term. While it is not possible to assess whether all this traffic was generated by upcoming Oxford English undergraduates, this form of targeted online 'outreach' activity does seem to indicate that it is never too early to start promoting our tailored library services to potential users of the English Faculty Library.

MEETING THE MODEL

In relation to the boutique library approach, the EFL's services and staff can claim to meet many of the recognised elements. We have a convenient location adjacent to the faculty teaching facilities, we offer significant subject specialism with our dedicated collections, and we are early adopters of new trends such as QR codes and LibGuides to help us to promote our collections. The customer focus illustrated by our syllabus specific guides, personalising materials for our new upcoming students and our highly tailored information skills programme all indicate that the EFL meets the criteria, while remaining an integral part of a centralised university library service.

REFERENCES

English Faculty Library. 2011. Welcome to the EFL [online]. At: http://www. bodleian.ox.ac.uk/english (accessed: 1 September 2011).
Oxford LibGuides. 2011a. English at Oxford: Guides to Resources [online]. At: http://libguides.bodleian.ox.ac.uk/english (accessed: 1 September 2011).
Oxford LibGuides. 2011b. Starting Out at Oxford: An English Freshers Guide to Using the Libraries [online]. At: http://libguides.bodleian.ox.ac.uk/english-freshers-guide (accessed: 1 September 2011).
Oxford LibGuides. 2011c. Welcome to LibGuides [online]. At: http://libguides. bodleian.ox.ac.uk (accessed: 1 September 2011).
Springshare. 2011. LibGuides for Academic Libraries [online]. At: http://www. springshare.com/libguides/academic/ (accessed: 1 September 2011).

BOUTIQUE INFLUENCES ON STRUCTURES AND LIFELONG LEARNING AT AUSTRALIAN CATHOLIC UNIVERSITY
TATUM MCPHERSON-CROWIE

Libraries and librarians can play a role in supporting academics as lifelong learners and enabling them to meet the changes and challenges of the evolving information resources and systems of access defined in, and required by, their work. Task-specific library-related literacies and broader information-related literacies, while distinct, are complementary and are better served when not used in isolation in higher education institutions and their libraries. A personalised library approach is able to fulfil an institution's requirements in the focusing of efforts and services and allocation of resources by librarians to respond to the most significant academic and institutional challenges of their members.

AUSTRALIAN CATHOLIC UNIVERSITY (ACU)

ACU is Australia's only university with quasi-national presence, operating on six campuses in three state capitals. In Australian higher education, ACU is characterised as a 'medium-sized university but, with six relatively small campuses, is able to offer personalised education to its students' (ACU 2010: 5). The university is recognised for its support of the education of indigenous students and endeavours to provide students with an infrastructure offering extensive support, which includes academic skills, counselling, equity and disability support, career development and student associations. Library services are underpinned and characterised by commitment to six core values:

- *Client focus:* We are attentive to the individual learning and educational needs of our diverse and dispersed clientele. We strive to provide equitable service to all clients.
- *Ethical conduct:* We commit ourselves to ethical behaviour, treating one another and our clients with respect, dignity and fairness.
- *Quality:* We evaluate what we do and strive for continuous improvement in service through the application of Quality Assurance systems and practices.

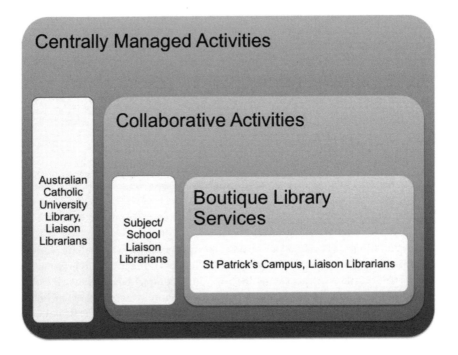

Figure H.1   Boutique library services at Australian Catholic University

We strive to deliver high quality services efficiently and cost-effectively.

- *Cooperation:* We foster a spirit of cooperation and collaboration within the Library, within ACU and beyond. We work collectively to achieve our goals, with each staff member taking personal responsibility for their role in the success of the team.
- *Professional rigour:* We set and attain high standards of professional performance. We ensure that all Library staff are enabled to fulfil their role.
- *Education and learning:* We value learning and, as professionals, contribute actively to the University's educational and research mission. (ACU Library 2011: 4)

ACU Library is centrally managed and operates as one national library across the six campuses of the university. In 2010 the central management structure of the library was significantly consolidated and has increased the number of staff working on central operations (ACU 2010: 24). A physical library, which provides local boutique identity by means of subject specialisation and carrying its own name, is located on all six campuses. Figure H.1 illustrates how the structure of ACU replicates the three broad aspects of the model: collaboration, centralisation and boutique, or personalised.

Centrally managed ACU liaison librarian activities include internal communication, external communication and marketing, core library functions, and learning and teaching. Collaborative ACU liaison librarian activities are organised by academic discipline and geographic location. The activities they undertake primarily address the domains of internal communication, core library functions, and learning and teaching. Boutique ACU library services provided by, for example, St Patrick's campus librarians have a prime responsibility to respond to the local needs of the campus, in the provision of core library functions, external communication and marketing, and learning and teaching.

During 2008 the role and programme of liaison librarians, also referred to as subject librarians, was nationally relaunched at ACU Library. Liaison librarians are required to collaborate closely with academic staff to help promote and achieve in graduates the specified university graduate attributes, and to ensure that the concept of lifelong learning is an integral component of university courses. Liaison librarians contribute specialist expertise in the Information Literacy Standards Framework (Bundy 2004) and work with academic staff to ensure that these competencies are embedded and promoted in the university curriculum. In offering this service, liaison librarians also develop and deliver learning opportunities to support the lifelong learning needs of academic staff.

One particularly prominent consideration was the need to personalise the national one-library structure for academic staff. In order to bring this about, a person (a liaison librarian) offered an identifiable face for the library and made a personal connection with the academic schools. The centrally managed communication and marketing of the library's revised policies successfully informed the university community. The campus-based liaison librarians reconnected our local communities with familiar information delivered by a different medium and endeavoured to manage and address member needs and expectations.

St Patrick's Campus Liaison Librarians

St Patrick's Campus is one specific example of a boutique service within the ACU structure. Engaging with campus-based ACU staff and students, through our school-based roles, provides the opportunity for librarians to gain a deeper knowledge of the context in which our academic groups learn, teach and research. The knowledge-base characterised by a local and personal approach to communication informs the task of managing and developing the collection at the St Patrick's campus library. It is from this collegial and well-informed position that liaison librarians shape our information literacy programmes to members' needs and provide personalised information services of increased value to our staff and students. The librarians of Raheen Library at St Patrick's campus work both collaboratively and independently to seek to understand, respond to and anticipate the needs of the schools for which we are responsible in order the better to determine and emphasise the availability of our most effective services.

LIFELONG LEARNING AT THE SCHOOL OF RELIGIOUS EDUCATION

The School of Religious Education (SoRE) is a national school that has a presence across a number of campuses. The SoRE develops both teachers and pre-service teachers for the Australian Catholic school system, and for that reason 'ACU has the largest group of religious education academics in the Australian tertiary education sector' (ACU 2011). The school offers undergraduate and postgraduate courses by face-to-face on-campus classes and in combination with online components, with enrolment by semester and intensive seasonal terms.

The interdisciplinary perspectives of the SoRE require that its academic staff be knowledgeable across a range of diverse subject areas. This necessitates that staff be well informed across a range of information resources, structures and services. The teaching and research foci of the school distinguish it from other interdisciplinary schools and this impinges on the work of their library liaison staff when they are considering the library-related provision and support required. There is a significant variation between the modes and means of working in these subject areas that, when combined with an individual's needs, strongly encourages an adaptable approach at both the school and personal level. This particular academic intersection of disciplines can be better supported by attending to the lifelong learning requirements and aspirations of academics.

Adopting a personalised library service approach to lifelong learning begins with any individual. Developing my own learning opportunities and capabilities helps to facilitate the confident instruction of my library members (Hahn 2009: 2; McKnight 2010; Tamarkin and The 2010 EDUCAUSE Evolving Technologies Committee 2010: 43; Whatley 2009: 30). The ways in which librarians learn is important, for example, how we consider information and operate within universities, as we combine forward-looking capabilities underpinned by traditional library science skills (McKnight 2010: 200; Siess 2010: 43).

We have felt that the library should offer lifelong learning opportunities that can be shaped to the individual's needs, without limiting the breadth and depth of options to what may be perceived to be of interest or relevance to our audience. Not all academic staff conceptualise a role for lifelong learning within HEIs, nor have the aspiration to be self-sufficient information seekers, and this impacts how you approach them (Doskatsch 2003: 118).

Scheduled classes, training and workshops for academic staff may be perceived as 'one-size-fits-none'. However, by exploring opportunities to connect with a group of academics, it is clear that these occasions offer insight into individual preferences, informal networks and research commonalities (Creighton 2011, Fister 2009, Tillman 2008). For academic staff, particularly non-teaching researchers, such networking offers the circumstances to connect and collaborate with other lifelong learners within their schools, faculties and the institution in general.

A key route into finding out the needs of academics is to make good use of attendance at faculty/school committee meetings and the reports that you submit to the committee, as representatives from other faculties and schools are often also in attendance. A boutique library service approach that engages in collaborative activities can enable the circumstances in which 'broadly focused libraries can become trusted consultants in the larger work of the institution' (Haynes and Kent 2010: 141).

REFERENCES

Australian Catholic University (ACU). 2010. Australian Catholic University Annual Report 2009 [online]. At: http://www.acu.edu.au/about_acu/publications/annual_reports/annual_report_2009/ (accessed: 1 April 2011).

Australian Catholic University. (ACU) 2011. School of Religious Education [online]. At: http://www.acu.edu.au/8076 (accessed: 1 May 2011).

Australian Catholic University (ACU) Library. 2011. Library Annual Report 2010 [online]. At: http://www.acu.edu.au/_data?assets/file/0004/333652/2010_Library_Annual_Report.html (accessed: 1 May 2011).

Bundy, A. (ed.) 2004. *Australian and New Zealand Information Literacy Framework: Principles, Standards and Practice*, 2nd edn. Adelaide: Australian and New Zealand Institute for Information Literacy.

Creighton, J. 2011. 21st Century Institutions [online]. At: http://futureready365.sla.org/02/02/id=944 (accessed: 1 April 2011).

Doskatsch, I. 2003. Perceptions and Perplexities of the Faculty–Librarian Partnership: An Australian Perspective. *Reference Services Review*, 31(2), 111–21 [online]. At doi: 10.1108/00907320310476585 (accessed: 1 April 2011).

Fister, B. 2009. Fostering Information Literacy through Faculty Development. *Library Issues: Briefings for Faculty and Administrators*, 29(4) [online]. At: http://libraryissues.com/ (accessed: 1 April 2011).

Hahn, K. 2009. Introduction: Positioning Liaison Librarians for the 21st Century. *Research Library Issues: A Bimonthly Report from ARL, CNI, and SPARC*, 265, 1–2 [online]. At: http://www.arl.org/resources/pubs/rli/archive/rli265.shtml (accessed: 1 April 2011).

Haynes, H. and Kent, P.G. 2010. Knowledge Management, Universities and Libraries, in S. McKnight (ed.), *Envisioning Future Academic Library Services: Initiatives, Ideas and Challenges*. London: Facet, 119–44.

McKnight, S. 2010. Adding Value to Learning and Teaching, in McKnight, S., (ed.), *Envisioning Future Academic Library Services: Initiatives, Ideas and Challenges*. London: Facet, 197–215.

Siess, J. 2010. Embedded Librarianship. *Searcher*, 18(1), 38–45.

Tamarkin, M. and The 2010 EDUCAUSE Evolving Technologies Committee. 2010. You 3.0: The Most Important Evolving Technology. *EDUCAUSE Review*, 45(6) [online]. At: http://www.educause.edu/EDUCAUSE+Review/EDUCAUSEReviewMagazineVolume45/You30TheMostImportantEvolvingT/218701 (accessed: 1 April 2011).

Tillman, C. 2008. Library Orientation for Professors: Give a Pitch, not a Tour. *C&RL News*, 69(8), 470–75 [online]. At: http://crln.acrl.org/content/69/8/470.full.pdf+html (accessed: 1 April 2011).

Whatley, K. 2009. New Roles of Liaison Librarians: A Liaison's Perspective. *Research Library Issues: A Bimonthly Report from ARL, CNI, and SPARC*, 265, 29–32 [online]. At: http://www.arl.org/resources/pubs/rli/archive/rli265.shtml (accessed: 1 April 2011).

CHAPTER 7

MARKETING PERSONALISED SERVICES
EMMA THOMPSON

Don't Sell the Steak – Sell the Sizzle!

Elmer Wheeler (1937: 3)

INTRODUCTION

As many of the valuable resources of a university library can no longer be shown during a tour, and promotion within the library is insufficient, the challenge for libraries is to promote effective use and full exploitation of electronic resources *as well as* the physical space and print collections. This has led to a need for marketing skills and imagination within library staff (Wisniewski and Fichter 2007, Donham and Green 2004, De Saez 2002). Our product has changed from being tangible (a physical book) to intangible. We cannot measure our success in terms of sales and profits, but if the students, staff and visitors do not know about the services we provide they may perform less well in their degree programmes or in their research and teaching. In short, we are in the business of selling 'sizzle' – that intangible benefit that delights when it is there and disappoints when it is not.

The Chartered Institute of Marketing's (2011) definition of marketing is: 'The management process responsible for identifying, anticipating and satisfying customer requirements profitably'. This particular definition dates back to 1976, and the business (and, of course, library) world has moved on considerably since then. More recently a new definition was proposed by the CIM to its members:

> *The strategic business function that creates value by stimulating, facilitating and fulfilling customer demand. It does this by building brands, nurturing innovation, developing relationships, creating good customer service and communicating benefits. With a customer-centric view, marketing brings positive return on investment, satisfies shareholders and stakeholders from business and the community, and contributes to positive behavioural change and a sustainable business future. (Chartered Institute of Marketing 2007)*

It is this second definition that has most relevance for personalised library services, as it puts the customer at the forefront: a 'customer-centric' view. This definition forms the structure of this chapter.

RESEARCHING YOUR MARKET

To many people working in libraries 'customers' is a difficult word; 'users' perhaps has negative connotations around drug abuse; and the term 'patron', though commonplace in the United States, does not have wide use and understanding in the United Kingdom. Many public and academic libraries use the term 'readers', although some use the term customers, but it has been a perennial problem in libraries (particularly in the UK). It is time to get over the problem with terminology for the people who use our service and buildings by abandoning attempts to label them all with one term. This is a book about *personalised* services, after all. We do not have a typical user of our services, so why have one term? Particularly with regard to boutique libraries, the users of the service can be a very well-defined group, by subject or faculty, or status as opposed to the homogeneity of the central library. It is essential to think very carefully about the different people who use your service. These categories of people may include:

- academic staff
- postgraduate research students
- online (perhaps distance learning) students
- undergraduate students
- postgraduate-taught students
- students on placement
- external visitors
- prospective students.

Your library will have a different list, depending on its function and location, so the first task is to generate a similar list to the one above for yourself. Segmentation of your market, your library users, is essential prior to designing and promoting new services. One size does not fit all. Within these categories are widely differing individuals. The seven ages approach to profiling researchers is a helpful way of approaching their differing needs (Webb, Gannon-Leary and Bent, 2007). This approach takes researchers from their initial stage, perhaps as a masters student, right through a potential academic career to the level where they are regarded as experts in the field. Clearly the needs of library users at different stages in their research career will change. Within these categories we need to think about the requirements and goals, and most importantly ask people what they want from your library service. Once we have this information then effective marketing is feasible.

In summary, the process of market research and segmentation will enable you to:

- identify gaps
- analyse strengths and weaknesses
- prioritise new services.

Do not second guess the needs of the different groups who use your library. We need to reach out from the library and talk to the university community. Involve students by reaching out to the Students Union and find out what their priorities are. This will also enable us to reach reluctant or lapsed library users who need to know of the direct benefits to them of using the services. It is quite likely that there are outdated views about the library that need to be challenged. Ask students and researchers about how they find information. You may learn some surprising things that can help you plan innovations. In the process of conducting market research you are in fact making the library visible to those who do not visit. Find out what your customers want by using surveys, focus groups or library reps, or monitor Twitter for mentions of your library and respond directly or indirectly. The results of the research and identification of the gaps in your service will enable your library service to come closer to being customer driven.

In an academic library it is easy to think of students as consumers; and in a climate of increasing undergraduate tuition fees in the UK students are, and will continue to be, demanding users of library services.

THE MARKETING MIX

All too often marketing is just seen as related to promotion. The well-known 'Marketing Mix' comprises four 'Ps': as well as 'promotion', there are three other related factors – 'product', 'price' and 'place'. These four elements must be balanced in order for successful marketing to take place. The four 'Ps' do not translate neatly into the library sphere because they do not consider the impact of 'service' and those who use services; rather, they are focused heavily on selling things. So in order to accommodate services marketing an additional three 'Ps' were added by Magrath (1986):

- people
- process
- physical evidence.

Marketing has moved on somewhat since then, and more recently Lauterborn (Yudelson 1999) proposed the four 'Cs' (see Figure 7.1), which seem much more suited to niche services like personalised or boutique services. The introduction of cost as an element instead of price helps us think about the cost of our time and the

Figure 7.1   The four Cs (after Lauterborn)

value for money of our services. Again, these aspects should be balanced in order for successful marketing to take place.

BUILDING BRANDS

Most people have a view of what a library is, which is shaped by the libraries they use or have visited in the past along with portrayals of libraries in the media. The library brand has always been an issue. Once it was so simple: a library was the building and the collection stored within it. A visitor, or new student or member of staff, would be inducted into the library with a tour and list of rules and regulations, and often that was it. The librarian would remain behind the reference desk to answer questions when prompted, and provide a 'shhh' when necessary. For many people this may still be the image of the library. How often do we hear academic staff say, 'I never use the library anymore...', when in fact they could not perform their role without using the services and collections that the library provides. The library must mean more than a building. If we are to achieve this we must brand and most importantly personalise the services we provide. This need not necessarily require a large budget, but of course is easier with money to back up ideas.

The library can be doing an amazing job, but if the service is so seamless it is invisible, it is in danger of being overlooked. Libraries and librarians must be proactive in shaping the library brand in general, but particularly the brand of their specific library. What makes your library or a personalised service within your library special? What are its strengths? What makes it interesting, quirky, fun, unique? Asking these questions will help define a brand. If there has been a success, shout about it; if a new database or resource is available to staff and students make sure they know about it, and how it can benefit them directly – and just as importantly – let them know who paid for it.

Some university libraries have made tremendous strides with their branding. The University of Warwick has engaged with the private sector, and has learnt and applied techniques to ensure that the mission and the brand are at the very heart of the service (Brewerton and Tuersley 2010). For smaller libraries this is eminently achievable, and arguably can be within easier reach where the high level of autonomy characteristic of the boutique approach is in place (Priestner and Tilley 2010). Another first step would be to think about branding a particular service within the library; for instance, the Discovery system, or the enquiry service, or the interlibrary loans service are all examples where branding could specifically be used. Ensure that when a member of staff or a student uses databases and electronic journals through your library they know who has selected and paid for the resource they benefit from. Almost all publishers and database providers allow library branding on their sites, but think carefully before just using the university logo. Instead, how about 'X is brought to you by the University Library', or alternatively use the library logo or brand.

In 2006 the BBC ran an advertising campaign, 'This is what we do', with the aim of raising awareness of the vast range of activities of the corporation in the various media (BBC 2006). Academic libraries also need to raise similar awareness, showing that the majority of the high-quality resources that users take for granted are in fact acquired and funded by the library, and making those users aware of the highly qualified individuals who can make their working lives easier. After all, people are often perplexed about just what is done in a library, and what roles the staff perform. By reaching out to users and engaging with them in a variety of settings misconceptions can be addressed and challenged and replaced with a more realistic perception of a modern library.

As the digital proportion of the library collection increases there is a danger that, as academic staff visit library buildings less frequently, they will have little perception of the role of the library service and staff, and not use the services. Internal marketing of the services of the library is vital, as are events and outreach activities.

Raising the profile of the library brand could be achieved in a number of ways:

- Publicity material and quick guides to key resources can be placed in faculty offices, staff rooms, the staff refectory and the library café.
- An event publicising key resources could be arranged to coincide with

faculty 'away days' or subject group meetings.
- Ensure that all specific service offerings have clear branding.
- Invite academic staff to contribute to library publications extolling the virtues of library resources and services.
- Use social media tools.

In short, the library must 'push' the publicity out to academics and students and not expect them to look for it online or in the library building, because this is clearly not happening. A creative, imaginative approach is likely to be memorable, and will encourage promotion of library services to others by the users themselves (whether this is a themed event, simply a well-timed promotion, or a poster placed appropriately for maximum impact). The importance of Word of Mouth (WOM) marketing in generating positive 'talk' about libraries cannot be underestimated.

While libraries embrace many new services, and all the possibilities offered by new technologies, it is vital that 'personalisation' is not forgotten. Universities are about people: the staff and students. To neglect the personal, the face-to-face contact, would be to miss a vital tool in engaging with our users.

BRAND OR BRANDS?

It is interesting that the CIM definition speaks of brands, plural. It is certainly very important to think of the library brand as a whole, but we must not stop there. How do we brand the complex matrix of services and collections that make up even a small library? We can communicate much more effectively with the people who interact with us if we brand our services too.

On his website focusing on library terms that users understand, John Kupersmith (2011) has brought together more than 50 studies that have evaluated terms that libraries use, like OPAC, Database, Journal, Interlibrary Loan. The studies consistently find that students, especially, just do not understand what these terms mean. They do not want to consult a database, they want to find an article; they do not want to weave their way through a series of links to find an e-journal, they want to find it on Google. When branding our services we must take care to look through the eyes of those who use the service; we are often just too close and too entrenched in library jargon to see beyond it. This is where good liaison with staff and student groups is essential and we should make sure that we test terms and signs and see whether they are understood. Once again we can learn from the retail industry here: most department stores no longer have a sign for a 'Cashier' – instead you see a sign saying 'Pay Here'. Adopt a similar approach in the library and on our websites, and we may find that our users start making better use of our resources, services and space. Whatever our adopted brand, or brands, they should have a consistent message. Consider using the same colour and name throughout your branding. Ensure that branding on e-services complements, and is consistent with, that used in the physical library.

NURTURING INNOVATION

The one constant feature in library and information work is change, and boutique libraries must adapt and tailor services and, where possible, buildings to meet the changing demands of students and staff. Innovation must be enabled and nurtured to meet and ideally exceed expectations of those users. Innovation does not always emerge from expected places. Perhaps you have staff in your library with hidden talents – provide opportunities where these might emerge, make sure they have an opportunity for these to shine, and make use of them. For example, you may have amateur illustrators, film makers and photographers within your team who can create exciting and unexpected web content, posters or leaflets. An example of this approach was undertaken at the University of Liverpool (2009) when a group of library assistants was given a wide brief to create imaginative and fun videos for the library. It is useful to think of marketing in terms of storytelling. Narrative can be a means of effective communication to and from users giving you an understanding of how they approach your library (Germano 2010). Think about the 'journey' of a student or a new researcher as they encounter your service, to help plan appropriate timing of help and promotion of appropriate resources.

There is also room for innovation in how the library itself is used. Make sure that the library is at the hub of the community it serves and, where space and time allows, open it up to that community as a venue for events and displays of student work, research posters, and other outputs from the academic department.

It is in this aspect of marketing that the boutique approach could excel. A smaller library could be the testbed for a new service or approach, which if successful could be adopted by the central service as well.

DEVELOPING RELATIONSHIPS

Relationships are at the heart of marketing for personalised and boutique libraries. By being close to the people who use our services we increase our understanding of their needs and can better communicate ways in which the library can enhance their working or studying. By being close to the user, staff in the boutique library can be more in touch with its customers, spotting trends in use and user requirements early and being able to liaise with central services if need be to plan effective innovations in service.

It makes good sense to plan relationship marketing carefully, but do not underestimate the chance encounter that may be crucial to building the profile of your library. By being active outside the library in informal and formal networking valuable contacts can be made and nurtured:

- Set up a drop-in display or help session in faculty staff rooms or staff restaurants.
- Get involved in the agenda of faculty away days.
- Display and promote material in student support offices.
- Walk the faculty corridors, coffee-mug in hand ostensibly en route to the kitchen to make a drink; it is surprising how many conversations you will have along the way.
- Encourage library staff to interact with the academic community in producing events that may not, on the face of it, appear to be library related. These are easy 'wins' and somehow the involvement of a few individual staff translates positively to include the library service.
- Seek out key stakeholders in your user groups and reach out to them. These could include: heads of department, committee chairs, student representatives/Student Union officers, librarians at other local libraries, support office managers. There will be many other stakeholders connected to your own specific institution.

Do not underestimate the importance of reaching out to administrative and technical staff as well as academics and students. These staff could become barriers to good communication if not kept well informed and up to date. For example, administrative staff are often responsible for general information on virtual learning environments (VLEs), student handbooks and newsletters – it is vital that the library is represented effectively in these.

If it is an academic member of staff, find out about their research interests before you meet them and show an interest in their work. Most researchers will not need much encouragement to talk about their research area, and you can learn about their needs. This sort of encounter can be formalised and offered as a desktop visit or 'book-a-librarian' or research consultation – another benefit to be communicated. Ensure you meet with new staff soon after they start working at your institution – ask them about the libraries they have used before, and tell them how you can help them settle into the institution they are joining. This can enable you to find a 'hook', or the key benefit, for this individual. These hooks might include one of the following:

- help with reference management
- keeping up to date with tables of contents
- using a personalised start page
- bibliometrics support such as the h-index, journal impact factors
- support for the Research Excellence Framework (REF) impact case study

data collection
* embedding information literacy in module assessment.

Running imaginative events can also develop relationships. The University of Plymouth Library provides an illustration of a creative approach that can be successful. In order to promote the Talis List electronic reading list facility, an event for academic staff was organised during the first week of the Wimbledon Tennis Tournament, advertised as 'Anyone for Talis?', with the tennis theme extending to the refreshments including strawberries, cream and Robinsons Barley Water. The event took the form of a drop in session with demonstrations of the service, and subject librarians were available to offer support and sign-up sheets for further training. Over 50 academic staff attended this event, and the light-hearted and fresh approach, which included the chance to try virtual tennis on a Wii games console, was in contrast with the previous 'Introduction to …' events, which were often poorly attended.

Staff must be considered not only as consumers in their own right, but also as the gatekeepers to students and therefore hugely influential. A fantastic campaign directed towards students can be undermined by mixed messages from academic staff. For instance, staff may be encouraging students to use services and products in the library that have been updated or replaced, or giving an impression that using services off campus is difficult, when in fact the service has been improved and upgraded.

In any institution there are fewer staff than students so it makes good sense to target them first, creating champions who can spread the word to students. Professional services or administrative staff in your institution, or liaison department, are easily overlooked, as they are not often direct users of library services and unless they understand the value of the library they can be a barrier in dealings with academic departments. Their view of a library is likely to be influenced by their own experience at school and university, and may well be outdated. Ensure that they know how libraries have changed and that the library is for them as well as for academic staff and students. Some ideas to get you started, for example:

* include news items in departmental newsletters
* attend coffee mornings
* find out if staff are part-time students as well – offer to help them find resources.

CREATING GOOD CUSTOMER SERVICE

A brand has value and takes time and effort to build but can be damaged very easily with a sloppy transaction. We are much more likely to tell others about a negative experience than a positive one, as a visit to Tripadvisor.co.uk can show. However, there is a fine line to be drawn between being helpful and frankly annoying. Some shops get this absolutely right, but others have staff latching onto customers as soon as they enter, which can have the effect (on this customer at least) of hastening an exit. A smile at the library entrance can go a very long way, and having the right staff on the front line in the library is essential to achieving a friendly and welcoming atmosphere. In a boutique service discretion and confidence are essential in frontline staff – no one wants to be passed from one member of staff to another for a simple enquiry. The importance of staff training and effective selection of frontline staff cannot be underestimated. All staff must know about the mission of the library and be able to give a consistent message to people visiting or contacting it. This is not just good customer service to visitors to the physical space, but also when students and staff contact the library by email, Twitter, Facebook, chat and other means of communication.

COMMUNICATING BENEFITS

Practical, time-saving benefits must be emphasised in the promotion of personalised services in order to be noticed among the ever-increasing amount of information delivered to academics' desktops.

Libraries are very good at communicating facts and figures about the building and collection. Leaflets and websites will provide careful detail about the number of books and journals, the date of the library's establishment, the opening hours. Compare this approach with examples from the commercial world. John Lewis does not tell you how many stores they have in the UK; they help you find one near you. They remember what you looked at last time you were at the site, in case you were undecided and are returning to finalise a purchase. They offer a variety of ways in to their products, with customer and expert reviews to help you make up your mind.

We also tend to be very good at telling users what is *not* permitted in a library building. In fact traditionally we are much better at communicating this than we are at promoting what is possible. Witness the proliferation in academic libraries of such signage as:

- No Food
- No Drink
- No Mobile Phones
- No Talking.

While it is important to maintain an environment conducive to study (and noise often tops the list of student complaints), there are more subtle ways of managing noise. Promoting a 'Quiet Zone', or a 'Laptop-Free Zone' is effective, as is signing places to use phones or introducing a library café. These are benefits to the users of the libraries, not a list of dos and don'ts.

Amazon.com communicates convenience and cost as major benefits. You know that postage is included on their products and you do not have to provide a lot of extra information to the website once you have logged in – just a few clicks and your item is ordered. This is a huge company, but it manages to personalise its services online. We can learn from such examples, even if our budgets represent a tiny fraction of theirs.

What are the benefits of your services? What does a library user want to know about your service? For example:

- Are you open?
- Can I save time?
- Can I get better marks in my assignments?
- How easy is it for me to browse and find that serendipitous discovery?
- Why would I use the library instead of using Google exclusively?
- Can the library help me to be more effective?

Ask these sorts of questions, and others like these, about your service, to help you understand what the benefits of your service are that you need to communicate to your groups of users.

Not only do we need to ensure that we ourselves understand what our users think are the benefits of our service, but we need to consider the terminology that we use in our communications. For example, if you are running a reference management software workshop, instead of advertising the session with this as a 'title' find other ways of selling the session that will appeal to the users – use one or more of the following:

- Save time!
- Create a personal citation library!
- Reduce errors in your bibliographies!
- Stop losing marks for poor citations!

Likewise, if you are putting together some promotional literature for a specific part of your collection, instead of an unappealing title such as 'The Library has a collection of thousands of e-books', try the following suggestion instead: 'Whatever your subject area, our collection of electronic books will enable you to find the information you need fast'.

Your market is captive in an academic library so, in theory, marketing should be easy. Indeed, there is no need for a huge budget, and TV advertising, but it is not enough just to print a few leaflets telling students and staff how many journals you subscribe to. So rather than promoting the number of books you have, how many PCs are in the building and how big a database is, use testimonials and key benefits to sell the niche services to students, staff and other visitors to the physical library and the website. We would not choose one supermarket over another just because of the number of products they stock; it is which products they are, and their price and convenience, that is more likely to sway our decision.

For a truly personalised service the library user must be at the heart of decision making, and understanding the needs and preferences of different groups of library users is key to successful marketing of your service. Make it easy for your users to spread the word about your services: add 'Share' buttons so that they can tell their friends and colleagues about the library. Social media offers a very low cost and highly effective means of communicating benefits and sharing news about your library (O'Connor and Lundstrom 2011).

The benefits to users can sometimes be like the elusive 'sizzle' – hard to pin down, but you know it when it is there. Often this can just be something that makes you smile. The online sports retailer and cycling specialist Wiggle sends a mini packet of Haribo jelly sweets out with every order. It is a bit of fun, and bought in bulk the cost per pack will be negligible, but it shows they know their market and want to make their customers smile.

CONCLUSION

It is essential that marketing is not down to one person or seen as an add-on in your service, but informs the development of the library and its services. Academic libraries used to have a monopoly within their institution, but now there are many competing information services. Librarians know that the high-quality information will benefit students and staff and help them achieve their academic potential. It is now more important than ever that this is known and properly understood by key institutional stakeholders as well. This involves getting out and about, being seen and being known; in other words, being a sales rep for your library.

TOP TIPS AND PRACTICAL ADVICE

- Make it your business to find out about the individuals who use your service.
- Know your market.
- Be confident about the culture and the niche that defines your service and allow this to influence all you do.
- Use testimonials from staff and students on your website and other materials quotes.

- Be responsive to demand, but use your knowledge to be proactive too.
- Do not be afraid to experiment.

REFERENCES

BBC. 2006. This is What We Do – New Campaign for BBC [online]. At: http://www.bbc.co.uk/pressoffice/pressreleases/stories/2006/03_march/23/whatwedo.shtml (accessed: 9 August 2011).

Brewerton, A. and Tuersley, S. 2010. More Than Just a Logo: Branding at Warwick. *Library & Information Update*, 9(9), 46–8.

Chartered Institute of Marketing. 2007. Tomorrow's World: Re-evaluating the Role of Marketing [online]. At: http://www.cim.co.uk/resources/understandingmarket/definitionmkting.aspx (accessed: 20 September 2011).

Chartered Institute of Marketing. 2011. Definition of Marketing [online]. At: http://www.cim.co.uk/resources/understandingmarket/definitionmkting.aspx (accessed: 20 September 2011).

De Saez, E.E. 2002. *Marketing Concepts for Libraries and Information Services*, 2nd edn. London: Facet.

Donham, J. and Green, C. 2004. Perspectives On … Developing a Culture of Collaboration: Librarian as Consultant. *Journal of Academic Librarianship*, 30, 314–21.

Germano, M.A. 2010. Narrative-based Library Marketing: Selling your Library's Value during Tough Economic Times. *Bottom Line*, 23(1), 5–17.

Kupersmith, J. 2011. Library Terms that Users Understand [online]. At: http://www.jkup.net/terms.html (accessed: 27 August 2011).

Magrath, A.J. 1986. When Marketing Services, 4 Ps are Not Enough. *Business Horizons*, 29(3), 44–50.

O'Connor, L. and Lundstrom, K. 2011. The Impact of Social Marketing Strategies on the Information Seeking Behaviors of College Students. *Reference & User Services Quarterly*, 50(4), 351–65.

Priestner, A. and Tilley, E. 2010. Boutique Libraries at your Service. *Library & Information Update*, 9(6), 36–9.

University of Liverpool. 2009. Goggle Vision: Using Electronic Resources [online]. At: http://www.youtube.com/watch?v=5slpJMRWKA8 (accessed: 11 September 2011).

Webb, J., Gannon-Leary, P. and Bent, M. 2007. *Providing Effective Library Services for Research*. London: Facet.

Wheeler, E. 1937. *Tested Sentences That Sell*. New York: Prentice Hall.

Wisniewski, J. and Fichter, D. 2007. Electronic Resources Won't Sell Themselves: Marketing Tips. *Online*, 31(1), 54–7.

Yudelson, J. 1999. Adapting McCarthy's Four P's for the Twenty-first Century. *Journal of Marketing Education*, 21(1), 60–67.

CHAPTER 8

THE COST-EFFECTIVE SERVICE: IS PERSONALISED POSSIBLE?
ELIZABETH TILLEY

INTRODUCTION: 'I'D LIKE TO GET MY SHOE BACK'

Whoever thought that a lost shoe in a restaurant in the Turks and Caicos would be found and returned – not by another customer, but by the owner of the restaurant? In the words of the owner of the shoe: 'Unbelievable ... Now that is what I call service!' (TripAdvisor 2011). It is useful to reflect on why this worked so well. The restaurant owner may have a special service in place just for customers who lose shoes, but it is much more likely that the owner has a built-in mindset that notices minute details about his customers and treats them as he would want to be treated himself. What were the costs of this spectacularly helpful service? Presumably a bit of time engaging with the user online and the effort required in handing the shoe to a middle man to pass on. Not a lot out of a day, mostly pretty much cost free, but earning massive amounts of 'goodwill'. Will that customer go back? Many people would! One of the most important aspects of this story that encapsulates the essence of the boutique approach is that this type of service is not a set of rules; rather, it is a mindset. Providing excellent service can be as expensive – or as cheap – as you want it to be; but if at the heart of the rationale for what you do are the people you serve, the service will be used and will become cost-effective.

Companies that are selling a product, whether it is a service or actual product, may well be more successful financially when they take such a customer-focused approach as the restaurant described above. Investment in excellent customer service reaps benefits for them. They will be judged on the quality of the good manufactured, or service sold, and will endeavour to differentiate themselves and their products in order to gain customers. A library service, meanwhile, is judged on the quality and effectiveness of the service provided, not the purchasing of a product. They may have indirectly paid for the product (for example, in advance via tuition fees), but we have to contend with users of libraries who, for the most part, do not see the cost implications of service provision. Despite this, in the 'value for money' organisations that we are based in, we find some stakeholders obsessed by the need for our services to be accountable and to demonstrate financial viability – at least according to their definitions. Institutions, dependent as they are on public funding, will inevitably feel the need to focus on certain criteria. Harper and Corrall note:

> *Academic libraries are particularly vulnerable to changes in the world economy because of their reliance on highly-priced globally-sourced information products and dependence on expenditure allocations from parent institutions that are heavily dependent on public funding. (2011: 96)*

Central administration increasingly holds services accountable for their expenditure and constantly looks to us to prove our worth. University administrators question their investment in library and information services, especially citing the internet as providing much of what subject specialist librarians can offer (for example, when subject specialists were threatened with redundancy at the University of Bangor in 2005, the media cited the internet as the alternative). However, this leads to a service culture that does not take the user into account and is therefore directly at odds with the personalised service of the boutique model. Markless and Streatfield comment that 'a narrowly finance-driven approach may create a managerial environment in which it is necessary to argue for funding based on "results"' (2006: 7). What those results are may be meaningless to our users as frequently the statistics collected simply measure resource allocations. It would be more helpful it there were other means of evaluating how effective that allocation has been, in order to determine its worth and impact on users. Part of the intrinsic issue of cost is to consider how we evaluate costs (dealt with in the next chapter), and promote the fact that the contributions we make to the success of the broader institutional mission are crucial.

An important question for librarians is whether we are able to translate a more simplistic company experience, where profits are what ultimately matter, to services such as libraries, where we are currently facing potential loss of staff and budgets in an economic recession. Companies aim to achieve a competitive advantage over those producing a similar product; in an ideal world, libraries are not competing with each other. If our services are sufficiently differentiated they often provide complementary services and resources that will appeal directly to certain segments of the user population – depending on subject, access, the feel of a specific place, as well as many other factors.

Our perception of what our service costs is driven by our experiences and what we choose to measure in order to address the issue of whether our service is too costly. We will each have perceptions about why a library service that is more heavily focused on one element or other of the boutique model will be more costly to run than another. This no doubt explains our desire to justify the inputs into the services we manage. But along with the costs, we need to explore the benefits or value of a library service. One way of doing this is to consider the economic benefits of customers using the library service. Matthews (2011: 2) suggests three possible economic benefits that, combined, result in the total value of the service:

- Direct use benefits: these are connected to the reasons that students want to use the library – that is, they save time by using the resources and services, they save money by not needing to purchase the information themselves, and the information should improve their knowledge, contributing to their studies.
- Indirect benefits of library use: these may include access to computers, space for study, building a sense of community, and so on. Contingent value studies may be employed to ascertain the value of non-market services.
- Non-use benefits: students who do not use the library may often still demonstrate in surveys that they are satisfied with the library service: there is a perception that the library's existence is valuable irrespective of its usefulness, but this type of benefit is inherently difficult to measure.

Economic benefits should not be confused with overall service quality as they are just one aspect of it. Attempts have been made to measure service quality, but much of it is rooted in the person, the user, and will vary from one time to another and from one part of the service to another. Putting a numeric value on a response by a user to a survey is potentially dangerous if that is all that we do. In order to fully understand value in reality we need to backtrack to the fundamentals of the goals of our service.

The aims and goals of our service are set firstly by the mission of the institution of which we are a part. If our institutional mission refers to 'excellence in teaching and research', our service must be driven by the need to provide services that will support that statement. In order to assist our students and staff to achieve this, our service must be of the highest calibre such that their use of it produces excellence in learning. This is irrespective of the model or framework underlying service provision. However, in this book, we would argue that service quality is really only possible where the boutique approach is considered seriously, because this is the style of service that allows for sufficient time, and knowledge, to understand the user and their needs, in turn fulfilling the institution's mission.

In this chapter I shall consider the myths that may be perpetuated about personalised services. Some definitions of the cost of service will be considered, followed by an exploration of an adapted model of cost-effective service excellence. A discussion of the implications of the significant costs for our services in the form of resources, staff and space will highlight some of the problems that any service faces and the solutions that personalised services can use to overcome these.

BOUTIQUE AND THE MYTHS

We probably approach the boutique model from one of two perspectives: either we are in a largely centralised, perhaps even converged service, or we are operating in a service that may, or may not, be specialised, where boutique or personalised service is the focus.

Perceptions about the costs of running a boutique service were clearly expressed via the SWOT analysis conducted at the Symposium on Personalised Library Services in March 2011. Delegates considered the boutique model and whether it was a valuable way of modelling library services. A number of suggestions (many were expressed as concerns) or myths arose from this. Ideas that are frequently referred to when considering centralised as opposed to local, specialised and personalised services and that continue to be referred to precisely because the evidence available to suggest anything to the contrary is limited include:

- Personalised services need a lot of staff, and staff are expensive. Therefore, personalised, customised service is too costly in the current economic climate.
- Centralised services cannot be personalised.
- Centralisation reduces costs more effectively than boutique services.
- Efficiency and money is what cost of service is all about – that is, the cost of service is not necessarily related to the quality of service.

Disentangling myth from reality is important. Spending time being a user, or building relationships with our users, in order to try to understand what it is they need is a first step. We quickly forget what it is like to be a user ourselves. While we cannot always give our users exactly what they want, as there will always be some constraints, if we take the time to focus on how we can best add personal value to our inanimate spaces and resources, we might find a way through the myths to reality. A salutary warning about the importance of relationships comes from an academic who recently commented that, for a library to be really effective, it needs those working on the (issue) desk to know who the readers are. Simple, you might think! He goes on to say, 'the difference between what I call a real library and a space which houses books is very analogous to the difference between good hotels and large pseudo-luxurious ones which are wholly anonymous' (Millar 2011: 6). The use of the word 'anonymous' is a good clue for us in understanding how our users often feel and appreciating that, whatever our services are like, it is relationships between user and service that are important.

Ultimately, whether or not these 'myths' represent reality, it is a pertinent fact to remember that any type of library service, whether centralised or boutique-style, converged or un-converged, information commons or not, will be an expensive service to run if its management do not understand how to maximise the resources available in order to ensure an effective and excellent service. While a poorly run boutique library may be closed more quickly, it is possible that the drain on resources of an institution with poorly managed centralised services may well be more damaging in the end.

'Cost' of Service

Sometimes an idea that looks wasteful can be amazingly efficient. (Tisch and Weber 2007: 75)

Costs can be defined as 'the consumption of resources to acquire, produce or maintain goods and services within a defined period' (Poll 2001a: 185). Figure 8.1 illustrates a simplistic relationship of costs to services:

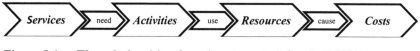

Figure 8.1   The relationship of services to costs (after Poll 2001a)

Cost-effectiveness can be defined as something that is *economical in terms of the resources and services made available for the money spent*. A number of issues arise in analysing cost-effectiveness:

- The products of libraries are not tangible objects or even a service that can be sold; they are non-material. The production process and the product are inextricably linked; so, for example, there is no point in having an expensive database full of quality information if it is not promoted, explained and demonstrated. It would not be used, and therefore would not be money well spent.
- Capacity costs – or fixed costs – take up much of a service's budget. Many of the costs are incurred independently of the numbers of people using the service: for example, insurance and basic utilities must be paid. Another such example might be the library management system (LMS); if circulation figures drop, it does not mean that the LMS will not be needed. What may of course vary instead will be the numbers of staff to man it and the technical service teams to support it.

Poll and Bryson provide a number of detailed analyses and description of cost types with additional summaries of costing techniques that are worth investigating further if you require specific tools and techniques (Poll 2001a: Annex A: 94; Bryson 2011: 90). One particular tool referred to by Bryson is 'activity-based costing', which considers the costs of an activity or service in relation to its outputs. We may wish to know how the inputs affect the outputs and to what extent there is a direct correlation between financial inputs and service performance. Exploring and investigating time and cost data will help provide assistance with this. As a tool that is used to enable libraries to understand their performance from a resource allocation perspective, it offers a means of providing data to enhance the decision-making process.

Productivity assessment is an alternative method that is concerned primarily with efficiency. Its focus is on improving the performance of services by demonstrating how they can become more efficient. Managers need to regularly evaluate the process and procedures of the workplace, encouraging staff to make changes that allow them to be more efficient and effective. The point of this is not so that jobs can be cut, but so that more time is available for enhancing service provision.

The main issue with models or any attempt to compare inputs and outputs is that the magic ingredient that tells us whether we are successful is not defined in units that we can easily measure. There has been much research conducted, notably with the Balanced Scorecard (Poll 2001b), examining whether outputs can be weighed against inputs (costs or resource allocation). However, demonstrating the effectiveness of an information service that attempts to promote and encourage use of that information is difficult. Crawford and McGuigan consider an option whereby a high level of activity, whether that be virtual or use of space and resources and services in a physical sense, is taken as proof that the service demonstrates effectiveness – that is, 'if patrons are using library services, the library is apparently fulfilling its mission of meeting user needs in the areas measured' (2011: 3). However, measuring this type of effectiveness is problematic. Further problems arise when services endeavour to measure the degree of added value or library goodness, which may or may not be apparent in a service. Most academic libraries conduct customer surveys in an effort to determine both quantitative and qualitative evidence for the effectiveness and performance levels of their services. From the recent CIBER survey on student satisfaction and library provision in the UK we find the following: 'Two particular aspects of library provision are strong predictors of overall course satisfaction: staff training hours per FTE and annual loans per FTE user' (CIBER 2011: 2).

Whatever the relative merits of different surveys, we need to conduct them in order to attempt to demonstrate whether the focus that we have, be it centralised or boutique, has any impact on the user. The crux of the problem remains: is it possible to assess accurately the financial expenditure and service activity of a library in order to provide sufficiently robust data that satisfactorily weighs up its cost effectiveness? Is this information addressing the issues that services are facing in academic institutions? Further to this, can a boutique service claim to be more cost-effective than its larger, centralised counterparts, and if so, can we persuade the powers that be that this is the case?

SIGNIFICANT COSTS

Library services require money for three main purposes:

- to buy the information that they lend
- to pay for, or buy, the personnel in order to assist with lending, and promoting the information purchased to ensure its successful use
- to pay for the physical or virtual space within which to house the information purchased and within which user and service may interact.

Services may have the same amount of cash per user to put into their service, but the way in which the cash is allocated will vary depending on what that service sees as priority and what its needs are. The recent Research Information Network (RIN) guide, 'Challenges for Academic Libraries in Difficult Economic Times', makes reference to the importance of working out the balance between content, staffing and services. The decisions that are made about the use of financial resources impact the user. The publication paints a fairly gloomy picture for libraries in terms of cuts in budgets over the next few years, and their analysis of how services should react states:

> In current circumstances we believe it is particularly important that libraries should be able to show not only that they are operating efficiently, but that they provide services with demonstrable links to success in achieving institutional goals. Return on investment is thus an increasingly important issue. Libraries therefore need to be more proactive in seeking to understand user behaviour and workflows; and in rigorously analysing and demonstrating the value of their activities in improving students' experience and in supporting teaching, learning and research. (RIN 2010: 16)

In a service that is structured along the lines of the boutique model, the service is tailored to match closely the needs of the user population that it services.

Before considering a model of cost-effective service excellence, and in the light of the warnings from the RIN about the future of library services, it is worth examining these significant costs a little further.

Purchasing 'Information'

In using the term 'information', I refer to all aspects of collection development. This includes print and electronic material, grey literature, audio-visual, and so on. It also includes access to the information, such as catalogues and Discovery systems. There have been different approaches to collection development, but it would be fair to say that in a research-intensive academic environment it is quite likely that there will be large sections of the collection that are not heavily used, or not even used at all. The concept of the 'long tail' is well known. Spending more on collections does not necessarily mean a cost-effective service. The advantage of a tailored, personalised service is that careful consideration is given to the resources and information that is purchased to make sure that it is useful and relevant. The CIBER report states that '[b]ook and other stock is being made to work very much harder, another success story for RLUK members, with a substantial uplift in loans per FTE user (and this on top of major investments in electronic content)' (2011: 18). Services are currently more aware of the need to be cost effective, but are also ensuring increased loans. Knowing the users means that you buy appropriately and that you buy in the knowledge that a greater percentage of the stock will be used.

Prudent managers in control of purchasing information resources for their users are essential. In the UK we are fortunate to have the Joint Information Systems Committee (JISC), who can negotiate on behalf of the UK academic community for obtaining the best deals for digital and periodical content. They have devised a national digital content strategy and undertook a periodical price survey in 2009. They share in the acquisition of resources, especially those in digital form, and have successfully run a programme assisting institutions switching to e-books for core texts (JISC National Observatory e-books project). It is an advantage to have negotiators working at a national level on our behalf, but it is also worth bearing in mind that, at a more local service level, there are advantages to be gained in team managers learning negotiation skills; in a tough economic climate, where every penny counts, there are always deals to be made and some information may be purchased relatively cheaply.

Tailored access to information is where added value may play a part in the user's experience of libraries. Users wish to control information and to navigate to what they need quickly and efficiently. They are independent searchers, and therefore need excellent search services to allow them to find the resources that exist. IT software and hardware tools that allow them to do this must allow for speedy interactions – if they are too slow or complex, the user will turn away and the added value of the collections is lost.

Service Personnel

Staff who run our services are a key cost. They are expensive, and we are exhorted to do more with less where possible. However, the damage that will be done to our services if we remove the human interactions with our users will be extensive. The level of service that users are provided with by staff is a key measure of service quality and excellence. This may range from instilling confidence in the user, demonstrating appropriate 'TLC', understanding their users' needs, or simply being efficient and dependable in dealing with service queries.

The CIBER report (2011) suggests that RLUK Library staff productivity, as indicated by a 28 per cent increase in the ratio of user FTE to each library post, has increased significantly over the last few years – that is, libraries are doing more with relatively fewer staff. This, from one perspective, is good news demonstrating increased productivity rates. However, staff can be expensive if not managed well and managers need to steward their human resources carefully. The relationships and behaviours, the processes and routines that help each person to work to their potential so that they can add the value for the people they serve is a crucial part of a manager's role. The cost of this *not* working is detrimental to service in many ways. Whatever the level of staffing, if staff are encouraged to maximise their potential and skills this will be responsible for a significant component of the added value of a service.

Space

A consideration of space includes several aspects: physical library spaces, virtual spaces and remote locations. The physical space used for a library service may be very costly. Real estate costs a great deal of money and cannot afford to be poorly used. So careful planning of space for collection development is required: the use of rolling stacks for collections may be used or, for large libraries, remote locations are utilised to store infrequently used materials. For example, the Bodleian Libraries are now making use of a remote location at Swindon for much of their stock. Changes in collection development policy, such as focusing on e-book purchasing, mean that space is freed up for other options.

The importance of designing cost-effective and useful spaces for library services has been very much in evidence over the last decade. New designs aim to maximise the use of the space for the user. If use of space is valuable to the individual users then the actual costs of maintaining and enhancing the space are more than justified. The JISC report 'Designing Spaces for Effective Learning' (2006) provides a list of case studies and key points to consider for those able to redesign their spaces.

Virtual space can be as costly or as cheap as is desired; cost has not as much to do with quality as it used to. It is important that services consider all the technical options that are available before spending vast amounts of money on website design and other mobile technologies. The user ought to be the focus of how virtual space is designed and used. If free web tools are used then it is also important to consider how robust the product needs to be and how much staff time can be allocated to the development of the site.

A final point about space as a significant cost is the potential problem of geography. If there are too many physical or virtual locations to visit to find the relevant information, a user may be confused, workload is likely to be duplicated, and the overall impression that they may have is of a service that is not high quality, time efficient or cost effective.

Undoubtedly there are many costs tied up in running a service such as an academic library. It has been established that analysing them to determine whether we are cost effective is problematic. Understanding how a cost-effective service can also be excellent is crucial but also harder to prove. In order to help us move away from the narrower focus of looking at the cost of inputs versus the potential value of the outputs, we shall next consider a model of cost-effective service excellence. The key to understanding how to be cost effective while maintaining service excellence boils down to the value the company puts on the customer. Similarly, the boutique approach is all about making a library service customer focused and personalised.

MODEL OF COST-EFFECTIVE SERVICE EXCELLENCE

The customer has to be delighted, but in a cost-effective way. (Heracleous, Wirtz and Johnston 2004: 38)

It is no doubt the ambition of any library service manager to achieve service excellence, and ideally in such a cost-effective way that all members of the institution are satisfied, users with the service and financial managers with the use made of the investment. Looking beyond our own type of service to other service industries is helpful in considering how to bring this about. Singapore Airlines and John Lewis are two examples of companies providing exemplary service. The latter has been largely impacted by the value that the company places on its employees.

Singapore Airlines has a model of service excellence containing components that strike a chord with what might best shape a personalised library service. Applying this model to library services can provide insight for services that are struggling to reconcile the desire to provide personalised services with the need to demonstrate cost effectiveness. Figure 8.2 illustrates their model, adapted for library services, to demonstrate their techniques for bringing about cost-effective, yet excellent, provision.

Ingrained Awareness of Mission and Customer Values

A mission statement sets out in a brief description the core purposes of the institution and level of information service. An awareness of the institutional

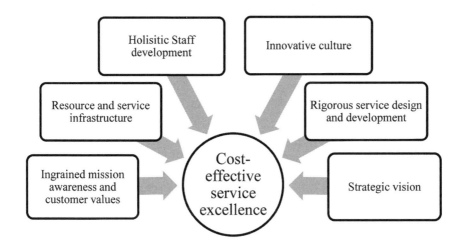

Figure 8.2   Activity system illustrating the development of cost-effective service excellence adapted from the Singapore Airlines model

mission is necessary in order to measure service performance. Asking ourselves whether the services we currently offer and run, or those to be implemented, focus on broader institutional mission goals as the focus is essential. Most academic libraries support teaching and research, but variations will exist and must be considered. At a more local, boutique perspective, the mission may include a specific subject or range of subjects, and/or focus on customer segmentation – that is, undergraduate or postgraduate, research or teaching.

By keeping the overall mission in mind, the services that a library offers should be considered alongside others within the institution. There are likely to be clear benefits from the interdependence and collaboration that occurs, and by putting the customer first we can focus on our priorities.

Strategic Vision

Strategic vision allows those managing the service to look both internally and externally, weighing up the current environment against potential for the future while providing clear, proactive, passionate leadership for the organisation. An integral part of the service, including knowledge of the stakeholders, allows them to advocate on behalf of the service, and negotiate for the necessary financial resources to enable the vision to be realised. To achieve service excellence, the implementation should endeavour to be proactive rather than reactive; this is inevitably more forward thinking and entrepreneurial in style.

In order to balance service excellence with cost efficiencies, it is crucial that management should demonstrate transparency and accountability with appropriate checks and balances on spending. An understanding of the global service 'spend', along with relevant tools to obtain and manage data on the use of the service, will give the visionary a clearer view of how to map out the future.

Networking and collaboration with related services in an academic organisation is an important feature for ascertaining ways and means of reducing cost effectively, while keeping service excellence at the forefront of strategic changes. Having a strategic mindset involves adopting environmental scanning, which considers both internal and external factors that could influence the service's ability to undertake activities planned; it will help identify competitors and, conversely, open doors to liaison opportunities. For example, if we were to consider technical Discovery solutions, it is clear that reinventing the wheel is expensive; and while one service's adaptations may not suit specific needs, it is likely that the basics can be reused and adapted.

Resources and Services Infrastructure

A rigid infrastructure in a library service will not assist managers in establishing a cost-effective service. We are operating in services that are experiencing rapid change: our customers' behaviour is changing, technology is rapidly changing, and the economic climate is constantly putting pressure on thinly spread services. Our resource and service infrastructures need to be flexible and fluid, able to change quickly as circumstances change. The hike in student tuition fees for 2012 in the UK is likely to have an impact on higher education – we have at least had plenty of warning about this and can consider how to change our services appropriately. The attempted jettisoning of the 'big deals' by higher education institutions in 2011 took up a considerable amount of key staff time across those institutions; the scale of the journals crisis and the timeframe involved meant that no other alternative was possible. The more flexible we are, the quicker we can adapt to a new service, and importantly suffer fewer financial losses – for example, staff time, technology, procedures, and so on.

The cost-effective service will aim to maximise the use of information purchased for its customers, in part via the expert knowledge of its staff. Interaction with customers through the use of traditional methods, as well as social media, provides varying options for users to acquire information. With a flexible mindset, however, the methods used to promote and advertise resources and services can be changed quickly and easily, adapting to changes in customer behaviour.

Establishing local infrastructures allows for greater diversification for the service as local input is often more reliable and its quality is a known quantity. Despite managing a relatively small unit of operation I qualify for a university credit card, which means that I can buy out-of-print material for the collections quickly and cheaply, and am not dependent on our agents. The relatively small amount of time that it takes to source the best possible purchase is insignificant.

It is a feature of the constantly changing environment in which we operate that workflow processes and procedures must be constantly evaluated for effectiveness. The smaller the service operation, the easier this is to do. The larger an organisation, the more rigid its infrastructure, the less well connected the parts of its operating machine, and the lesser its ability to shift gears quickly and smoothly – for example, in the redesign of a service website. However, larger organisations may be able to make decisions about changes with an initial cost that cannot be afforded by a much smaller operation – for instance, the change to shelf-ready books. In theory, the latter example would release staff for more diverse tasks; in reality, in the past this has often meant reduction in staff working for the service.

Holistic Staff Development

In Singapore Airlines (SIA), training of staff is considered as 'next to godliness' (Heracleous, Wirtz and Johnston 2004: 38). Input into extensive training is considered essential, and it is perhaps a salutary warning to library services in their pursuit of service excellence that SIA's new stewardesses undergo four months of training. It is unlikely that we could afford such focused and in-depth training for our library staff, but it gives an indication of the importance that the company puts on having well-trained and qualified staff. In libraries, irrespective of the size of organisation, we need to balance cost with quality of service. The example serves to remind managers that library staff inductions could, and perhaps should, be considerably more extensive and in depth than may currently occur. Time invested in staff training will rarely be wasted. It would be fair to say that staff talents and skills are one of the most valuable resources of the organisation, and focusing on constantly improving these will further enhance the service.

The issue of training is not just about the induction process for new staff; it is also about having a work environment where all staff have a training and development programme. In some ways there is a tension between this and more focused succession planning where staff with particular potential are given opportunities to develop – some might say, at the expense of others. All staff need the opportunities to develop and acquire new skills, especially in the rapidly changing environment in which we work. Some of the key skills that well-trained staff working in a personalised service environment will possess include:

- functional skills
- soft skills including personal interaction, personal poise
- emotional intelligence
- technical expertise

- analytical skills
- innovative, creative skills.

As a firm believer in the dynamic nature of a service that is run by small autonomous teams, I am encouraged to find that there is plenty of evidence to suggest that working in small teams is motivating for staff, while also being productive. The camaraderie of working in such a team cannot be underestimated.

Turnover rates of staff may have a negative impact on service. A high rate proves costly for the service, not just financially but in terms of continuity and relationship building that has an effect on the service delivered. Too low a rate may appear to be less costly financially, but could result in a weakened service with few new skills and innovative ideas coming in with new staff. It is tempting in the current economic climate to advertise for staff to fill short-term or temporary contracts. This is, however, short-sighted, and it is important for managers to be strong advocates of the need for permanent positions. Lack of job security, and time spent on induction and training, is all a waste – not just of money, but of people's skills and productivity; in essence, it is cost ineffective.

Management of services and resources based on the autonomous small team model tends to have a flat management hierarchy. Reporting lines will be clear but minimal. Effective services require information to travel quickly, efficiently and openly. Service excellence requires information to be disseminated clearly and personably. The cost-effective excellent service is heavily reliant on collaboration that facilitates growth and increases adaptive behaviour. Interpersonal networking should be given value and can be seen as a means of improving the flow of information both between staff members and between users and staff.

Rigorous Service Design and Development

To provide an excellent service, the user needs to be the fundamental resource for the development of new services or products. This is not just for the concepts or ideas that stem from their high expectations that will generate designs, but because of their crucial role in the feedback mechanism of the development cycle. Extensive feedback mechanisms should be employed. Making careful use of surveys and focus groups is one way of gathering information; surveys can be expensive to conduct, however, and if not carefully thought through may ultimately steer service development in a costly direction. Alternative techniques such as appropriate benchmarking, competitive intelligence, new services trialled and tested with users, tailored and quick turnaround, and value chain are important.

Here are aspects of service design and development that have an impact on related costs:

- A compromise needs to be struck between the system being tested enough to stand user scrutiny and the escalating costs associated with further refinement and subsequent delays in deployment.
- The other extreme is where innovations continue to exist long beyond their expected shelf life simply because there is insufficient investment for change, or lack of management will. In order to avoid this, focus on continual improvement. This need not be expensive, and the advent of many free, readily available and continually improving web tools is proving to be a key to sustainable personalised small-scale services.

Culture of Innovation

A service that is innovative is likely to be one that is effective. We want people to use our service, not just for the numbers through the door but for the added value that our resources, services and space offer. Logically, therefore, the more people that use the service productively, the better it is. We are not trying to compete with each other as one retailer might compete with another; instead, we are aiming for optimal use of the service in which we work. As users change, and their needs for resources and services change, so the innovative library service must be one that is marked by continuous change. Innovation helps to create value for user communities.

The argument goes that if the service is one that demonstrates incremental development in all aspects of delivery and resource provision then it will be cost effective. Heracleous, Wirtz and Johnston comment on SIA's 'Total Innovation' strand:

> *Continuous incremental development comes at a low cost but delivers that necessary margin of value to the customer. It is the totality that counts. This also means that is does not need to be too expensive ... this allows us to make a small profit ... to enable us to innovate without pricing ourselves out of the market. (2004: 36)*

Innovation, in organisations such as libraries, could be considered using the following four criteria (based on Bessant and Tidd 2007):

- products: changes to products and services
- processes: changes to processes and procedures
- position: changes in the context within which products are used
- paradigm: changes to the organisational business model.

Innovation has a positive impact on creating cost-effective services that are also personalised and scream 'excellence'. Barriers to innovative practice might include:

- Larger organisations. These tend to be much more risk averse than their smaller counterparts; they tend to be more bureaucratic and lack the structure to support effective innovative activity. SIA aims to put 30 per cent of its resources into creating new product and service ideas, which seems a staggeringly high percentage, and yet its story in a competitive market bears out the success of the strategy.
- Management structures. An innovative, creative environment not only requires sufficient resources; it needs sympathetic support from managers, incentives, training, time, autonomy and excellent communication. Innovative institutions should inspire their staff to actively seek creative solutions and have the flexible structures in place to allow for ideas to be effectively communicated.

The long-term investment in people is a crucial aspect of creating not just cost-effective services but ones that are excellent and also serve to 'delight'.

Application of SIA's Model to the Boutique Approach

SIA's model of cost-effective customer excellence, adapted here for library services, demonstrates that underpinning truly effective, efficient and personalised services are, first and foremost, relationships and, secondly, the communication infrastructure that fosters this. Whatever the size of the organisation, be it centralised or not, the personalised boutique approach can work. SIA's workforce is guaranteed to be larger than most of our library services, and yet its emphasis on staff development, training, innovative practice, the positive climate of design and development, all triggered by the mission and strategic vision of the management, has led to its success. In the small specialist library the impact of such an approach is as much needed as in the bigger, centralised counterpart. SIA recognised that the customer's needs were paramount, and it managed to maintain this alongside cost efficiency. If we can come close to this in our libraries, this surely destroys the myth that subscribing to the boutique approach must necessarily be expensive.

HIDDEN COSTS AND BENEFITS

What of the hidden costs and benefits of services? These are not so much 'hidden' as very difficult to measure, and consequently may easily be forgotten. Hidden costs must be weighed alongside the other significant costs of resources, staffing and basic infrastructure needs. We need to be aware that there is a cost attached to not providing excellent service. We therefore need to recognise and shout about the benefits!

Impact of Irritants

McKnight and Booth (2010: 27) refer to 'irritants' that may completely detract from the service excellence that we have spent time and money on developing. Irritants may take the form of poor transactions, unfriendly staff–user interactions, login issues for online resources, a banging door, a badly lit study space, and so on. The irritant may well cause the user of the service to decide that the service is just not worth using. This clearly is detrimental to our service and especially to the focus we want on excellence. Critically, our irritated user is more likely to tell ten people about the cause of their frustration than they are to tell the same ten people about the excellent service they may have had from the same library a week ago. We may wish to resolve all the complaints that come our way. Library services, however, must be grounded in the reality of financial boundaries. We cannot always satisfy every customer whim or resolve every user complaint. Ironing out all the irritants of user A will inevitably end in creating a problem for user B.

Time Wasting

Time wasting must be one of the biggest hidden costs for any service. There are two aspects to this: firstly there is the staff member who does not use their time productively, appears to be especially lax at tasks, or perhaps has to constantly redo a simple task. It is important to build a relationship with such a person to discover what are the underlying causes for the behaviour. It is often the case that there are straightforward issues that can relatively simply be resolved. Secondly, there is the staff member who is carrying out a task extremely well, but the task is no longer relevant, it could be done twice as quickly, and the whole procedure and process needs an overhaul in order to increase productivity. Until services are determined to engage with their staff at these levels, it is quite possible that they will never be cost effective. The tactic may be to reduce costs by not replacing staff when they leave.

Added Value

The added value of a service is an important benefit to be aware of and to make much of via testimonials in reports to stakeholders. A value-added service is likely both to gain library champions who are usually strong advocates for library services and, via word-of-mouth marketing, to help to continue to increase the worth and value of the service offered. The extent to which our service adds value will differentiate us from other services; further strategic marketing of our services will help produce a cost-effective service.

Goodwill

Accountants often add a line item in their accounting procedures to allow for 'goodwill'. This is inevitably imprecise. So far it has been assumed that all aspects of service provision and delivery will cost the service something. However, it is possible for an excellent service to cost very little and to achieve much goodwill. There are many ways to do this:

- Employ frontline staff who are empathetic: the restaurant owner from the story at the beginning of this chapter understood the importance of the shoes to the customer. The more we understand our users' needs, the better our service will be.
- Allow front line staff to take responsibility and to demonstrate enterprise.
- Do not just survey students for evidence; ask the frontline staff what they hear the customers say.
- Make sure that library staff are experts. They should be able to help with confidence.
- Entice people into the virtual world of libraries; but whatever is promoted online, ensure that users know who to contact straightaway if there is a problem.
- Create physical environments that people want to spend time in: a bunch of flowers at an issue desk, if you still have an issue desk, works wonders as does the attention to little details that do not cost a lot of money – for example, a poem of the week. Make multipurpose spaces available and do not underestimate the importance of the stimulus for use that a change in furniture (or collection location) can bring about.
- Use your personal email address (not a generic library address) to send a message around a group of students.
- Allow a little bit of fun into the system. Put up a humorous story on Facebook and follow it with something useful; it will almost certainly be looked at.

These are just a few examples of how to provide excellent service relatively cost free. It requires a particular organisational mindset to know that this is what can be done and also to implement policies that encourage this, but the end results will be effective.

CONCLUSION

A cost-effective service that is known for its excellence is worth striving for. Throughout this chapter the one key element that consistently has the potential to undermine this ideal state is the management of library service staff. Cost reduction in times of economic crisis through streamlining procedures and centralising tasks invariably results in losing staff. Streamlining procedures in and of itself is no bad thing; a truly innovative service would constantly be on the lookout for ways of doing this. However, replacing staff with self-service terminals or e-books, for example, should not be so that they can be made redundant, but so that they can be trained and up-skilled, motivated and inspired to create a better, more useful service for their users. Ultimately it does not matter what size of service we are in. If the pressures on the service to cut costs mean that we lose the staff who build relationships with users, who promote and explain how to use the resources, who make our physical and virtual spaces convenient and pleasant places to be, then our services may appear, on paper, to be cost effective, but will rarely be excellent. Personalised services need personalised touches.

TOP TIPS

- Strategic planning focused on user needs leads to cost effectiveness.
- User input is key. Money is wasted on services librarians think users need.
- Pressure to demonstrate economies of scale often leads to generic service delivery; avoid it!
- Adapt, rather than reinvent, the wheel.
- Consider carefully adopting expensive technology; there may be cheaper open-source alternatives, and expensive outlay ties you to specific technology for too long.
- Anonymity is costly.
- Build relationships with users.
- A smile, a pleasant manner and alert staff do not cost money and yet provide effective service.
- Employ at least one innovative person in your team.
- Keep an eye out for the detritus in your service and remove it quickly – it has a significant impact on effective use.
- Focus staff time towards services that enhance the user experience and weed out time that is carelessly and unproductively spent.

REFERENCES

Bessant, J. and Tidd, J. 2007. *Innovation and Entrepreneurship*. Chichester: John Wiley.

Bryson, J. 2011. *Managing Information Services: A Sustainable Approach*, 3rd edn. Farnham: Ashgate.

CIBER. 2011. RLUK Library Trends: Data from Sconul, the Association of Research Libraries, LibQual, the International Student Barometer and CIBER [online]. At: http://www.rluk.ac.uk/files/RLUK-library-trends%20tg%201.pdf (accessed: 26 March 2012).

Crawford, G.A. and McGuigan, G.S. 2011. An Exploratory Quantitative Analysis of Academic Library Services: An Examination of Performance Based Metrics. *Library Leadership & Management*, 25(3) [online]. At: http://journals.tdl.org/llm/article/viewFile/1997/5592 (accessed: 10 June 2011).

Harper, R. and Corrall, S. 2011. Effects of the Economic Downturn on Academic Libraries in the UK: Positions and Projections in Mid-2009. *Review of Academic Librarianship*, 17(1), 96–128.

Heracleous, L., Wirtz, J. and Johnston, R. 2004. Cost-effective Service Excellence: Lessons from Singapore Airlines. *Business Strategy Review*, 15(1), 33–8.

JISC. 2006. Designing Spaces for Effective Learning: A Guide to 21st Century Learning Space Design [online]. At: http://www.jisc.ac.uk/media/documents/publications/learningspaces.pdf (accessed: 16 March 2012).

McKnight, S. and Booth, A. 2010. Identifying Customer Expectations is Key to Evidence Based Service Delivery. *Evidence Based Library and Information Practice*, 5(1), 26–31.

Markless, S. and Streatfield, D.R. 2006. *Evaluating the Impact of Your Library*. London: Facet.

Matthews, J.R. 2011. What's the Return on ROI? The Benefits and Challenges of Calculating your Library's Return on Investment. *Library Leadership and Management*, 25(1) [online]. At: http://journals.tdl.org/llm/article/viewFile/1861/1623 (accessed: 10 June 2011).

Millar, F. 2011. Fostering Real Libraries. *Oxford Magazine*, 313(fifth week, Trinity), 6–7.

Poll, R. 2001a. Analysing Costs in Libraries. *The Bottom Line: Managing Library Finances*, 14(3), 83–94.

Poll, R. 2001b. Performance, Processes, and Costs: Managing Service Quality with the Balanced Scorecard. *Library Trends*, 49(4), 709–17.

Research Information Network (RIN). 2011. Using and Accessing Information Resources [online]. At: http://www.rin.ac.uk/our-work/using-and-accessing-information-resources/challenges-academic-libraries-difficult-economic-times (accessed: 10 June 2011).

Smarta. 2011. Five Lessons in Customer Service from John Lewis [online]. At: http://www.smarta.com/advice/sales-and-marketing/sales/five-lessons-in-customer-service-from-john-lewis (accessed: 10 June 2011).

Tisch, J. and Weber, K. 2007. *Chocolates on the Pillow Aren't Enough: Reinventing the Customer Experience*. Hoboken, NJ: John Wiley.

Trip Advisor. 2011. I'd Like to Get My Shoe Back [online]. At: http://www.tripadvisor.com/ShowTopic-g147399-i213-k2845697-I_d_like_to_get_my_shoe_back-Providenciales_Turks_and_Caicos.html (accessed: 10 June 2011).

CHAPTER 9

EVALUATING THE IMPACT OF THE BOUTIQUE LIBRARY
DAVID STREATFIELD

INTRODUCTION: WHAT IS IMPACT?

What do we mean when we think of the impact of the boutique library? The definition of impact that we have applied to libraries and information services for the past decade is: 'Any effect of the service (or of an event or initiative) on an individual, group or community'.

This definition, which we adapted from the work of leading educational evaluator Carol Fitz-Gibbon (1996), is fairly straightforward, but deceptively so. Teasing out the effects and attributing them to a specific service is always challenging, and to do so with sufficient rigour to satisfy the adherents of experimental evaluation designs may be impossible. Fortunately, most evaluations can be accomplished by choosing good proxies or surrogates for impact and by conducting the evaluation with sufficient rigour to meet the requirements, whether these are to enhance service development or to provide external accountability evidence.

The problems do not end with deciding how vigorously to pursue impact – unlike most traditional library service measurement, which shows greater or lesser efficiency in providing services but always shows *some* use, impact evaluation may show that a service is *not* doing what is intended (since the focus is on whether the service is effective, not whether it is 'ticking over'). It is also fairly common for provision of services, especially new services, to have consequences that were not foreseen – and these too may be positive or negative. And even though we usually think about impact evaluation of academic library services in terms of the student users, there may also be important effects on academic staff and researchers, library staff, senior managers and, occasionally, other people, as well as on the interactions between any of these groups. Altogether, as we shall show below, impact evaluation can be a very slippery concept, but one that *can* be successfully applied to the boutique library without disproportionate effort.

WHY EVALUATE IMPACT?

Over the past decade we have run a series of workshops for a total of more than 800 library service managers who were attempting to evaluate the impact of their services. In this chapter, 'we' refers to work done with my colleague Sharon Markless, which began with national UK research into the effective school library (Streatfield and Markless 1994) and then the effective further education library (Streatfield and Markless 1997, Markless and Streatfield 2000), continued into action research conducted with several university library teams intent on evaluating the impact of aspects of their services (Markless and Streatfield 2005, 2006), and has expanded to encompass consultancy on evaluating the impact of international library and information programmes (Streatfield and Markless 2009) and exploring concerns about the ethical and political aspects of evaluation (Streatfield and Markless 2011, Markless and Streatfield 2011). We are also working jointly on a new edition of our book on impact evaluation for LIS managers (Markless and Streatfield 2012).

Many of the participants in the workshops, especially in the earlier years, were in a position to choose whether and how to get involved in impact evaluation. They could decide to stick to their existing activity measurement processes or to aspire to look beyond service efficiency and try to gauge the effectiveness of their services from a user perspective. Since they were not being pushed into this work, we were intrigued to find out why people wanted to evaluate the impact of their services. They offered us a variety of reasons for getting involved, from securing additional resources to meeting the requirements of internal or external accountability, and from raising the profile of the library service in academic settings to enhancing staff job satisfaction or providing a focus for continued development of the service. More recently, some participants were also concerned about making a case for survival.

You may have all or any of these motives for adopting the boutique approach and for evaluating what you do. However, once you have chosen the route that focuses on personalised services you do not have the same element of choice. If you are aiming to provide an effective boutique library service you need to constantly look at what you are doing, what effects this is having on your customers or users, and what you can do to develop unique services and resources, as well as to continually tailor your services to their needs. Without these efforts you will not be able to sustain the idea of the boutique library, which is essentially about providing responsive and proactive services based on understanding of user concerns and requirements.

What are the pressures that move services towards impact evaluation? These are several. Traditional performance measurement in academic libraries has concentrated on the collection of data about levels of use of services, such as volume of loans or computer occupancy rates. What we tend to refer to in passing as 'busy-ness statistics' are important to tell library service managers whether their services are running efficiently and to provide a rough basis for comparison with the performance of other similar services. The need to go beyond limited performance measures begins to arise when usage patterns change. If there is a significant rise, or especially a fall, in usage rates, library staff may be able to speculate about possible reasons but they will not really know what has caused the change without further investigation at the user end of the process.

Turning to specific academic library services, as the activities provided and supported by the library move closer towards the core teaching and learning activities of the institution, traditional library performance measurement becomes less useful. Library managers may be able to draw some messages about their stock management from the number and range of loans over time (although these measures are becoming less relevant with the spiralling uptake of e-publications). Taking a common example of a library-based teaching intervention by way of contrast, counting attendance rates tells the provider little or nothing about whether and how an information literacy workshop is contributing to student learning.

In floating the idea of the boutique library, Priestner and Tilley (2010: 38) asserted:

> *The purpose of the collections of an academic library, at whatever level of specialism, is research and learning, fulfilling the mission of the institution. The key is focusing on the service provided for the people who make use of the resources, rather than the collections per se. Subject specialists know that, at the heart of successful service delivery, are the relationships that they build with academics and students alike. They are vital in understanding the needs, and wants, of the user and in evaluating the impact of service development.*

One of the international library development programmes with which we are involved, chooses to focus its impact work on 'changing people's lives'. In essence, impact evaluation for boutique libraries is about looking at whether and how these library services contribute to changing the lives of students, academic staff and researchers, as well as the library staff involved.

WHY IS IMPACT EVALUATION MESSY?

In the first few years of running workshops for library managers we found that at the beginning of each event most of the participants struggled to get to grips with how to evaluate the impact of services. This is hardly surprising because library school researchers in the same period had similar problems, as we discovered when we were called on to review the Value and Impact Programme funded by the Library and Information Commission (Streatfield and Markless 2002). Six out of the eight projects funded under this programme shared several characteristics:

- little attempt to define terms
- lack of a framework through which to explore value and impact
- a tendency to slide into national surveys of activities or policies
- poor choice of methods to gather evidence about impact.

It is hardly surprising that most of these faults were also apparent when library service managers attempted similar tasks for their own services at that period, although it is fair to say that library managers are now more aware of the issues and possibilities for evaluating service impact.

In our view, the stumbling block was, and to some extent still is, the strong action focus of library service managers. Judging by the library development plans we have seen recently, these still tend to concentrate on what services will be provided over the following year and how delivery will be monitored, rather than taking a step back and looking at what each service is trying to achieve. This step back is an important one, because if you do not know what you are trying to do, how can you tell whether you are succeeding? For this reason we recommend that people should start to evaluate impact by clearly stating the objective of the service under review for a specified time period (usually of one to three years) – which brings us to our impact evaluation sequence.

A SEQUENCE FOR EVALUATING IMPACT

There are four main steps in our sequence for evaluating the impact of library services, as modified and developed over the past ten years. These are:

- Find the focus: use research evidence and professional expertise to decide where the services can make a difference.
- Articulate: specify service objectives in these areas of impact.
- Identify impact indicators that will tell you if the objectives are being met (whether you are making a difference).
- Collect evidence to show whether the impacts are occurring (and what else is happening).

These four steps are elaborated below.

1. Find the Focus: The Research Evidence and Professional Judgement

Some key questions to ask when beginning to apply this sequence are:

Case Study Phase One

The university library team is concerned that students are struggling to find information from a range of sources and that they are running the risk of plagiarism because they do not provide adequate references to what they use. Accordingly the staff organise a series of 'library workshops' on effective information searching (trying to show how various search engines can help) and on how to cite different types of information. They keep **records of attendance** at these events and ask participants to complete a **'reactionnaire'** at the end, using rows of tick boxes to gauge participant satisfaction with the session, the presenters and the environment. Spaces are provided for comments after each set of boxes, but most respondents only tick the boxes. Participants are generally satisfied with what is offered, but the overall attendance level is disappointing. The subject librarians are conscious that students are still struggling and think that some of those in most difficulty are not attending. They open a dialogue with some lecturers who confirm their fears about student weaknesses in handling and using information but feel that most students will not engage in this type of skills training unless they see it as directly relevant to their own course.

Figure 9.1   Case study phase one (early days)

- Where can the boutique approach make a difference? What significant contribution can the boutique library make and how far can its services reach into core areas of teaching, learning and research?
- What is achievable and feasible within current constraints?
- What does the research tell us about where and how personalised services can be effective?
- How much part should professional judgement play in deciding where to focus service provision and where to look for evidence of impact?
- To what extent should the different perspectives of service users, providers, institutional leaders, funders and others guide the choice of focus?

The answers to these questions will vary according to the setting and circumstances of the library and its home institution, but there is some common ground.

When we try to use research evidence to help decide on potential areas of service impact, people developing boutique library services are relatively well placed. There have been few systematic reviews of what we know about the impact of libraries and their services in general, and these have shown patchy and partial evidence about what works in different library domains (Wavell et al. 2002, Poll 2011). The academic library known for utilising the boutique approach is something of an exception to this generalisation: if we take Priestner and Tilley's already-quoted comment about the core role of the boutique academic library as our point of departure, there is substantial and growing research available to help decide where to focus service efforts to support research and learning in general and to proactively help the student learner in particular. A few of the most pertinent research areas are identified below with some examples of what is being researched in each (this is of course only a selection from a rich research literature). Unfortunately, there are also some crucial gaps in the research.

Information Literacy and Academic Libraries in the Twenty-first Century   Various optimists have attempted to predict how information literacy work is likely to evolve (for example, Andretta 2007) and where academic libraries fit into the picture (Godwin and Parker 2008; Markless 2009), or have tried to reconceptualise the scope and focus of digital and information literacies (Martin and Madigan 2006). Several information literacy models or frameworks have been devised to support higher education work in this area, drawing more or less strongly on relevant research and pedagogic theories. The best known of these models in the UK academic library context is the Seven Pillars model, originally devised by SCONUL in 1999 as a guide to teaching information skills and now in the process of revision for the changing world of information literacy (SCONUL 2011a, 2011b). A critique of the most widely used models, including the first version of the Seven Pillars, was offered by Markless and Streatfield (2007).

Information-related Behaviour of User   Two of the leading international LIS researchers (Bruce 1997, Limberg 1999, 2005) have independently pursued research into the information-related behaviour of students from a phenomenographic perspective and are now collaborating on aspects of information literacy research.[1] Limberg's work is being continued through the EXACT Project (2008), led by Olof Sundin, which is focused on how people come to grips with the transfer of formal expertise and control of information from libraries (and other institutions) to the end users in Web 2.0 resources, and how end users justify and uphold trust in the authority of resources used. The phenomenographic tradition in this field has been upheld by Heinström (2003) in her study of information seekers using the internet, which offers helpful characterisations of users based on how they search.

---

1   See http://iilresearch.wordpress.com/2011/03/ (accessed: March 16, 2012) for an outline of Swedish–Australian research collaboration.

Other work focused on the search behaviour of information users in e-environments has been contributed by members of the CIBER team formerly based at University College, London (CIBER 2008; Nicholas and Rowlands 2008; Gunter, Rowlands and Nicholas 2009).

The Disciplinary Context of Information Seeking and Use   The CIBER team has also contributed to our understanding of aspects of the behaviour of information users in different academic disciplines (Nicholas et al. 2009, 2010; Nicholas, Rowlands and Jamali 2010). The other main benefactor in this field is the Research Information Network, which has funded case studies of information use by researchers in the life sciences (RIN and British Library 2009) and humanities (RIN 2011a). It has also conducted a study of the information-related training of postgraduate and postdoctoral researchers (RIN 2008; Streatfield, Allen and Wilson 2010) and another of the role of the research supervisor in fostering information literacy among those being supervised (RIN 2011b).

Towards a Theorised Pedagogy of Information Literacy   Ross Todd (2011) recently drew attention to the need for a pedagogic theory of information literacy to illuminate work in this field and to provide direction for future research. He suggested that this could be based on the research-grounded guided inquiry work of Carol Kuhlthau (which has much to offer although it is based in US schools practice). Other valuable research-based work includes Christine Bruce's conceptual framework aimed at linking information literacy theory and practice (Bruce, Edwards and Lupton 2007), Louise Limberg's three theoretical perspectives on information literacy (Limberg, Sundin and Talja 2012) and her work with colleagues constructing the information literacy roles of librarians working with nurses (Sundin, Limberg and Lundh 2008).

Beyond the Research: Professional Expertise   One of the depressing aspects of the 'accountability culture' introduced into the public sector in recent years is that all the emphasis on meeting arbitrary targets and 'consulting with the users' has tended to devalue professional expertise (as argued, for example, by O'Neill 2002, Macfarlane 2009). We think that it is important for library managers to review evidence about what has happened up till now and then make professional judgements, in this case about where to focus the service to achieve maximum effect and what to concentrate on when evaluating the impacts of the services.

2. Articulate: Specify Service Objectives in these Areas of Impact

Once you have decided where you want to focus your service efforts, the next stage is to specify what you are aiming to enhance, improve or change by delivering each specific service – why you are providing that service. The aim should be to specify service objectives sufficiently clearly that you will be able to take stock in a year's time (or at the end of an agreed period) and say to what extent you have succeeded

> **Case Study Phase Two**
>
> Building on evidence from Phase One, library subject specialists approach various lecturers and suggest that library staff deliver information seeking and use sessions at the beginning of appropriate assignments. Subject librarians are invited to 'perform' at a number of sessions in different subject areas. In addition to **reactionnaires** administered at the end of a sample of sessions, lecturers are asked to **compare student bibliographies and citations** with pre-intervention efforts. They generally report a marked improvement in both areas. Using the SCONUL *Seven Pillars model* (1999 version) as a guide, library staff prepare a **questionnaire for students and academic staff** asking whether students need help on other aspects of information literacy. Student responses are equivocal but staff point to aspects of managing information and information use in problem solving. **Focus groups** are organised for students to explore this issue further, and a clearer picture emerges of aspects of IL where many would like help. (Students start to engage when they see that IL might help them to improve their assessments and exam results.)

Figure 9.2   Case study phase two (becoming proactive)

in getting there. For this reason, the objectives should be time limited (what you hope to achieve in one to three years, depending upon the scale of your challenge) and should take account of the resources of time, materials and money available to deliver the service and meet the objective. Too many service development plans are unrealistic about what can be achieved with limited resources – this is again where professional judgement comes into play.

To repeat a point made earlier, you need to have a set of clear impact objectives, so that you know what you are trying to achieve and are then in a position to gauge whether you are succeeding. Since libraries with recognisable boutique services will more than likely be focused on making a direct or indirect contribution to teaching and learning, most of the objectives are likely to be in the area of independent learning, such as:

- improve levels of competence (students can...)
- enhance the quality of student or research work
- build student and academic, staff and researcher confidence when engaging

---

Case Study Phase Three

Subject specialists now deliver IL sessions on various courses and collaborate with some lecturers to prepare IL e-guidance, as well as to plan IL interventions, team teach, and sometimes jointly assess assignments. IL is included within **PDPs** and IL questions are included in the university **annual student survey**. **Pre- and post-IL intervention questionnaires** focused on the students' self-assessments of competence, confidence and knowledge are administered for a sample of interventions, and **focus groups** are held with samples of students to gauge the effectiveness of IL work (including informal support offered by library staff) and to identify other potential support needs. **Focus groups with new academic staff** have exposed the need for IL training, as well as the potential to provide IL support for postgraduate and postdoctoral staff and their supervisors. A strategic shift by the university in response to the widening participation agenda and increased student numbers has raised the possibility of an i-skills framework to expand the e-guidance work across the institution. External consultants **interview staff** to assess the scope for such a framework and recommend that library staff work with academics to develop IL learning support materials in all subject areas (this really happened!).

Figure 9.3   Case study phase three (recent developments)]

with information
- change the nature of student enquiries
- help students and researchers and academic staff to extend and develop skills.

You may also have objectives that focus on the library services themselves, but from a user standpoint, such as:

- students, academic staff and researchers know how the services can help them
- a wider range of people use the services
- people are more confident in using the full range of information, reading and contributing to service development.

Since we have proposed a sequence to work through in order to evaluate service impact, it is important to stress that impact evaluation should complement 'traditional' service monitoring, not replace it. When you have specified your service objectives you still have to ensure that the service is delivered so that you will have impacts to evaluate! Traditional library performance measures will tell you whether the specified activities have been carried out and whether services are functioning efficiently. The impact evidence should go beyond this to look at the effectiveness of what you are doing.

3. Identify Impact Indicators that will Tell you if you are Making a Difference

The next step in the sequence is to choose impact indicators that will tell you whether you are meeting the objectives. We usually suggest that you identify two or three impact indicators for each objective and that you review these regularly so that you keep them to the minimum required to tell you whether your service is succeeding. When doing this it is important to focus on *what* evidence will tell you what you need to know, not on *how* to gather the evidence (focusing too early on how to collect the evidence may lead to premature ruling out of important indicators).

For our definition of an indicator we have again borrowed from Carol Fitz-Gibbon (1996: 5), who suggests that an indicator is a statement around which you can collect evidence on a regular basis to show a trend. No single indicator will give you definitive evidence of the actual impact of any service. Human beings are complex and are affected in many subtle ways by each experience. Impact indicators are usually surrogates for impact: pieces of information that provide good clues, telling part of the story. Your challenge is to design the strongest surrogates possible. For example, if you ask people who attended a workshop on citing publications how good they found it, this offers a weak surrogate for the impact that you are trying to record. People might have liked the workshop because they found the speakers entertaining or enjoyed the activities. A stronger surrogate, and therefore a better indicator, is whether the participants begin to cite references more appropriately after attending the workshop. Indicators should be:

- directly linked to what you are trying to achieve in the key areas where you have chosen to deploy resources and to evaluate the effects. This is why we give so much attention to articulating objectives before getting any further into evaluating impact.
- clear and understandable (check with colleagues to make sure).
- generally accepted as reasonable and fair. You need to agree that the indicators really do tell you about the impact of your services. Are they evaluating something where other parts of the institution have a bigger role, or things of secondary importance in the eyes of your staff or managers?

Are they up to date? You may be providing invaluable online support for students, but this may result in declining use of your physical space or reference material. Do your indicators reflect such changes?

- valid – do they evaluate what they say they are evaluating?
- informative, providing significant information. They should illuminate your successes, highlight changes and alert you to problems or issues.
- as few in number as possible. They should cover the most significant parts of the services (what really matters) – sometimes an indicator will serve for more than one area of impact. However, you also need to make sure that the indicators are balanced. You do not want to choose a very small number of indicators and then find that they focus your attention in the wrong place.

If you have consulted over your objectives and prioritised them, it is reasonable to confine your impact indicators to the priority areas in which you are trying to make a noticeable difference and to rely on traditional process and output performance indicators to monitor other areas. There are several ways in which indicators can fail to do their job. They can be:

- corruptible: easily used to create a false impression.
- corrupting: provide an incentive to disruptive or counterproductive actions – your indicators should always encourage positive services. In the boutique library, corrupting indicators might focus on one or two aspects of the overall service to the detriment of others. Indicators should reflect the competing priorities that all services have to struggle with.
- inflexible: and unable to reflect diversity and change in your services. Indicators are provisional. It is very rare to get indicators completely right at the first attempt. We do not usually know enough at the outset about the complex relationships between different factors and different elements of any service. The first time you work through the measuring impact process you may find that some indicators do not tell you what you really need to know while others distract you from the real issues. Change them.

It is difficult to measure some tangible benefits that libraries can bring – for example, personal development or enhanced quality of student work. However, indicators of impact do not have to be quantitative and therefore easily measured. Qualitative indicators can be equally valid and may be more illuminating.

Impact indicators can be expressed in various ways, such as:

- The proportion or percentage of researchers who use the library as a first port of call when needing information for their work.
- Researchers use the library as a first port of call.
- Do researchers use the library as a first port of call …?

Case Study Phase Four

Subject specialists continue to collaborate with lecturers on IL sessions and these are now part of the **peer observation** programme. Combined teams of subject librarians and teachers are developing e-materials to help students deal with IL issues as they arise. Students are recruited to **test and critique materials** before they become part of the i-skills framework, **pop-up surveys** are used to obtain student feedback and the **university student survey** now includes a question on the usefulness of the framework. Library staff began to offer IL workshops as part of the generic skills training offered centrally to postgraduate and postdoctoral researchers initiated with Roberts funding. These workshops were **observed** and the tendency for library contributions to adopt a behaviourist approach to teaching rather than the constructivist learning approach favoured by the rest of the training was noted. **Surveys of researchers** found some dissatisfaction with the generic approach to skills training. As a result, library staff are now working with trainers and with academic development units to develop subject-based situated IL learning opportunities for researchers (including lecturers in their research roles) as well as for research supervisors, supported by an adapted version of the i-skills framework. Regular **focus groups** are held with students, academic staff and researchers to evaluate current offerings and consider further developments. Library staff are currently negotiating with the university ethics committee to secure a **research study** of library-initiated IL support for students and researchers.

Figure 9.4   Case study phase four (current picture)

4. Collect Evidence to Show whether Impact is Occurring

The last step in the sequence involves deciding what information to collect to tell you whether your services are having the anticipated impact. When you focus on the impact of services on people, you are looking for changes in their attitudes or behaviour that can be attributed to these services. This takes us directly into the world of social science research. For practical purposes, you will often be combining 'traditional' efficiency measurement data with impact evidence gathered using the social science repertoire. Borrowing from the social scientists, most of the evidence you can gather is collected in one of three ways:

- Observe: through structured observation, informal observation, self-recording by service users or other means.
- Ask people questions: through questionnaires, interviews, focus groups, and so on.
- Infer that relevant change is happening: two commonly used methods are to:

  1. examine documents or other products created by your target groups to see whether your interventions have made any difference. (The aim here is to look for changes that can be fairly directly linked to what your services offer. For example, if you offer students an introduction to systematic searching for information you could look for general changes in the quality of student assignments. However, more direct evidence of progress can be found by looking at the quality of bibliographies or seeing whether a wider range of sources is cited.)
  2. monitor the activities of the target groups using output indicators (for example, participation in events, levels of service use, examination results). The drawback with using this traditional method is that you may find it difficult to show that these changes are influenced by your services.

Again, libraries where personalised services are their focus are a special case when it comes to evidence collection. Since the boutique library is predicated on the idea of excellent services that are tailored to the requirements of users and constantly adapt to their needs, the best way forward is likely to be through the action research route. This involves using the three methods of evidence-collection outlined above, but as part of a systematic cyclical process. This process involves gathering evidence of impact, then collective interpretation of this evidence by library staff and a representative range of users, who then make modifications to the services in the light of the evidence, before going back round to evidence gathering and so on until no significant improvements are found. There is no space here to elaborate this approach, but there are a number of accessible books that describe action research more fully (for example, Stringer 2007; Coghlan and Brannick 2009; Mcniff 2010).

How Much is Enough?   How much evidence should you collect? The pragmatic answer to this question is 'as little as you need to make good decisions'. When considering this it is important to remember that impact evidence is not a distinct category of information, but information applied to a specific purpose. It follows that how much information you need to gather depends upon the purpose. If you want to assure yourself that your work is making a difference or to check on how you are doing compared with other similar services then you need to collect enough information to be comfortable that you have a good picture of what is going on. One way to check this is to see whether your evidence resonates with your colleagues – do they recognise the picture that your evidence presents? If they are uncertain about the evidence offered, you may have to gather further impact information to amplify the picture.

On the other hand, if you are trying to convince other people beyond the library about the effectiveness of your services, you will have to take account of what they regard as convincing evidence even if your own views are different. Enough qualitative information will be required to convince a reasonable reviewer, but you may have to supplement this evidence with quantitative data (usually process data) if this is what the people who oversee or fund your services expect to get. You will then have an education job to persuade people why your evidence offers an in-depth and nuanced picture of what is happening that may well tell you more than performance data. This should not be too difficult in a higher education setting where much decision making is based largely or wholly on qualitative evidence (at best!). Sophisticated quantitative data and good quality impact information should complement each other strongly.

However, if the concern is to convince government, you are likely to have to conform to arbitrarily prescribed targets and data collection methods that may have only tangential connection to service impact. If you are making a case for securing funds, stronger evidence may be needed again, if you are competing with other agencies or services. Your evidence gathering will have to be at least as convincing as theirs, even before you report on the effectiveness of your service as shown through that process.

Reliable Evidence   When looking at the reliability of your evidence, we suggest that you consider three criteria (based on Thomas 2004):

- Relevance: does the evidence constitute information for (or against) a proposition? In impact evaluation terms, does it tell you whether or not the chosen success criteria are being met, or is it actually evidence of something else?
- Sufficiency: is there corroboration with other instances of the same kind of evidence, or other kinds of evidence? In other words, is the picture consistent or are you making too much of one-off instances?
- Veracity: is the process of gathering evidence free from distortion and as far as possible uncontaminated by vested interest?

We are not seeking to transform you into an academic researcher with a strong philosophical bias at this point! Instead, we suggest that you use these three criteria as a checklist when you have decided what evidence-gathering methods to use and again when you look over the evidence that you have gathered.

Of course, you do not always have to generate your own evidence in order to argue a case or to take management decisions. As already noted, such libraries are relatively well placed to exploit a range of relevant research in proposing courses of action.

Choosing Collection Methods   Deciding how to collect evidence is not as simple as saying, 'If you want to find out about changes in people's attitudes – interview them', or 'Observation is the best way of noting changes in behaviour', but there is a relationship between what you are looking for and how to find it. This can be seen if we look at four key dimensions of change in the teaching and learning context (affective, behavioural, knowledge based and competence based):

1. Affective changes (attitudes, perceptions, levels of confidence, satisfaction with services)   You may be able to observe changes in people's attitudes, but getting evidence usually involves asking the people who may or may not have changed. In particular, asking questions through short and tightly focused questionnaires should work, because they are impersonal, but at the same time you are showing interest by asking the questions. If you are looking for evidence about people's confidence (for example, when using ICT), questionnaires administered before and after your service intervention give people the chance to register changes without any pejorative overtones.

Taking a broader impact area, if you are looking at the role of the boutique components model in life enhancement, you might construct a well-focused user questionnaire to gather information on:

- the quality of student communication with library staff (for example, freedom to ask questions, get support in seeking information)
- the quality of ongoing student relationships with specific library staff
- the extent to which the library provides a positive study environment (for example, appearance and comfort, noise level, and so on)
- the extent to which the library provides more direct support for study and research (for example, whether materials can be obtained when needed, whether there are adequate photocopy facilities, and so on).

On the other hand, you might want to explore these issues more fully through a structured focus group.

2. Behavioural changes (people do things differently)   Here, observation comes into its own, but you can also infer changes by looking at people's work. For example, to see change after an information-seeking input to an education assignment, you can look at completed assignments to check the number and range of sources cited, how the sources are presented and used, and how the work compares with previous assignments. It should also be possible to track changes by analysing enquiries and requests for documents.

3. Knowledge-based changes   To find out if people have learnt anything, you have to ask them questions. This questioning can take many forms including tests, questionnaires or focus groups. Take care not to become over-reliant on post-event questionnaires by participants. These are sometimes called 'reactionnaires', because they only really gauge whether people are positive about the experience. As Burrow and Berardinelli note: 'While learner interest and motivation are certainly factors in the outcomes of training, there is not a direct relationship between the learner's perception of training and actual learning, especially at the time when the learner has just completed the training experience' (2003: 9). If you really want to find out whether your training interventions have made a difference it is probably best to contact some of the participants a few months later and ask.

4. Competence-based changes (people do things more effectively)   How can you tell whether people are more competent? You can ask them questions, but also ask other people who observe them doing things. To pick up on what other people see, it depends who the people are and whether they are willing to give you feedback. Potential respondents may be other students or teachers. Interviews are usually the most viable method for evidence gathering of this sort, because informants may feel uncomfortable about making judgements on other people in writing.

An alternative way to throw light on the level and variety of user skills (or of skills weaknesses) is to analyse a sample of enquiries recorded by your service. Service records are typically used to review the demands on the service, but they can also be used to tell you about what your users are struggling with. An analysis schedule could be constructed for this purpose.

SOME OTHER METHODS OF GATHERING IMPACT EVIDENCE

In the first year of a recent impact-evaluation programme, ten teams of UK university library staff used the following methods to gather impact evidence in relation to e-information services and e-learning innovations (Markless and Streatfield 2006):

- When the focus was on the impact of services on students:
    a) tests (including online diagnostic tests)
    b) questionnaires and embedded questions
    c) focus groups
    d) interviews conducted while students were conducting searches

e) student diaries
f) progress files
g) student bibliography analysis (adopted in five universities).
- When the focus was on academic staff the choice of methods depended on the purpose:
    h) to gather staff perceptions about service impact: structured face-to-face or telephone interview (four universities)
    i) for more specific baseline evidence: focus groups
    j) to evaluate cooperation or collaboration between academic and library staff: records of contacts between these groups
    k) for evidence of change in academic staff: analysis of their lists of recommended reading and e-links for students. (One team also undertook an information literacy teaching audit covering the whole university.)
- When specific information literacy inputs were made by library staff:
    l) monitoring of information literacy outcomes or of assignments that required students to deploy a research strategy
    m) observation of student engagement by other library staff.

A useful observation made by the library staff involved in this programme (particularly if you are considering adoption of an action-research approach) is that interviews produce 'fairly instant results' – that is, the evidence can be used almost immediately to improve service delivery.

This list of collection methods is not exhaustive – to give two other possibilities, you might consider:

- conducting critical incident interviews, where the incidents in question are encounters with your service and where the interviewer seeks to build up a picture of the information-seeking and use practices of the respondent by asking a sequence of questions (for example, from what triggered an enquiry through to what happened as a result of using any information acquired).
- collecting a representative range of stories of successes and failures when using the library or its services by interviewing users or requesting their own accounts. Although this type of testimony can be powerful there is an obvious danger of cherry-picking the successful narratives. This can be avoided by passing the selection task to an independent panel (for example, student and academic staff users), who will decide whether to target contributors or how to seek volunteers (and on what basis), what criteria to use in selecting stories and which ones to feature to illustrate the impact of particular library services.

USING IMPACT EVALUATION RESULTS

Once you have begun the process of baseline data collection and have some results, you are in a position to prescribe service delivery targets in your impact areas (if you want to go in this direction). But in what zone do you want to pitch your targets? A study for the National Foundation for Educational Research in England and Wales (Arnold 1998) sums up the idea of target zones:

- The historic zone: Targets in this zone are those that lag behind current performance, which is hidden to the extent that others are not aware of this. By this means, standstill can be represented as improvement – it is a means of 'domesticating' any threats that targets may offer.
- The comfort zone: Targets in this zone seek to keep improvement very much within reach. They often reflect a belief that there is really no need to improve.
- The smart zone: Targets in this zone are sufficiently ahead of the present state of play to make a difference.
- The unlikely zone: Targets in this zone seek large improvements through 'determination and high aspiration, or recklessness'. They can be a recipe for high risk and high stress.

It needs no guesswork to identify which of these zones is the ideal, although in practice library services show very different aspirations in their target setting. You may also want to compare your impact evaluation findings with those of other boutique libraries. Benchmarking of services has acquired a slightly sinister reputation because of the enthusiasm with which the New Managerialists have embraced the concept as a means of generating comparative performance 'league tables', but benchmarking need not degenerate into a competition to get into the 'top' quartile.

At an impact evaluation workshop for health library managers, we asked whether they felt that there was scope for benchmarking based on service impact. They went into a huddle and came back to say that they felt that this type of benchmarking could be useful for service development, providing that it drew upon:

- commonly shared impact evaluation evidence-collection instruments (for example, interview schedules, questionnaires, or banks of questions) – both core instruments and extension tools designed to evaluate additional dimensions of service provision.
- shared techniques – using the same activities in the same way at the same time in the curriculum cycle (that is, agreeing a common methodology, timing, impact areas and impact indicators).
- benchmarking with like services (services of a similar scale operating in broadly similar types of university and where the library shares a common

philosophy – such as aspiring to provide boutique services).
- Benchmarking as the *start* of the learning, not as the means of measuring success or failure. If there are differences in the relative impact of services it will be useful to try to find out why.

Some tools and methods for impact evaluation are available at the SCONUL Vamp Project (Impact Initiative) website (2011).

MANAGING IMPACT EVALUATION

The impact evaluation sequence is designed to take you through the main processes to be planned for when evaluating the impact of the library, but there are some management issues that are likely to arise.

A drawback with systematic impact evaluation is that it is unlikely that you will already have good-quality information about how well your target audiences are doing in your chosen impact areas at the outset. Assuming that you decide to introduce new services to meet your impact targets, the two basic options are to establish a baseline before you start innovating and then do regular (for example, annual) evaluations, so that you can see whether the situation changes over time, or to simultaneously start innovating and gathering impact evidence so that you will soon have information against which to compare later results. The same options are open when evaluating existing services. Neither of these approaches is likely to sit comfortably within the annual planning cycle.

The same discontinuity is likely to occur with evidence collection, especially for new services, because it is likely to take longer than one year for the full impacts of any new service to show up. Faced with this problem, some library services have chosen to focus on short-, medium- and long-term impacts, with the short-term impacts linking into the annual planning and service delivery cycle (and tending to lean towards process indicators rather than impacts), the medium-term impacts focusing on changes in people's behaviour that may be attributable to service changes, and the long-term impacts trying to show the overall effects of specific service developments, including long-term changes in user behaviour.

The impact evaluation sequence will not necessarily work well with highly innovative services, such as experimental e-services offering novel service delivery options. This is because the simple logic model (which is how the impact evaluation sequence can be described) is not designed for situations where you do not know what the impacts are likely to be when introducing the service and where there will probably be unintended consequences of innovation. A more complex approach is needed here, sometimes described as emergent evaluation (Rogers 2008) or developmental evaluation (Patton 2011), in which you simultaneously innovate and evaluate potential impacts until you have built up an understanding of where changes are occurring, so that you know where to focus your evaluation work and to apply the other steps in our sequence. This evolutionary approach to evaluation does not fit comfortably with organisational plans, although it does sit well within the action-research cycle, which is one reason why we have advocated this approach.

To conclude by drawing on our experience of working with teams of university librarians to help them to evaluate aspects of their own services, one key message from those involved is that implementation requires time for planning – and time to carry out the plan. They recommend that managers thinking about innovation and evaluation should build on current innovations and projects, and conclude that 'influencing the University and negotiating committees is harder than doing the evaluation!' (Markless and Streatfield 2005: 8).

TOP TIPS

- If you want a proactive service focused on research and learning, you need to evaluate its impact on users.
- Focus is vital: be clear about what boutique libraries *can* do and *what* you want to do so that you are well placed to see whether you *are* doing it.
- Look at the research on what works and how.
- Generate clear and time-limited service objectives – so that you can see if you are meeting them.
- Find impact indicators that tell you whether you are 'winning' (making an impact on users).
- Be rigorous in collecting your evidence – even if you do it on a small scale.
- Decide how much evidence will be convincing.
- Choose collection methods to get the evidence you need – do not get wedded to one method.
- Be flexible in managing impact evaluation – everything is provisional.

REFERENCES

Andretta, S. (ed.) 2007. *Change and Challenge: Information Literacy for the 21st Century.* Adelaide: Auslib Press.

Arnold, R. 1998. *Target Setting: School and LEA in Partnership.* Education Management Information Exchange, National Foundation for Educational Research, Slough.

Bruce, C.S. 1997. *The Seven Faces of Information Literacy.* Adelaide: Auslib Press.

Bruce, C.S., Edwards, S. and Lupton, M. 2007. Six Frames for Information Literacy Education: A Conceptual Framework for Interpreting the Relationships between Theory and Practice, in Andretta, S. (ed.), *Change and Challenge: Information Literacy for the 21st Century*. Adelaide: Auslib Press, 37–58.

Burrow, J. and Berardinelli, P. 2003. Systematic Performance Improvement: Refining the Space between Learning and Results. *Journal of Workplace Learning*, 15(1), 6–13.

CIBER. 2008. Information Behaviour of the Researcher of the Future: A CIBER Briefing Paper. University College London CIBER Group [online]. At: http://www.jisc.ac.uk/media/documents/programmes/reppres/gg_final_keynote_11012008.pdf (accessed: 18 October 2011).

Coghlan, D. and Brannick, T. 2009. *Doing Action Research in Your Own Organization*. Thousand Oaks, CA: Sage.

EXACT Project. 2008. EXpertise, Authority and Control on the InterneT (EXACT): A Study of the Formation of Source Credibility in Web 2.0 Environments for Learning [online]. At: http://www.lincs.gu.se/digitalAssets/1030/1030712_EXACT_abstract.pdf (accessed: 18 October 2011).

Fitz-Gibbon, C.T. 1996. *Monitoring Education: Indicators, Quality and Effectiveness*. London: Cassell.

Godwin, P. and Parker, J. 2008. *Information Literacy meets Library 2.0*. London: Facet.

Gunter, B., Rowlands, I. and Nicholas, D. 2009. *Is There a Google Generation?: Information Search Behaviour Developments and the Future Learner*. Oxford: Chandos.

Heinström, J. 2003. Fast Surfers, Broad Scanners and Deep Divers as Users of Information Technology: Relating Information Preferences to Personality Traits. *Proceedings of the American Society for Information Science and Technology*, 40(1), 247–54.

Limberg, L. 1999. Three Conceptions of Information Seeking and Use, in Wilson, T.D. and Allen, D.K. (eds), *Exploring the Contexts of Information Behaviour: Proceedings of the Second International Conference on Research in Information Needs, Seeking and Use in Different Contexts*, 13/15 August, Sheffield, UK. London: Taylor Graham, 116–35.

Limberg, L. 2005. Experiencing Information Seeking and Learning: Research on Patterns of Variation, in Macevičiūtè, E. and Wilson, T.D. (eds), *Introducing Information Management: An Information Research Reader*. London: Facet, 68–80.

Limberg, L., Sundin, O. and Talja, S. 2012. Three Theoretical Perspectives on Information Literacy. *Human IT* [accepted for publication].

Macfarlane, B. 2009. *Researching with Integrity: The Ethics of Academic Enquiry*. London: Routledge.

Mcniff, J. 2010. *Action Research for Professional Development: Concise Advice for New (and Experienced) Action Researchers*. Dorset: September.

Markless, S. 2009. A New Vision of Information Literacy for the Digital Learning Environment in Higher Education. *Nordic Journal of Information Literacy in Higher Education*, 1(1), 25–40.

Markless, S. and Streatfield, D.R. 2000. The Really Effective College Library, Library and Information Commission Research Report 51. Information Management Associates for the Library and Information Commission, Twickenham, Middlesex [Phase 2 project report].

Markless, S. and Streatfield, D.R. 2005. Facilitating the Impact Implementation Programme. *Library and Information Research*, 29(91), 10–19 [special issue devoted to the Impact Implementation Programme].

Markless, S. and Streatfield, D.R. 2006. Gathering and Applying Evidence of the Impact of UK University Libraries on Student Learning and Research: A Facilitated Action Research Approach. *International Journal of Information Management*, 26, 3–15.

Markless, S. and Streatfield, D.R. 2007. Three Decades of Information Literacy: Redefining the Parameters, in Andretta, S. (ed.), *Change and Challenge: Information Literacy for the 21st Century*. Adelaide: Auslib Press.

Markless, S. and Streatfield, D.R. 2011. Evidence – What Evidence? Methodological Fundamentalism, the New Managerialism and LIS Evaluation [paper]. Third Information: Interactions and Impact Conference, Aberdeen.

Markless, S. and Streatfield, D.R. 2012. *Evaluating the Impact of Your Library*, 2nd edn. London: Facet [awaiting publication; 1st edn. London: Facet, 2006].

Martin, A. and Madigan, D. (eds) (2006). *Digital Literacies for Learning*. London: Facet Publishing.

Nicholas, D. and Rowlands, I. 2008. *Digital Consumers: Reshaping the Information Professions*. London: Facet.

Nicholas, D., Rowlands, I. and Jamali, H.R. 2010. E-Textbook Use, Information Seeking Behaviour and its Impact: Case Study Business and Management. *Journal of Information Science*, 36(2), 263–80.

Nicholas, D., Clark, D., Rowlands, I. and Jamali, H.R. 2009. Online Use and Information Seeking Behaviour: Institutional and Subject Comparisons of UK Researchers. *Journal of Information Science,* 35(6), 660–76.

Nicholas, D., Williams, P., Rowlands, I. and Jamali, H.R. 2010. Researchers' E-Journal Use and Information Seeking Behaviour. *Journal of Information Science*, 36(4), 494–516.

O'Neill, O. 2002. Called to Account, in *A Question of Trust: 2002 BBC Reith Lectures*. Cambridge: Cambridge University Press, 41–60.

Patton, M.Q. 2011. *Developmental Evaluation: Applying Complexity Concepts to Enhance Innovation and Use*. New York: Guilford.

Poll, R. 2011. Bibliography: Impact and Outcome of Libraries. The Hague: International Federation of Library Associations [online]. At: www.ifla.org/files/statistics-and-evaluation/publications/Bibl_Impact_Outcome-Jan 2011.pdf (accessed: 18 October 2011).

Priestner, A. and Tilley, E. 2010. Boutique Libraries at your Service. *Library & Information Update*, 9(6), 36–9.

Research Information Network (RIN). 2008. Mind the Skills Gap: Information-Handling Training for Researchers [online]. At: http://www.rin.ac.uk/our-work/researcher-development-and-skills/mind-skills-gap-information-handling-training-researchers (accessed: 18 October 2011).

Research Information Network (RIN). 2011a.. Reinventing Research? Information Practices in the Humanities [online]. At: http://www.rin.ac.uk/our-work/using-and-accessing-information-resources/information-use-case-studies-humanities (accessed: 1 April 2011).

Research Information Network (RIN). 2011b. The Role of Research Supervisors in Information Literacy [online]. At: http://www.rin.ac.uk/news/role-research-supervisors-information-literacy (accessed: 1 November 2011).

Research Information Network (RIN) and British Library. 2009. Patterns of Information Use and Exchange: Case Studies of Researchers in the Life Sciences [online]. At: http://www.rin.ac.uk/our-work/using-and-accessing-information-resources/patterns-information-use-and-exchange-case-studies (accessed: 18 October 2011).

Rogers, P.J. 2008. Using Programme Theory to Evaluate Complicated and Complex Aspects of Interventions. *Evaluation*, 14(1), 29–48 [online]. At: http://evi.sagepub.com/cgi/content/abstract/14/1/29 (accessed: 8 November 2011).

SCONUL Vamp Project. 2011. Impact Initiative [online]. At: http://vamp.diglib.shrivenham.cranfield.ac.uk/impact/impact-initiative (accessed: 8 November 2011).

SCONUL Working Group on Information Literacy. 2011a. The SCONUL Seven Pillars of Information Literacy: Core Model[2]. Society of College, National and University Libraries, London [online]. At: http://www.sconul.ac.uk/groups/information_literacy/publications/coremodel.pdf (accessed: 18 October 2011).

SCONUL Working Group on Information Literacy. 2011b. The SCONUL Seven Pillars of Information Literacy: Research Lens[2]. London: Society of College, National and University Libraries [online]. At: http://www.sconul.ac.uk/groups/information_literacy/publications/researchlens.pdf (accessed: 18 October 2011).

Streatfield, D.R. and Markless, S. 1994. Invisible Learning? The Contribution of School Libraries to Teaching and Learning, Library and Information Research Report 98. British Library Research and Development Department, London.

Streatfield, D.R. and Markless, S. 1997. The Effective College Library, British Library Research and Innovation Report 21, Developing FE Series, 1(8). Further Education Development Agency, London.

Streatfield, D.R. and Markless, S. 2002. *Critical Evaluation of the LIC Value and Impact Programme: Report to Resource: The Council for Museums, Libraries and Archives*. London, Resource.

Streatfield, D.R. and Markless, S. 2009. What is Impact Assessment and Why is it Important? *Performance Measurement and Metrics*, 10(2), 134–41.

Streatfield, D.R. and Markless, S. 2011. Impact Evaluation, Advocacy and Ethical Research: Some Issues for National Strategy Development? *Library Review*, 60(4), 312–27.

Streatfield, D.R., Allen, D.K. and Wilson, T.D. 2010. Information Literacy Training for Postgraduate and Postdoctoral Researchers: A National Survey and its Implications. *Libri*, 60, 230–40.

Stringer, E.T. 2007. *Action Research*. Thousand Oaks, CA: Sage.

Sundin, O., Limberg, L. and Lundh, A. 2008. Constructing Librarians' Information Literacy Expertise in the Domain of Nursing. *Journal of Librarianship and Information Science*, 40(1), 21–30.

Thomas, G. 2004. Introduction: Evidence and Practice, in Thomas, G. and Pring, R. (eds), *Evidence-based Practice in Education*. Maidenhead: Open University Press, McGraw-Hill Education.

Todd, R.J. 2011. Uncovering Information Literacy: Mythology, Myopia and Movement. Third Information: Interactions and Impact Conference, University of Aberdeen, June [keynote paper].

Wavell, C., Baxter, G., Johnson, I. and Williams, D. 2002. Impact Evaluation of Museums, Archives and Libraries: Available Evidence Project, School of Information and Media, Faculty of Management, Robert Gordon University, London: Resource [online]. At: http://www.mla.gov.uk/documents/id16rep.doc (accessed: 18 October 2011).

CHAPTER 10

IMPLEMENTING AND MANAGING BOUTIQUE
ANDY PRIESTNER AND ELIZABETH TILLEY

INTRODUCTION

Whether you are reading this final chapter having read all of the preceding chapters or, more likely, having dipped in to some of the chapters of specific interest, you may well now be thinking: 'So what?' Certainly, when we first presented our boutique model and advocated a more personalised approach in our *Update* article (2010), there were responses from some quarters suggesting that a few librarians strongly felt that they already 'do all this stuff'; after all, librarianship is all about the user, isn't it? And all librarians know this and act accordingly, don't they?

While we accept that, yes, most information and library services strive to be user-centric and, moreover, that we are by no means reinventing the wheel with our boutique, or personalised, approach, our purpose in putting together the initial symposium and thereafter this book was not only to explore how personalised we already are, but also how much *more* personalised we can be. And the answer we have unanimously and independently arrived at is *far more* personalised. It is our assertion that we may think that we are putting user needs first, but we are not actively seeking to find out what they are. And that instead of actively listening to our users, we are assuming that we – as professional librarians, or experienced library staff – know better and that they 'don't know what's good for them' or, worse still, that they 'don't know how lucky they are' to have resources and services that we could scarcely have dreamed of in our day. There is also a clear danger that we are making assumptions about what our users need by drawing on scant evidence and filling in the blanks ourselves. And finally, that we are neither recognising, nor embracing, the fact that we are now living in the 'Age of the Individual'.

TRUE PERSONALISATION

Naturally while expounding our 'new thinking' we ended up examining our own services closely and, despite the fact that we both felt our libraries were heading in the right direction, in terms of offering a truly personalised experience we decided that they both fell short of the mark. We might make impassioned points in presentations about communicating appropriately and connecting with our users, but when it came down to it neither of us was really 'working' personalised hard enough. In fact it took writing chapters for this book for us to recognise that we were not following through and 'putting our services where our model was'. However, once we recognised this state of affairs it did not take us all that long to put this right. Some simple changes implemented at Judge Business School's Information and Library Services were as follows:

- A characterless blog was rebooted as a more friendly, relaxed destination with shorter blog posts, which recognised both the limited time of users and the need to invest content with more voice and personality.
- As detailed in Chapter 2, each user group was assigned a designated support librarian (many of which are library assistants who are more than equal to the task) responsible for connecting with these users, in order to establish their stresses and unique needs and, more importantly, to simply build rapport.
- We followed up personally with student representatives after committee meetings both to ensure that their voice was heard and to dig deeper to see if we can be doing more for them. This has also involved contacting non-attendees, not to scold but to encourage.
- We identified stressful times and made student lives easier by extending a helping hand and dispensing advice at these points of need.
- We abandoned generic inductions and training in favour of targeted sessions that focused on the audience and interactivity, rather than on the presentation and ticking the content boxes.

At the Faculty of English similar changes have taken place, but the users are different both in age and subject, and so are the services provided. A couple of recent examples include:

- sending all new fresher students a handwritten postcard with a photo of the library staff to welcome them when they arrived for the first time in Cambridge
- providing what is now a popular service in exam term for students: tea@ three is free and supplied in the library space, providing students a chance to stop work for a short time, chat with friends, or work on a puzzle or crossword.

All of the above measures at each library prompted a perceived higher engagement and improved feedback from users suggesting that the extra effort had been recognised and was very worthwhile. What is more, none of these changes costs money; if anything, in terms of staff time they proved more efficient.

HONESTY AND REALISM

These alterations and tweaks at Judge and the English Faculty revealed something else to us too, something that might seem obvious but that we nevertheless had almost blithely ignored in our respective careers thus far: the need for honesty. Neither of us had been honest enough about our users' needs and had either pretended, or assumed, that they wanted something more complex or finely tuned. In fact, when we got down off our professional pedestals and talked to our users we discovered that the most pressing needs were simple and easily resolved. To give two examples:

- Why did a certain set of management students never fill in our annual user surveys? Because, they told us, they are confused by its generic references to e-resources when all they use for their course are the books on reading lists. They could only answer a few questions and understandably did not complete the surveys due to irrelevance to them. We have since resolved to give them a separate survey in future.
- Why did another group of fourth-year students seem so disengaged and confused by our approach every year? Because, they told us, having already spent three years at Cambridge during which they were largely ignored, they were overwhelmed and didn't know how to react to our wide smiles and our offers of help. With this group, we have backed off and have started to only send them information when they really need it.

Further above, these changes were described as 'tweaks'; it was a deliberate choice of word. For our experience is that the majority of the time 'going more personalised' only requires slight alterations to the services we were already offering. We also feel that hand in hand with this honesty comes a need to be more realistic about user needs. You may only have one hour with a group of students each academic year and, as a result, be tempted to spend it detailing everything there is to know about your library service, in the desperate hope that some of it will go in. The reality, of course, is that *none* of it will go in and furthermore the audience will have the impression that you don't have the facility or the will to understand that their group and indeed individual users have specific needs. Taking a generic approach does not go unnoticed. We also need to be realistic about the type of information users need and how they want to receive it and therefore about what is a good use of our time.

NO AGENDA

Another simple truth that is well expressed in Margaret Westbury's case study, and that we have also embraced in our respective services since we started on this journey, is a definite need for some of our approaches to our users to have no agenda, hidden or otherwise. Is it not high time that we librarians stopped informing and advising at every available opportunity and instead revealed ourselves to be human beings with the same hopes, fears and dreams as everyone else? Instead of behaving like cocked pistols ready to go off at any moment, surely we just need to relax a bit more and get to know our users on a personal unconditional level first? Twenty minutes spent talking to a PhD student over a coffee about what they and you are doing for Christmas is time very well spent, as it expresses your interest in them as a person rather than a PhD student and reveals you to be – shock, horror – a person rather than a librarian. As Chris Powis powerfully relates, we need to move beyond the labels and the preconceptions and connect as equals, and this works both ways. If we manage this, either naturally or, less ideally, with a bit of an unnatural effort, then we have a relationship on which we can build. The next time that the same PhD student needs library assistance, you will be the first person to whom they will turn. To use an analogy, the way we have become programmed to behave as librarians is not unlike those first Christian missionaries who went off to deepest Africa and Asia in order to educate and evangelise the natives, because it was zealously believed that the natives needed it. Regardless of the heritage, culture and thinking that the missionaries encountered there, some of which was highly complementary to Christianity or which could have been usefully embraced, it was all categorised as heathen. Just as they felt the natives were in badly need of, and would benefit from, better Christian morals, so too do we sometimes assume of our users a dire need of instruction in information and library matters, before we even begin to establish whether they need it or stop to consider their previous experience. Communication remains the key, backed up by a healthy intention not to make assumptions or generalisations.

MOMENTS OF TRUTH

To recap on a point made in Chapter 2, to borrow from Jan Carlzon (1987), what we need to foster with our users are 'moments of truth', moments when we connect with them, interact with them, share with them – moments that will make them come back for more. If our users recognise that we are there for them by virtue of our customer focus, or simply our willingness to stop and have a chat with them, then they will not only feel supported by us, but also connected to us.

We also need to make sure that the approach we take to customer service in our libraries is sufficiently personalised. The following may be simple tenets of any customer service business, but they can and should apply to librarianship too:

- Eliminate the sales pitch and listen to your customers, and afterwards prove that you are listening by making appropriate changes.
- Help your users even when they're asking for something that is not directly related to the library – the impression and goodwill this will generate pays

dividends.

- Train your staff to be knowledgeable, courteous and approachable, and empower them to make customer-pleasing decisions where and when it is appropriate to do so – ditch the black-and-white approach and bring in the grey so that you are judging on a case-by-case basis.
- If you receive a complaint, deal with it immediately.
- Honour your appointments and always have time for your customers however busy you are; promising and not delivering can be very damaging.
- Answer emails and your phone in a timely manner.
- 'Go the extra mile' – don't just point vaguely in the direction of a PC or the bookshelves, but escort the user to the resource they need.
- After you think that you have finished dealing with a user's request, always check whether they have any other questions or needs – they invariably do.
- Make them feel like they're getting something more, whether it be a smile, a sweet, a pencil, a badge – these little things also have the potential to build a connection or spark a conversation.

Further to this last point, as we have embraced personalisation we have also recognised just how much small things do matter and how long they are remembered: a particular slide on an LCD screen that amused a user; a mini-basketball hoop-and-ball freebie from a database provider; a tray of sandwiches from a training session brought to the issue desk for anyone to help themselves. All of these cost little but generate a great deal of goodwill.

Good customer service boils down to seeking a relationship with your customers. A good experience, or moment of truth, can instantly build a relationship, and that is where we absolutely need to start. And of course the resultant pay-off of the creation of such a relationship can be far-reaching, not just in terms of that individual coming back for more of the same, but due to their subsequent sharing of the experience, meaning that others will be encouraged to connect too. A single moment of truth can promote library use far more effectively than any poster campaign.

MANAGING A PERSONALISED SERVICE

If you are not sold on going personalised yet, you probably never will be, but if at least some of this is prompting you to nod encouragingly, underline or (heaven forfend!) write in the margin then you probably want to know how as a manager you can take this to the next level; or if you are reading this at an earlier stage of your career, how you as a library assistant can hope to persuade your colleagues to embrace this approach.

More than anything else we have come to recognise the boutique or personalised approach as a mindset rather than a strict set of rules that Must Be Obeyed. We have found it both refreshing and enlightening to examine and develop our services through this lens, as it has been an activity that has regularly alerted us to new ways of thinking about user needs. So this has to be our first piece of advice: consider everything you currently do from a slightly different angle, an angle that is perhaps more honest and realistic, more open to conversation rather than consultation, but most of all more intent on really finding out what's going on inside our users' heads and in our users' academic lives.

While conversations over coffee, friendly chats at the issue desk and chance meetings in corridors all have their place, we do feel that the approach needs to be managed in order to be truly effective, as initially you will need to implement some practical changes and develop some new ground rules for you and your staff. There are of course many other ideas and suggestions elsewhere in this book, but we thought it would be useful to provide a list of key actions:

- Find out from a cross-section of users of your service what they think of your service. This is best conducted in person and could use a focus group model or involve one-to-one meetings. It is vital that you don't just talk to library 'friends' and champions, as they are already won over; it is more important to establish from non-users why they don't use your service. When you get the 'face time' it's also important that you don't structure or restrict the conversation too much; some of the best ideas begin in unexpected, if not, downright wacky places. Inevitably you will discover through these focus groups that many users who don't think they use your service actually do, but this is no bad thing.
- Draw up a list of things your services do less well and things you do less well, derived from survey data and qualitative opinion as well as from your own personal assessment. For each of these elements consider how they might be addressed or improved by taking a more personalised approach. If you want to undertake this using a more formal method, carry out a SWOT analysis or similar.
- Analyse all your activities and consider which of them actually add value to the service for your users. In order to 'kick-start' personalised, you may need to make some room in the staff schedules by ditching those that do not. This might feel a little reckless at first, but you will be amazed at how little some services are missed and at how freeing this process can be.
- Gather your team or your colleagues together to explain why you think this new approach is a good idea, as you will need their dedicated buy-in. Success or failure of the strategy will stand or fall with your team members and your management of them. You will need to invest sufficient time into getting them up to speed with what personalised will actually mean in your environment and how you expect their interactions with users to change

(especially in terms of customer service tenets as listed further above). Our experience is that going personalised will dramatically increase team engagement as members will have more frequent and more rewarding interaction with users – even more so if you elect to devolve responsibility for specific user groups to them.

- Go personalised incrementally. Trying to adopt this strategy in one fell swoop would be too much to take on; besides, the mindset may take some time to feel natural. Perhaps start with an outpost intended to connect with users outside the physical library, by fulfilling the needs of a specific user group derived from a focus group, or by revising a training session that was previously more generic in approach.

- Sell the new strategy to key stakeholders by detailing the benefits of the approach. Not only will it make your dedication clear, but it will reinforce the library's focus on customer service and meeting user need and perhaps remind those less far-sighted stakeholders that this is what we librarians are here to do.

- Try to eradicate as many generic emails to all users as possible and replace with emails to specific user groups. Your users will thank you for it.

- Don't fear failure – there is really nothing to lose. Some things might not work as well as others. Some things might not work at all, but the great thing is that you will be learning all the time and, what is more, being seen to be trying to improve the service. However, it is important to remember that if an activity or service isn't working make sure you don't scrap it solely on the basis of your perception of its success – find out from users what they think. You may be surprised to find that their view is contrary or that they might have a suggestion as to how it might be improved.

- After Dale Carnegie (2006), seek to become more interested in your users rather than trying to get them to become more interested in your service. The latter will flow from the former.

- Above all else, as detailed in Chapter 2, explore more opportunities for communication to take place and actively listen to your users. This is at the heart of the approach and you really cannot go wrong if this is your overriding goal.

Of course, not all of the above is achievable if you are not in charge; however, by suggesting some of these approaches and recording positive feedback to such endeavours you could build a strong case for adoption to present to those who are. Responding to user need is part and parcel of librarianship, so your argument should prove convincing. As detailed further above, small changes make all the difference, so start small and build from there once the benefits become more readily apparent.

Our overall finding has been that, as there is so much more to recommend the approach than to discredit it, once you start along the personalisation path it takes on a momentum all of its own and more often than not the next step ends up volunteering itself to you unbidden.

BOUTIQUE CENTRALISATION?

As touched on elsewhere in this book, personalisation strategies may have the potential to be curtailed due to the inevitable constraints of centralisation – the size and structure of large centralised services can limit flexible work practices – and/ or the lack of autonomy of the librarian wishing to implement it. However, there is no reason why a central senior management team should not adopt, or at least encourage, such approaches to flourish. Centralised services are, of course, very much interested in proving that they offer added value and are also in a position to widely promote successful personalised services. We do not see boutique as the province of the small separate library alone but as a mindset with considerable potential for wider application across an entire library service. After all, the approach is about prioritising user needs and offering them the most relevant service possible; and, as we have seen, there is increased efficiency and engagement to be derived from adopting a personal rather than a generic approach. Personalisation offers opportunities for users to feel valued, understood and switched on to what library services are offering them today. Also don't fail to neglect that other key element of our original boutique library model: collaboration. Sharing and utilisation of resources beyond your own service can not only save you time, and therefore money, but it can be professionally rewarding too. Share the load in order to generate quicker results.

PERSONALISING IN AN IMPERSONAL WORLD

The Age of the Individual, first coined around 2007, is a trend towards consumer-generated content, products and, more crucially for us, services. The growing expectation of many individuals, and particularly younger people, is that all of these can, or will, be tailored 'just for them'. In market research terms consumers are therefore becoming more 'sophisticated' as they seek to take more control of each and every aspect of their lives. Although this could be viewed negatively by librarians as our users simply becoming more demanding, another take on this is that it presents us with a tremendous opportunity. If academic libraries are to continue to be relevant, it seems obvious that we have to key into this mindset and actively tailor our offering in order to meet these individual needs and wants.

However, there is another opportunity here and that relates to a parallel trend of these times: our increasingly impersonal experience of the world, as we – and definitely our users – communicate more via social channels, or by email, rather than in person, typically via smartphones. This is another door waiting to be pushed open. Even if our users do not articulate this need, there is a high possibility that they, like the rest of the planet, are seeking identity and community in an increasingly uncertain and impersonal world. The trade-off of our current way of life is an absence of real human interaction, a void that we can and should gainfully fill. In this way a personalising approach can be seen as something of a backlash, if you will, against an aspect of the Age of the Individual that has the capacity to make us and our users feel lost and lonely. It is here that we return to the idea of those agenda-less conversations, those connections that remind us that we are human and need personal interaction in our lives.

A FINAL WORD ON 'BOUTIQUE'

We do hope that you have gathered some practical and applicable ideas from this book, even if you do not end up immediately rebranding your service as a 'boutique library'. In fact, we'd be rather surprised if you did. While we have found it useful shorthand for our model and our message, our experience has been that it may not be the ideal word off which to hang our approach due to its retail and hotel connotations. Spending five minutes explaining, or even defending, why we have called our model 'boutique', rather than on the reasons why we need to build relationships with our users by personalising our approach, is time clearly wasted. Whatever we and our chapter authors have called this mindset, we hope that our message has been clear. Personalising library services in higher education *does not* have to be costly and it *does not* have to take up more time. It has the potential to deliver highly rewarding – and occasionally surprising – change, at a time in information and library work when we need to adopt a new approach more than ever.

REFERENCES

Carlzon, J. 1987. *Moments of Truth: New Strategies for Today's Customer-Driven Economy*. Cambridge, MA: Ballinger.

Carnegie, D. 2006. *How to Win Friends and Influence People*, new edn. London: Vermillion.

Priestner, A., and Tilley, E. 2010. Boutique Libraries at your Service. *Library & Information Update*, 9(6), 36–9.

INDEX